Sharing Our Lives Online

Sharing Our Lives Online

Risks and Exposure in Social Media

David R. Brake
University of Bedfordshire, UK

First published 2014 by
PALGRAVE MACMILLAN

Palgrave Macmillan in the UK is an imprint of Macmillan Publishers Limited, registered in England, company number 785998, of Houndmills, Basingstoke, Hampshire RG21 6XS.

Palgrave Macmillan in the US is a division of St Martin's Press LLC, 175 Fifth Avenue, New York, NY 10010.

Palgrave Macmillan is the global academic imprint of the above companies and has companies and representatives throughout the world.

Palgrave® and Macmillan® are registered trademarks in the United States, the United Kingdom, Europe and other countries.

ISBN 978–0–230–32029–1 hardback
ISBN 978–0–230–32036–9 paperback

This book is printed on paper suitable for recycling and made from fully managed and sustained forest sources. Logging, pulping and manufacturing processes are expected to conform to the environmental regulations of the country of origin.

A catalogue record for this book is available from the British Library.

Library of Congress Cataloging-in-Publication Data
Brake, David, 1966–
    Sharing our lives online : risks and exposure in social media /
    David R. Brake.
        pages   cm
    Summary: "Most of us know someone who has inadvertently revealed something shameful or embarrassing online about themselves or someone else. With the growth of social media like Facebook and Twitter, we are heading towards a radically open society. In exploring this phenomenon, David R. Brake first provides an overview of the harms that can be posed by unwary social media use – not just for children but for all of us, young or old. He then draws on in-depth interviews, a range of related theories of human behaviour and a wealth of other studies to analyse why this happens. He explains in detail the social, technological and commercial influences and pressures that keep us posting what we should not and stop us fully appreciating the risks when we do so. This is an invaluable book for students, parents, policy-makers and any social media user." — Provided by publisher.
    ISBN 978–0–230–32029–1 (hardback)
    1. Online social networks.   2. Self-disclosure.   3. Privacy.   4. Risk perception.   5. Computer crimes.   6. Interpersonal communication– Psychological aspects.   7. Social media—Psychological aspects.   I. Title.
HM742.B73 2014
302.23′1—dc23
                                                        2014025119

Contents

Acknowledgements

All works of scholarship stand on the shoulders of others – this one is certainly no exception. I am grateful for the generosity of the many researchers who have shared their work and given my own a critical hearing as it has developed. The Association of Internet Researchers in particular has over the years provided both a stimulating and congenial venue through its conferences and mailing list for this scholarly collaboration to take place. Some of those whose advice and guidance were particularly helpful at various points include Maria Bakardjieva, Lois Scheidt, Lynn Schofield Clark, and Elisabeth Staksrud. The starting point for this book was my thesis research, and both then and subsequently my supervisors at the LSE, Robin Mansell and Nick Couldry, have played a key role in guiding and supporting me. I also benefitted greatly from working with Sonia Livingstone on related publications and from her own advice as part of my thesis committee.

I could not have managed without the help and encouragement of my fellow PhD grads in the LSE's media and communications programme – Ellen Helsper, Patrick McCurdy, Elizabeth Van Couvering, Zoe Sujon, Ranjana Das and many others. Last but not, of course, least, I would like to thank my family and in particular my wife, Delphine – for many, many reasons.

1
Introduction

The contradictions and complexities involved in the increasing sharing of personal information on social media are neatly encapsulated in this *New York Times* piece on a teenage personal weblogger:

> He wanted his posts to be read, and feared that people would read them, and hoped that people would read them, and didn't care if people read them. He wanted to be included while priding himself on his outsider status. And while he sometimes wrote messages that were explicitly public – announcing a band practice, for instance – he also had his own stringent notions of etiquette. His crush had an online journal, but J. had never read it; that would be too intrusive, he explained.
>
> (Nussbaum, 2004)

Profiles and entries on Facebook, Twitter and many other such services can contain diaristic or confessional material that looks as if it is only for the author to read or perhaps for trusted friends and family – but although social media services often include tools to keep such writings private, many are visible to a large number of people or even published openly on the web with a potential audience of millions. In this first, stand-alone chapter I will summarise the evidence and arguments I will further develop in the rest of this book. In Chapter 2, I outline the risks of disclosing personal information online on social media and who is at risk. In Chapter 3, I provide a detailed exploration of the academic theories which have informed my research. Chapters 4–6 draw on my own social media experience and research and on studies and statistics from researchers around the world to analyse some of the reasons why we reveal what we do on social media. The concluding chapter looks ahead at how the social media landscape may change and suggests some ways educators, policymakers and the social media industry itself can and should influence this approaching future.

Digital media have been used as social media from their beginnings, of course, and risky self-disclosure went alongside the development of digital media itself. For example, Usenet newsgroups, the first discussion forums to be provided on the internet, featured a group about homosexuality (net.motss) as early as 1982, even though those who participated would be likely to be easily identifiable through their email addresses – anonymous email was not common at the time (Pfaffenberger, 1996). What makes this phenomenon particularly noteworthy now is an explosion in the scale of such activities. Early Usenet users probably posted messages in the belief that their only likely readers would be a few thousand people who were students or scientists like themselves.[1] Now not only has internet usage spread dramatically across the developed and developing world, but the technologies to enable sharing of a variety of personal information have become much more available and a variety of easy-to-use tools have sprung up and attracted large followings.

Some are designed around sharing one kind of data – for example, Delicious enables sharing of internet bookmarks and Foursquare enables location sharing. Many others started focused on a single task but developed additional functionality over time. Blogging tools like Blogger, Wordpress and Tumblr for example (and 'microblogging services' like Twitter) started as means to share text and later added the ability to embed a variety of multimedia forms. Flickr, Photobucket and Picasa were designed primarily around photo sharing but also enable discussion and video sharing. Social network services (SNSes) like Facebook and Google+ are umbrella services that enable (and encourage) the sharing of many different media forms.

At the time of writing, Facebook is the biggest and best-known social networking site. It claims that 727 million people use the site daily – 80 per cent of them from outside North America (Facebook, 2013a), but across the world one source found five other SNSes that are leaders in certain countries – Qzone, VKontakte, Odnoklassniki, Cloob and Drauglem (Cosenza, 2012) – and many other smaller and specialist sites. While outside developed countries the overall proportion of internet users is lower, the proportion of those connected who use SNSes can be very high. In China, for example there were 401 million bloggers – two in three internet users – 288 million users of SNSes and 330 million users of 'microblogs' (CNNIC, 2013, p. 27).

Not only are SNSes growing in size and variety across the world – viewing and participating on them is becoming a dominant element of internet use for many. For example, of the approximately 40 hours per month the average UK internet user spends online from a laptop or mobile device (Ofcom, 2013, p. 276), the average Facebook user spends eight hours using that site – longer than on any other site or set of related sites; Google's sites together amounted to 7.6 hours (Ofcom, 2013, p. 289). Social media are no longer solely or even primarily a youth phenomenon either. In the US in 2013, 71 per cent of all online adults had used Facebook, including 60 per cent of online 50–64 year olds and 45 per cent of those 65 and over (Duggan & Smith, 2013, p. 5). In the UK, the distinction between age groups is more marked but while 94 per cent of online 14–17 year olds use social networking sites, the proportion of 45–54 year olds, while lower, is still just over half (Dutton & Blank, 2013, p. 39).

A series of high-profile cases has highlighted the dangers of the kinds of online self-disclosure that can take place on sites like these. Much of the concern that has been raised to date about revealing information about oneself online – in the US and UK at least – has been related to the risks to children and teens of exposing themselves to older sexual predators. US media have reported that there are 50,000 sexual predators online at any given time (Hansen, 2005). A study which found that one in five young internet users in the US between 10 and 17 had been sexually approached on the internet is widely cited (Finkelhor, Mitchell & Wolak, 2000), and an advisor to a national children's charity in the UK asserted that at least 300 children had been sexually abused between 2002 and 2007 after being 'groomed' online (Brown, 2007). As I will argue in Chapter 2, however, academic research conducted to date suggests that while the abuse of children and teens using the internet is clearly shocking and should be minimised, it has been exaggerated in the public mind, while harms to reputation, interpersonal relationships and employability due to revelations made in the wrong context have received insufficient attention.

Imagine the plight of Stephany Xu, who in mid-2008 wrote an ill-advised would-be humorous posting to the Facebook group for the Princeton class of 2012. It was publicly mocked on a weblog about Ivy League colleges (Yu, 2008), and this in turn was picked up by Gawker (Tate, 2008), a gossip website which claims to have 5.3 million readers per month (Gawker, 2012). As a result (and in part thanks to her unusual name), more than five years later a search for her name on Google still offers the articles as the first two links (which quote extensively from the original semi-public posting) and photographs of her.

Abby Margolis wrote a pseudonymous weblog, 'Girl with a One Track Mind', about her sexual activities, which she turned into a book, but her identity was revealed by a newspaper (Mikhailova, 2006) and she had to abandon her career as an assistant film director. Brooke Magnanti, who wrote a pseudonymous weblog, 'Belle de Jour', about being a part-time sex worker while finishing her PhD – subsequently published as a book and made into a television series – was similarly exposed (Ungoed-Thomas, 2009). Dr Magnanti says that having been pushed into revealing her 'double life... it feels so much better on this side. Not to have to tell lies, hide things from the people I care about' (Magnanti, 2009). Ms Margolis, who has had longer to contemplate the consequences of her blogging, was not as sanguine:

> Having to keep up a facade with everyone in your life is exhausting. I wonder, though, if she's ready for the inevitable media blitz and prepared for every part of her life to be held up to public scrutiny. Things will die down in the press once the story is no longer fresh news, but with one quick click on Google, Magnanti's legacy as the formerly anonymous prostitute Belle de Jour will continue to live on; sadly that may impact her life in ways she could not possibly predict.
>
> (Margolis, 2009)

These two were blogging pseudonymously, but even on SNSes where people generally use their real names they sometimes reveal very damaging information about themselves. A wanted fraudster had a former US justice department official on his friends list and led the police to himself after boasting of his exploits through his Facebook updates (BBC News Online, 2009), and one study of the public profiles of adolescent MySpace users found that 8 per cent revealed alcohol use, 3 per cent showed or talked about smoking tobacco and 2 per cent revealed marijuana use, although these would be illegal activities for most of these young people (Patchin & Hinduja, 2010).

Of course writing online about your sex life or criminal activity is at the extreme end of the spectrum of self-disclosure. People have lost their jobs or had their lives turned upside down because of much less obviously highly charged material. Sometimes social media users' carelessness is manifest – one news site simply collected and displayed public social media postings tagged '#ihatemyjob' (Kotenko, 2013).

Companies often lack coherent and well-publicised policies about what their employees can write, however – as a result, bloggers can find themselves fired simply for maintaining a blog in which they mention work or in which they share comments about customers or conditions that would be innocuous if shared around the water cooler. This phenomenon is sufficiently widespread that a new word has been coined to describe it – being 'dooced' – after the pseudonym of one of the best known early bloggers to be fired under these circumstances (Armstrong, 2002). Ellen Simonetti, an airline attendant with Delta Airlines in the US, appears to have been fired because she posted (non-sexual) pictures of herself in uniform on her blog (BBC News Online, 2004b), and Michael Hanscom was fired from a contract at Microsoft after posting a picture on his blog of some Apple Macintosh computers that the company had ordered (Hanscom, 2003).

A survey of the public and of human resources (HR) professionals across the US and Europe (cross-tab, 2010) reveals a potentially serious gap in perceptions of what companies should be able to look at online when they are considering people for employment. In the US, 79 per cent of HR recruiters searched for candidates online before hiring, and in Europe numbers ranged from 59 to 23 per cent. Yet although 43 per cent of Americans surveyed (and 56 per cent of 18–24 year olds) thought that recruiters judging their social networking sites was somewhat or very inappropriate, 63 per cent of recruiters *did* look at candidates' profiles, and the numbers are similar for examining video- and photo-sharing sites. What causes candidates to be rejected can be worryingly broad – the survey also found that in the US, 43 per cent of recruiters found 'inappropriate comments or text written by friends and relatives' could encourage them not to hire someone, and in France a similar proportion might reject a candidate because they showed 'poor communication skills'.

As the survey suggests, it isn't just self-disclosure that presents potential problems – social media users can also get others into trouble whether deliberately or inadvertently. Because our social actions are often bound up with and implicate others, greater self-exposure leads to greater exposure of others – whether intentional or incidental. For example, the well-known Olympic swimmer Michael Phelps found himself exposed in a tabloid newspaper after pictures of him using a cannabis pipe at a private party were circulated online (Dickinson, 2009), and the newly appointed head of UK overseas intelligence found the location of his home and other family details were accidentally revealed to anyone in London because his wife's Facebook settings had made her profile visible (Evans, 2009). One survey found that between 60 and 80 per cent of bloggers never ask permission before writing about co-workers, employers, family or friends (Buchwalter, 2005). The situation of children in this respect is under-studied. Many are now growing up in a world where parents are increasingly documenting their lives in ways over which they have no control and which could result in future embarrassment. According to one UK study, two-thirds of newborns were pictured online, on average within an hour of their birth, and only 6 per cent of parents say they have never uploaded their children's pictures to social network sites (Press Association, 2013a).

Exposure in the media or being shamed in front of friends or employers may not be the only harms people face after ill-advised online comments or actions. Some find the traces they leave of their lives online collected and used against them by online vigilantes. In China and across Asia, where this appears particularly prevalent, the process of collective data gathering for public shaming is known as the 'human flesh search engine'. When Gao Qianhui posted a video online mocking the victims of an earthquake in the Sichuan region of China, her comments were distributed widely across online forums along with her personal contact details and information about her parents, culminating in her arrest by local Chinese police (Fletcher, 2008); and when a woman in South Korea subsequently dubbed 'Dog Poo Girl' left excrement from her dog on the subway, her action was exposed by a third party whose photos were put on a blog and subsequently picked up first by the local and then international press (Volkenberg, 2005).

Away from the headlines there is reason to believe that more and more people are likely to encounter other problems because of self-disclosure – for example, harm to their reputations and damage to their interpersonal relationships. Unfortunately research to measure these impacts is limited. One online survey of bloggers in 2004 found 36 per cent of respondents said they had encountered trouble because of things they had written on their blogs, and a similar number knew other bloggers who had encountered such problems (Viegas, 2005); another survey found just under 10 per cent had been 'in trouble' over something published on their blog (Buchwalter, 2005). US survey data (Pew Internet & American Life Project, 2006) hint at the scale of the problem – 13.7 per cent of US bloggers surveyed had had 'bad experiences because embarrassing or inaccurate information was posted about them online', compared with 2.8 per cent of non-blogging internet users. Moreover, focusing on the harms of which respondents are aware in studies that have been conducted to date may understate the problem, as friends or employers may disapprove of what they read on someone's blog or profile without telling the authors. This also does not take into consideration harms that may result from the persistence of personal information visible online years into the future when individuals' life circumstances or public attitudes have changed, an issue that will be discussed in more detail in Chapter 5.

Why focus on the online?

Problems with inappropriate self-presentation and miscommunication are hardly unique to the online world. Why, then, focus on the online? Because, this book will argue that these services allow new forms of risky behaviour and the nature of the technologies used often conceals the potential consequences of such behaviours. Moreover, as I will explore in Chapter 6, there is a market imperative that encourages those who provide such services to underplay these risks both to maximise usage generally and because the advertisers who fund these services can more effectively target users who have revealed more (or too much) about themselves.

Throughout human history, society has accommodated itself to a succession of new technologies, adopting them selectively and building new norms of behaviour around them (Bakardjieva & Smith, 2001; Lally, 2002; Lie & Sørensen, 1996; Silverstone & Mansell, 1996). Undoubtedly this will happen again, but there are two issues that must be addressed. Firstly, while social media have been adopted very broadly very quickly, the norms that will enable societies to adapt to them emerge more slowly, and while there is uncertainty about how we should adapt there is an increased likelihood of conflict and disruption. Secondly, precisely because these norms emerge more slowly, we might be at a pivotal moment where we may be able to influence their development. It does not appear likely that at this point we can (or should) stop the adoption of social media, but there are several potential ways in which we can adjust to their existence. Some suggest that they are inevitably making the idea of personal privacy obsolete and that this is broadly to be welcomed (Jarvis, 2011). However, if societies were to reach a new equilibrium of comfort with greatly increased and promiscuously recirculated online self-expression, we should seriously consider the potential consequences of this accommodation. If this future does not appeal, we must consider what alternative ways of coping with social media we should be advocating – a subject I will return to in the concluding chapter.

Why do we reveal what we do online?

Why then, given the risks which appear inherent in online self-expression that could reach a broad audience, do people continue to expose themselves to such risks in large numbers? Some have suggested that a new generation of young people – the heaviest users of these new tools – have a new, more relaxed culture of sharing their lives that this software helps them to express (Palfrey & Gasser, 2008). However, as I will show in Chapter 2, this new kind of self-disclosure does not seem to be limited to 'digital natives', and indeed social media use is rapidly spreading through most of the population who are online. No single factor can explain this change in behaviour, but I have identified several different levels of influence that I will describe below and that will be explored in greater detail in the remainder of this book – macro-level influences are those that appear to apply across whole societies or across a broad range of technology users, while micro-level influences are those that affect people based on their individual outlooks, motivations and the particular interactions they have when using technologies and services.

Macro-level influences

First and fundamentally, the technology services that enable these practices are increasingly *easy to use* and *popular*. Thanks to what have been termed network effects, they have become sharply more attractive as more people go online and start using them (M. L. Katz & Shapiro, 1985). Indeed, once these tools have become sufficiently commonplace, it becomes increasingly socially awkward to opt not to use them (Baumer et al., 2013; Portwood-Stacer, 2013). Moreover, as the companies that run SNSes become larger and wealthier, they benefit from a variety of forms of media exposure. This typically begins with coverage of these services as novelties, and then rapidly journalistic coverage tends to reinforce the notion that 'everyone' is using them. This may be exacerbated because journalists are natural 'early adopters' of social networking technologies since they are middle-class, urban, networked knowledge workers. And, of course, the largest of these companies like Facebook and Google have the financial power to promote and advertise the benefits of the use of their products widely.

The technological tools used to access and contribute to these services are also increasingly *inexpensive* and *ubiquitous* – at least in the developed world, where a large majority of people under 65 access the internet regularly. Across much of Asia, mobile phones have for some time been a leading means of accessing the internet – 78 per cent of Chinese internet users do so via mobile devices compared with 69.5 per cent who use desktops (CNNIC, 2013, p. 18). Using social media from one's mobile phone is also rapidly moving from a novelty to a commonplace activity elsewhere – 48 per cent of Facebook's users in 2013 were accessing it only via their mobiles (Lunden, 2013). This means that maintaining and updating one's online presence can be done anywhere. And thanks to GPSes built into mobile phones and other means of location tracking, the sharing of certain personal details like one's whereabouts can be done *automatically* without the user needing to lift a finger (and therefore without giving them the opportunity to consider the consequences). In Chapter 6, I will set out some of the ways in which business imperatives and technological developments appear set to further encourage the growth of online self-disclosure, while the harvesting (and potential misuse) of such information by governments and corporations seems also likely to increase.

The enabling technology and the companies that provide and support these services are not the only overarching factors that may be encouraging online self disclosure. There is a long-standing but increasing *media interest in self-disclosure*. This has been noted since the mid-1990s, with the growth of the talk show on television, increasingly personal newspaper and magazine columns and the cult of celebrity across all media fuelled by personal revelations (whether real or PR-inspired) (Calvert, 2000; Niedzviecki, 2009; Rosen, 2005). As noted earlier, the media have publicised the increasing amount of personal revelation online and the services used to enable this and have also profited from it, as a steadily increasing proportion of published revelations about the daily lives of ordinary people and of celebrities has come to light online.

There are also factors working together that can make it difficult for people to use the tools available to protect their privacy when they post online. For users to employ privacy tools effectively they need to be aware of them and their capabilities, the tools must be sufficiently easy to employ, the users need to have used them correctly and, once they have been set in a certain way, the settings need to be effective and to remain so over time. There is ample evidence that a significant minority of users of social media services have difficulties with one or more of these stages. The fact that the technical capabilities, user bases and policies of these services often change rapidly does not help matters. Facebook, for example, started in 2004 as a service used by adult members of a small group of Ivy League universities in the US, whose profiles were visible only to other members. Now it is used by hundreds of millions of people, and its policies – including default privacy settings – have changed repeatedly.

The services themselves that are available tend to 'nudge' users in the direction of increased self-exposure because of the way they present themselves, though each one to different extents and in different ways. Partly this is because of the choices that they offer users – for example, default settings that encourage information sharing and discourage the use of privacy controls where these are offered. Partly also, this is a reflection of what such sites fail to do – for example, they often don't provide their users with a good sense of how many people read what they write or who those people are, though the data are probably collected by the site owners for their own commercial uses.

I suggest two principal reasons why this is the case. Firstly, there is an ideology of openness online. Many of the early users who first discovered and then wrote about and publicised the internet saw it as a technology that first and foremost enabled free expression – 'we are creating a world where anyone, anywhere may express his or her beliefs, no matter how singular, without fear of being coerced into silence or conformity', to quote John Perry Barlow's 'Declaration of the Independence of Cyberspace' (1996). In addition to beliefs and political views, many of these same pioneering users began to publish what would conventionally be considered very personal details of their lives online, and as will be explored in Chapter 6, many early pundits have suggested it is not merely possible but imperative to do so. Mark Bernstein, for example, advised fellow bloggers to 'be sexy... If your writing is a personal journal, and if it is honest, you will have to write about things that you find embarrassing to describe, feelings you might not want to share, events that you wouldn't mention to strangers (or, perhaps, to anyone)' (M. Bernstein, 2002). Tony Pierce, another blog-writing pundit, said, 'out yourself. tell your secrets. you can always delete them later' (Pierce, 2004). To some extent, these writers and others may have been influenced by countercultural anti-individualistic ideas that were popular among influential figures in San Francisco's tech community.

Lastly, such sites also have a financial interest in encouraging use and discouraging caution, and Facebook in particular is unembarrassed about this. Mark Zuckerberg, the founder of Facebook, told a journalist, 'Facebook has always tried to push the envelope, and at times that means stretching people and getting them to be comfortable with things they aren't yet comfortable with' (C. Thompson, 2008).

The broad societal and technological shifts that have been outlined above do contribute to the growth of online self-disclosure, but a central argument of this book is that there are other important and less visible factors that also play a role. The micro-level influences I explore below – and particularly in chapters 4 and 5 – refer to the often complex and even contradictory ways individuals using these services decide what it is that they wish to do and what it is that they believe they are doing in their interactions with potential and real audiences.

Micro-level influences

A central part of this book, drawing on in-depth interviews with a range of personal bloggers,[2] is a detailed examination of the way in which individuals' perceptions of what it is that they are doing and their varying motivations can influence their choices to reveal personal information online.

As will be discussed in more detail in Chapter 3, sociologists studying interpersonal interaction suggest that we present ourselves in different situations in different ways, taking into consideration those who might be watching us and our relationship with them. Erving Goffman, one of the best-known scholars in this field, suggests we have one 'face' we 'perform' for our friends when we feel ourselves to be 'backstage' and another we show to the rest of the world 'frontstage' (Goffman, 1959). In order to study online interpersonal interaction using this theoretical approach, I have divided the writer's conception of their audience into three aspects: the number and character of the audience, the audiences' reaction to what has been written and the potential changes in both of these over time.

Who's reading?

There are many tools available to writers online to track the number, locations and even potentially the identities of their readers. Commercial sites of course have long exploited features like cookies to track the demographics and locations of users but free tools like Google Analytics are available to anyone. In addition, some social media tools provide more information about readers to those who publish through them, particularly when people have to register themselves with these sites in order to read or view what they publish.

As we have already noted, a great deal of what is produced online on social media sites appears to be the kind of personal information that would normally be shared only 'backstage', but it is being exposed online to large numbers of people, and indeed very often to any internet user who could search for or stumble across it. Users of SNSes may restrict access to some or all data about themselves to 'friends only', but the protection this provides may be more perceived than real. According to Facebook's own data, the median Facebook user registered 99 'friends' (Ugander, Karrer, Backstrom & Marlow, 2011, p. 3) as of 2011, but other studies show wide variation in friend numbers – particularly depending on the age of the user – US survey research based on self-reports suggested that while 66–74 year olds had a mean of 78.4 Facebook friends, 18–34 year olds had 318.5 friends (Goo, 2012) and the median number of friends reported by those aged 14–17 was 350 (Madden et al., 2013). One UK survey from a consumer research firm reported the average 22 year old claims 1000 or more social network friends (Intersperience, 2011).

One might expect those who disclose personal details regularly to be regular users of reader-tracking tools in order to ensure that they have the kind and number of readers that they intend to have. As will be discussed in Chapter 4, however, it appears that a significant number of these writers don't track their readers and even when they do they are often not particularly interested in the results.

What are they thinking?

Normally, in Goffman's analysis, people adjust their face-to-face 'performances' as they go in light of the reactions of those with whom they are communicating – either those 'given off' (spontaneously and involuntarily revealed, for example through frowns or other forms of body language) or 'given' (Goffman, 1959). While the internet can transmit 'given off' impressions when using videoconferencing services, in most cases the only way writers online can know how their works have been received – in particular, if what they say is upsetting or embarrassing – is through 'given' feedback, whether in the form of online comments to a posting, email or even conventional face-to-face discussions with readers. Because of the uncertainty about readers' views in regard to what they are writing, one might also expect those who disclose personal details about themselves to try to find out as much as they could about who might be reading, might solicit feedback and to be sensitive to the feedback that they do receive. As will be discussed in Chapter 4, however, writers' attitudes towards what readers might think of what they've said vary widely, and some don't appear to consider their readers at all.

When are they being read/heard?

Goffman mainly wrote about face-to-face interactions, which are instantaneous and transient, but although online writing is distributed instantly and responses to it can also appear very quickly, what is written online may be saved indefinitely, even if the texts may not always be as visible later as they are at the time of publication. When a post on a weblog is old enough to disappear from that site's front page, for example, it is nearly always stored in archives sorted by date (together with any associated comments from others). Even when these texts are not viewable online, they may be archived privately by the providers of online services, and anyone who has read them at any point could have saved what they had read on their own computers. Lastly, where texts are available online without some form of privacy protection, they will normally be saved and indexed on a variety of search engines and specialist archives such as archive.org.

As Chapter 5 explores, this longevity makes the calculation of risk from online revelations much more uncertain. A revelation that is seen by its author and its present-day audience as innocuous may nonetheless come to have serious consequences in subsequent years, for three reasons. Firstly, new technologies, changes in the way that services make what users have produced visible or changes in the population and practices of the internet-using population might expose what a social software user had published to different audiences to those that they had intended – the proportion of online Americans who had read a weblog rose from 17 per cent to 32 per cent between 2004 and 2010, for example (Pew Internet & American Life Project, n.d.-a). Secondly, social attitudes about what is written may change over time – for example, today's boasting about visiting distant holiday resorts could be taken tomorrow as evidence of irresponsible attitudes towards climate change. And lastly, thoughts and behaviour appropriate to one stage of life – say, adolescent experimentation with alternative lifestyles – may come to be viewed differently at a later stage – for example, if the author should wish to become a politician.

What happens next?

In Chapter 7, I will consider some of the possible ways in which different societies may adapt to present and future social media technologies and practices, and the implications of these potential shifts in attitudes. While the focus of most of this book will be on the harms to which social media users may be exposed, this concluding chapter will also attempt to set out some of the benefits of social media use and thereby enable readers to reach a balanced assessment of risks and benefits. While incautious social media use is indeed risky, that chapter argues that trying to minimise such risks by indiscriminately banning or restricting the use of such tools by young people is likely to be both ineffective and, in the long run, harmful. Those without experience in using social media may be those most likely to make mistakes when they do escape parental control. Moreover, just as 'soft skills' of self-presentation are deemed important in the workplace and daily life, and are an important reason for (or justification for) middle-class privilege, so social media where used mindfully and appropriately may be a prerequisite for future success for many, helping them to build and maintain social capital (Steinfield, Ellison & Lampe, 2008).

This book concludes with some suggestions aimed at all the groups involved in the debate around the future of online self-expression including parents, governments, educators and the social media industries themselves.

2
What Is Risky about Online Self-Disclosure and Who Is at Risk?

Early hopes

When the internet began to attract the attention of the public in the mid-1990s, early reactions tended to be hyperbolic – taking the form of 'dystopian rants or utopian raves' (Silver, 2000). Some cultural critics, as Silver suggests, 'blamed the Net for deteriorating literacy, political and economic alienation, and social fragmentation' (2000). Early arguments raged between those who saw interaction in virtual communities as being a (lesser) alternative to face-to-face interaction and social participation (Nie, 2001) and those who saw it as a supplement to such interactions (J. E. Katz & Rice, 2002; Wellman, Quan-Hasse, Witte & Hampton, 2001).

Most politicians, journalists and pundits, however, lined up around the world to hail the coming of the internet – in the words of another observer:

> extolling not just the potential, but the reality of the internet as an agent of an unprecedented social transformation: a new economy, a new politics, a new world order, indeed a new and advanced species of men and women who were weaned on the computer and transported across all borders of space and time by the power of the internet.
>
> (Carey, 2005, p. 445)

The focus of attention initially was the possibility of limitless access to information, but as the number of users rose, it became apparent that the internet would be used just as much for interpersonal communication.

Although as Silver points out, one of the earliest popular accounts of shared life online was about an online 'rape' (Dibbell, 1993), the advent of what Howard Rheingold famously described as virtual communities (Rheingold, 2000) was widely seen as an advance, at first. A new breed of cyberculture scholars emerged to describe this new form of interaction and they largely greeted it with enthusiasm. Sherry Turkle was one of many who suggested that the forms of identity play then observable in the multi-user domains (MUDs)[1] were enabling some to experiment with their identities and learn about themselves:

> We don't have to reject life on the screen, but we don't have to treat it as an alternative life either. We can use it as a space for growth. Having literally written our online personae into existence, we are in a position to be more aware of what we project into everyday life.
>
> (Turkle, 1996a, p. 263)[2]

Other scholars suggested that people with identities or points of view that are 'marginalised' or 'stigmatised' could find and interact with one another online, leading to greater self-acceptance (McKenna & Bargh, 1998).

Encouraged by politicians, and enthusiastic media and a plethora of exciting (and excitable) internet companies, the public in the developing world flocked online. Around the turn of the millennium, however, the public's view of the internet in the UK and US seemed to darken, just as the dot-com bubble burst and some of the optimism about the transformative economic benefits of the internet also began to fade.

Hitherto, internet use was principally seen as problematic if it was excessive. Now, as children and teenagers began to be increasingly visible online and as it emerged that teens were becoming the most active group of internet users, concerns began to be raised about what they were doing online. In the US, the first worry was access to pornography. This was spurred by a high-profile study of pornography to be found on the internet and bulletin boards (Rimm, 1994) which was featured on the cover of *Time* magazine (Elmer-Dewitt, 1995), despite numerous methodological concerns (Hoffman & Novak, 1995). In response to this, US lawmakers proposed the Communications Decency Act[3] in 1996 – the first of many governmental attempts to control online content deemed obscene or indecent.

There are many potential harms that have subsequently been associated with computer and internet use. These include obesity (from excessive time in front of a screen or exposure to advertising for un-nutritious food), violent behaviour (from exposure to violent games and video shared online), exposure to harmful or offensive content (pornography, and hate speech among others), availability of (and potentially addiction to) online gambling in countries which normally restrict gambling, addiction (to online games or other online activities) and a range of other issues (Hargrave & Livingstone, 2007; Livingstone & Brake, 2009; Livingstone, Haddon, Gorzig & Olafsson, 2011; Livingstone & Hargrave, 2006; Subrahmanyam, Kraut, Greenfield & Gross, 2000; Widyanto & Griffiths, 2006).

Arguments continue to rage about all of these potential problems – this book cannot attempt to address all of the potential risks (nor does it go into detail about the many potential benefits of internet use which, it can be reasonably argued, more than compensate for these risks in many cases). As the title of this book indicates, my focus here is on the risks that are associated with what we reveal about ourselves either publicly or to defined groups of 'friends' through our social online use, whether deliberately or unwittingly. Public concern about *these* risks did not come to a head – at least in the US – until some years later, with the growth of social network sites and the rise to prominence in the media and public discourse of the 'online predator' – people who used the internet to find and seduce children.

Birth of the 'online predator'

In the US at least, concern about online predators appears to have exploded in 2006, driven by two factors. Firstly, by the growing popularity among young people of SNSes like MySpace – launched in 2003 and bought by media mogul Rupert Murdoch for $580m in 2005 (Siklos, 2005). Secondly, by a network TV show – *To Catch a Predator* (Dateline, 2008). Between 2003 and 2007 it featured a series of dramatic exposures of would-be sex offenders who contacted their would-be victims (actors) online. As Marwick notes, instances of major newspapers' use of the term 'online predator' rose from fewer than 20 each year between 1995 and 2005 to 58 in 2006 and 457 in 2007 (A. E. Marwick, 2008), and this rising concern helped spur the attempted introduction of a Child Online Protection Act (COPA[4]) in the US, backed by rhetoric like this:

> Social networking sites...have become a haven for online sexual predators who have made these corners of the Web their own virtual hunting ground.
>
> (Fitzpatrick, 2006)

In both the US and the UK, parental concern about the risks to their children from unauthorised contact with strangers and inappropriate revelation of personal information remains high. While two-thirds of UK parents maintain that the benefits of internet use for their children outweigh the risks, their leading concern in one survey was over their children giving out personal details online to inappropriate people (28 per cent were very or fairly concerned), and a similar proportion (24 per cent) were concerned about who their child might be in contact with online (Ofcom, 2011, pp. 78–82). In a US poll, figures were dramatically higher – 82 per cent of adults and 92 per cent of parents said they were concerned with children sharing too much information about themselves online (Common Sense Media, 2010).[5]

This degree of concern does appear to be culturally determined to some extent. In Scandinavian countries, for example, although there is considerable variation in parental concern between the different nations, only between 5 and 16 per cent of parents' chief concern about their children's internet use was that they might meet strangers or dangerous people online (compared with between 15 and 32 per cent most concerned about them visiting pornographic sites and between 3 and 23 per cent most concerned about the amount of time spent online) (Staksrud, 2013).

Risks to children from online self-disclosure

There are many ways in which anyone's release of information about themselves online, intentional or inadvertent, can lead to harm – I have outlined some of these below. Not all of these are easily measured, and the degree to which they are studied at all varies between countries around the world both because of different degrees of concern about different risks for cultural reasons (already alluded to in the case of online predators) and because of differing levels of resource available for research in different countries. The chief risks of online use on which parents, educators, policymakers and the industry tend to focus are sexual predators and cyberbullying.

Sexual predators

There are paedophiles who have used and continue to use the internet to find and seduce or 'groom' children. Each time a new such crime is uncovered or a would-be paedophile is caught by the police, journalists or vigilante groups, there is generally widespread media coverage and understandable revulsion (BBC News Online, 2003, 2004a; Brown, 2007). Nonetheless, I would suggest – as others have also argued

(d. boyd, 2014; Cassell & Cramer, 2007; A. E. Marwick, 2008) – the reaction to these shocking crimes amounts to a 'moral panic'. To say that a concern is a 'panic' is not to say that the problem identified is not real, but – as Goode and Ben-Yehuda define the term – that the level of concern is disproportionate to the scale of the problem (Goode & Ben-Yehuda, 2009, p. 2).

There is certainly evidence that young people are receiving sexual messages online, but the results from EU Kids Online, a pan-European study of children between 11 and 16 years of age, suggest the proportions encountering serious problems are low. Of those interviewed, 85 per cent had not received a sexual message of any kind in the previous year and, among those who had, 75 per cent were not bothered by them. Of those who were bothered, half 'got over it straight away' and just 6 per cent were bothered for more than a few days – and 55 per cent of bothered children said they were 'a bit' or 'not at all' upset. When dealing with low proportions, it is hard to be precise but this suggests that in the course of a year around two in a thousand children received a sexual message that bothered them for more than a few days. While 11–12 year olds were more likely to be bothered by any sexual messages, only 7 per cent of them had received any (Livingstone, Haddon, Gorzig et al., 2011, pp. 79–82). Although the survey did not attempt to determine the origin of such messages, other evidence suggests that those young people are corresponding with are largely those they know already. One US study found that 'About three quarters of the youths surveyed had not sent personal information online to people they did not know in person; only 5 per cent talked online to unknown people about sex' (Wolak, Finkelhor, Mitchell & Ybarra, 2008, p. 116).

Figures from the EU Kids Online survey (Livingstone, Haddon, Gorzig et al., 2011) about young people encountering individuals they had first met online tell a similar story. The majority of children (70 per cent) said they had never had contact with anyone they had not met face to face previously. Overall, 9 per cent of children had met someone face to face that they had first met on the internet, but these numbers vary strongly by age – 15 per cent of 15–16 year olds had had such a face-to-face encounter but only 2 per cent of 9–10 year olds and 4 per cent of 11–12 year olds – and the kind of person they met also varied. Except in the case of 15–16 year olds, the majority of such meetings were with people who were a friend or family member of someone else they knew in person (Livingstone, Haddon, Gorzig et al., 2011, pp. 85–87). Overall, eight in nine of those who had such meetings encountered nothing that bothered them (though for the few 9–10 year olds 31 per cent had been bothered in some way by a meeting), and of those who had been bothered, half were not upset or only a bit upset. So perhaps half a per cent of children had had an upsetting face-to-face encounter in the last year with someone they met online.

Taken together, surveys in the US and across Europe tell a similar tale. As the report's authors concluded,

> Of those who were bothered, most (63 per cent) met someone their own age, half of them took someone their own age with them and most told someone their own age where they were going. This suggests that the majority of offline meetings, even if upsetting, happen with peers...It seems, therefore, unlikely that the internet is responsible for a substantial increase in the likelihood of face-to-face meetings with strangers.
>
> (Livingstone, Haddon, Gorzig et al., 2011, pp. 94–95)

The problem of sexual solicitation online remains a real one, but a more nuanced one than the encounter with a paedophile stranger who stalks children on Facebook often focused on in the media. As a summary of the evidence in the US concluded, SNSes don't seem to have increased the risk of victimisation (at least as of 2007) and those most vulnerable to online sexual solicitations are those who were already vulnerable for other reasons – 'youths with histories of sexual or physical abuse...delinquency, depression, and social interaction problems unrelated to abuse also may increase vulnerability' (Wolak et al., 2008, p. 117). One indication that concern over a link between young people's internet use and sexual victimisation may be overblown might be the fact that US government figures show that the rate of sexual victimisation by strangers was basically unchanged between 1995 and 2005 (Chaffin & Jones, 2011, p. 5). A different US survey focused specifically on youth internet safety found that, between 2000 and 2010, the rate of unwanted sexual solicitations reported by those between 10 and 17 more than halved (from 19 per cent to 9 per cent (Mitchell, Jones, Finkelhor & Wolak, 2013)). Better still, the proportion of pre-teens declined more sharply (from 12 per cent to 5 per cent) and the proportion of incidents where the source of solicitations was someone previously met online declined from 97 per cent to 68 per cent over the same period.

Since the focus of this book is on social media, the key question is whether disclosure of personal details online in particular increases risk of unwanted sexual solicitation. While intuitively this appears to be a potential issue, and certainly this appears to be an article of faith for the cybersafety community, the connection if it exists is not clear. One early study concluded that 'sharing personal information, either by posting or actively sending it to someone online, is not by itself significantly associated with increased odds of online interpersonal victimization once a youth's pattern of internet risky behaviour is taken into account' (Ybarra, Mitchell, Finkelhor & Wolak, 2007, p. 142). As part of the study by Wolak et al., 400 police officers in America were interviewed in 2007 about internet-related sex crimes – strikingly, the authors noted: 'we have yet to find cases of sex offenders stalking and abducting minors on the basis of information posted on social networking sites' (2008, p. 117).

Another larger and more recent study found that children using SNSes were 46 per cent more likely to have received sexual messages than those that did not. However, 'which children experience online as harmful and which do not appears unrelated to the fact of their using SNS' (Staksrud, Ólafsson & Livingstone, 2012, p. 9) once you take into consideration demographics and children's amount and kind of usage. The study also found that just having a public profile by itself increased the chances that young people would meet people face to face whom they had first encountered online, but had no effect on other risks or on harm by itself.

Given the very small numbers of children encountering serious harms, it remains difficult to acquire more detailed, statistically significant information on what kinds of online self-disclosure behaviour lead to serious harm – especially, if as Wolak et al. have suggested (2008), online risky behaviour may be a symptom of offline vulnerabilities that are the main underlying cause. For example, the report by Staksrud et al. found that children who display their telephone number or address on their social network profile were 29 per cent more likely than other social network users to have received sexual messages (2012, p. 7), but since many online safety messages and parents discourage this practice it might be that this is simply a symptom of a general willingness to act in a risky way rather than being a risky behaviour in itself. The media-led discourse around online safety suggests that online disclosure of one's age and location enables strangers to find, contact and lure away unsuspecting young people. As noted earlier, this form of harassment is extremely rare. The most common case is that of teenage girls who meet and sleep with adults voluntarily, knowing they are adults – half of whom said they were close to or in love with the offender (Wolak, Finkelhor & Mitchell, 2004).

As noted at the beginning of this section, there can be no denying that cases of sexual abuse and harassment linked to the use of social network sites do occur. The internet and other digital technologies do provide potentially vulnerable young people with new ways to explore their sexualities, sexually harass others or flirt with anonymous strangers. However, as many scholars are now suggesting, it is not participation in SNSes per se that normally leads to such harms but particular (and thankfully rare) ways of behaving online and offline (Holmes, 2009; Staksrud et al., 2012; Wolak et al., 2008). We do not know enough about what are the most risky forms of online behaviour, what leads certain young people to engage in them and the extent to which the availability of new online technologies may exacerbate existing problems. Understandably, however, the very sensitive nature of this issue makes it difficult to conduct ethical research that would shed light on these details.

Cyberbullying

The issue of online bullying – or 'cyberbullying' – has some similarities to sexual interactions online, as outlined above. Notably, although it can take place at any age, scholarly and popular concern tends to be focused on its prevalence among children and young people. In addition, while some forms of cyberbullying clearly take place using a variety of online means alongside 'traditional' bullying and there's a burgeoning body of research examining it, there are at least three lingering problems with such research. Firstly, there are problems of definition which are reflected in part in significant variations in measures of the prevalence of cyberbullying. For example, Olweus criticises the media and (unnamed) scholars for suggesting that cyberbullying is a major and growing problem, when his surveys in the US and Norway between 2006 and 2010 found one in 20 or fewer children reporting having experienced cyberbullying in the previous two or three months – 'only 25 to 35 per cent of the level of traditional bullying by direct verbal means' (Olweus, 2012, p. 9) – and both levels are broadly static over that time while mobile and internet use rose. Hinduja and Patchin responded that, from their own studies and an analysis of others' research (Patchin & Hinduja, 2012), 'approximately one in four teens have experienced some form of cyberbullying' (Hinduja & Patchin, 2012, p. 2). Of course, Olweus was measuring children from grades 3–12 – not just teenagers – and asking about recent and repeated bullying while Patchin & Hinduja's own surveys include 'when someone posts something online about another person that they don't like' as an instance of cyberbullying (Hinduja & Patchin, 2012, p. 2). EU Kids Online's large-scale European survey appears to lend credence to Olweus' point of view – it found that while one in five 9–16 year olds said that someone had acted in a hurtful and nasty way towards them, only 6 per cent experienced this via the internet and 3 per cent via mobile phone (Livingstone, Haddon, Gorzig et al., 2011).

Secondly, research has yet to demonstrate conclusively that cyberbullying represents a significant additional or subjectively more severe harm to young people than bullying that already occurs in other ways. On the one hand, by its nature online bullying does not permit the kind of direct physical intimidation of violence or shouting. On the other hand, a number of scholars of cyberbullying suggest potentially harmful long-term effects of even isolated cyberbullying episodes for a number of reasons outlined by Kowalski et al.: 'A single act may be forwarded to hundreds or thousands of children over a period of time. From a victim's perspective, he or she may feel repeatedly bullied' (Kowalski, Limber & Agatston, 2008, p. 62).

> A child who is bullied at school is at least free from the actual bullying when he is away from school...The public nature of cyberbullying increases the potential negative impact...and instead of knowing who the bully and the observers were, cyber bully victims walk around often unsure of who bully is and most definitely unsure of how many campus people are aware of, or contribute to, their humiliation.
>
> (Kowalski et al., 2008, p. 86) – see also Willard, 2006;
> Ybarra & Mitchell, 2004

While in principle the internet is a practical way to practise anonymous bullying, and while it has been argued that 'relative anonymity, the lack of social status cues, and opportunities for disinhibited behaviour may promote greater risk-taking and asocial behaviour' (Finn, 2004), in Sheridan & Grant (2007) it does not appear that most cyberbullying is in fact anonymous. One early study found nearly half of those surveyed did not know who had cyberbullied them (Kowalski & Limber, 2007) but this seems to have been an outlier – many subsequent studies have confirmed more than four in five of those cyberbullied knew who had done it (Patchin & Hinduja, 2012, p. 27).

Olweus argues that cyberbullying should be merely considered another manifestation of traditional bullying, not least because he found in both his US and Norwegian data that nine in ten of those who were being cyberbullied were also being bullied conventionally – a factor echoed though not as strongly by Patchin and Hinduja's work, which found two-thirds of those cyberbullied in the previous month said they had been bullied in other ways at school over the same period (Patchin & Hinduja, 2012, p. 26).

Thirdly, the causal connection between online self-disclosure and cyberbullying remains even more unclear than the connection between online self-disclosure and sexual harassment and abuse. The research of Staksrud et al. into SNS use and harm to children is initially even more damning in relation to bullying – compared with children who do not use SNSes, those who do so are 114 per cent more likely to have been bullied on the internet (Staksrud et al., 2012, p. 9). However, as with the case of sexual harassment above, this should be seen in a wider context – once demographic and overall internet usage and risk factors are considered, SNSes are no longer a significant factor in cyberbullying risk. As noted above in the case of sexual harassment, people do not appear to be generally victimised by strangers, so in that limited sense the publicness of their profiles is not important. However, the more personal information – particularly of a sensitive character – that someone makes available – whether to all internet users or to their peers – the more potential ammunition they are providing those who might mock what has been revealed or recirculate it to unintended audiences.

The 'digital native'

If children were the subject of the 'first wave' of concern about online self-disclosure, those a few years older – teenagers and young adults – subsequently came to be the subject of a 'second wave' of concern and fascination. This group has been sometimes dubbed 'digital natives' (Prensky, 2001). In Prensky's terms, they are those who have grown up with computers, video games and the internet and are thereby 'native speakers' of their 'digital language' (2001, p. 1), compared with earlier generations depicted as 'digital immigrants' who 'always retain, to some degree, their "accent," that is, their foot in the past' (2001, p. 2). This group is presumed to be both more proficient with digital technologies and more inclined to use them – and most relevantly to this book there's often a presumption that 'digital natives, who live so much of their lives in networked publics, are unlikely to come to see privacy in the same terms that previous generations have, by and large' (Palfrey & Gasser, 2008, p. 101).

Three distinct problems arise with this conception. Firstly there is a basic definitional problem. Studies and depictions of 'digital natives' generally focus on young people, but since the term was coined those who could be considered 'natives' are no longer universally young. Prensky suggested that college students were 'digital natives' when he coined the term in 2001 – a group that is now entering middle age. If young people are still more willing to self-disclose online than their elders, this would increasingly suggest that such behaviour may be more attributable to their age than their familiarity with technology. Secondly, the presumption that young people are active and skilled technology users has also been questioned. As Marwick, Diaz and Palfrey suggest, the 'generational' rhetoric of the popular media 'flattens the diverse experiences of young people in different contexts, countries, class positions and traditions' (A. E. Marwick, Murgia-Diaz & Palfrey, 2010, p. 4). Those with low education or income are more likely not to use the internet or to use it less, regardless of age. Studies do tend to show that younger people use a broader range of social media for longer than their elders, but the gap between the young and middle-aged is narrowing. For example, while 83 per cent of online 18–29 year olds used Facebook in the US as of August 2013, so did 79 per cent of 30–49 year olds and 60 per cent of 50–64 year olds (Brenner, 2013).

Lastly, while more active use of the internet tends to be linked with more confidence and more 'skill' in use, there is room for debate over how in turn this might be linked to online risks. On the one hand the comfort that digital natives purportedly feel online might make them more inclined to release information about themselves online. As will be discussed further in Chapter 6, pressure to participate from peers who are already using services that enable and encourage self-disclosure, and direct and indirect commercial marketing of these tools targeted primarily at young people, may reinforce this tendency.

On the other hand, it can be argued that more skilled users are more aware of and able to use the tools and settings that are available to protect their privacy. However, it is possible that compared with older people, younger adults' greater skill (or confidence) with online tools may be partially offset by their relative lack of life experience. A study by van Deursen, van Dijk and Peters, for example (2011), suggests that although overall older people are less capable of internet search than younger ones, they are better at assessing the quality of the internet information they get, and a study of online privacy attitudes comparing 18–24 year olds with 40+ year olds concluded: 'the 40+ age group are more knowledgeable about privacy in general (offline and online), so lack of knowledge rather than lack of concern regarding privacy may be a reason why the 18–24 group act in Facebook in a seemingly unconcerned manner' (Brooks & Anene, 2012, p. 1).

Moreover, a survey of UK teenagers found that those who believed themselves to be more skilled on computers were more likely to take part in a broad range of activities online and that the broader the range of their use the more online risks they appeared to expose themselves to, regardless of their skill level (Livingstone & Helsper, 2010). The greater level of exposure may therefore outweigh any greater knowledge of the tools to monitor and control access – although this particular study was looking at a wide range of online risks not just those that relate to self-exposure.

What about the 'rest of us'?

What children and the 'digital natives' have in common is that discursively they can be presented as 'others' who must be protected because of their vulnerability or criticised for their irresponsibility. Young 'digital natives' have also been convenient objects of academic research, as those who are undergraduate students are easy for researchers to access and study. But what about the situation of older internet users?

In some respects, although receiving less attention from scholars, this cohort may in some ways face more potential harm from their online self-disclosure than younger people. Having lived longer they have a larger amount of personal material which might be problematic if revealed. They have probably accumulated a larger number of friends and acquaintances over the years that could be aware of and deliberately or inadvertently share this material. In some cultures, adolescents and young adults are tacitly permitted to experiment with risky behaviours (Erikson, 1956) (see, e.g., the behaviour of US college students during spring break), and their indiscretions if unearthed may therefore be considered pardonable – older people may not be given the same degree of latitude. Moreover, as norms of behaviour change over years and decades, conduct that was previously acceptable or at least condoned may come to face condemnation. We have already seen this in the re-evaluation of the reputations of authors like T. S. Eliot (Julius, 2003) or Enid Blyton, whose works exhibited casual prejudice that was normal or at least acceptable at the time. Facebook only dates back to 2004 and widespread public adoption of blogging back to the late 1990s, so the consequences of this longer-term risk may not yet have been fully appreciated. Lastly, as older people are in more responsible work positions, may marry and have families, the consequences of harm to their employment, reputation or personal relationships (for example) may be more severe than for more unsettled younger people. There is some evidence from Nosko, Wood & Molema (2010) that self-disclosure on Facebook declines by age, so it is possible that middle-aged and older people are more aware of potential problems.

A national US survey of teens' social media use found 19 per cent said they 'posted updates, comments, photos, or videos that they later regretted sharing' (Madden et al., 2013), and another survey of US adults found that 29 per cent of social media users said they had posted 'a photo, comment or other personal information that they fear could someday either cause a prospective employer to turn them down for a job, or a current employer to fire them if they were to see it' (Findlaw, 2013). An earlier survey found that 9.5 per cent of US bloggers who responded said they had been 'in trouble' because of something they had written on their blogs (Buchwalter, 2005). Another survey conducted early in blogging's diffusion relied on a convenience sample, but found that '36 per cent of respondents have gotten in trouble because of things they have written on their blogs' (Viegas, 2005). All of these measures rely on respondents being aware that what they have written had caused them difficulties (and remembering such incidents), but it is in the nature of much mediated communication that negative reactions can occur without the author's knowledge. These surveys also do not indicate the cause, frequency and severity of such 'difficulties', or their longevity. One way to complement the few available statistics might be to ask internet users about the frequency with which they make negative judgements about others because of what they had posted online, but I am not aware of any such studies, although one recent study indicated that the phenomenon US Facebook users most disliked was 'people sharing too much about themselves' (Smith, 2014). We also do not know about the extent of harm caused to others by revelation of personal information by friends and acquaintances.

To some extent all internet users are vulnerable to the risks outlined below, but in each case I will outline how self-disclosure on social network sites may link to increased risk, and how the severity and incidence of risk may vary between different groups.

Risks to adults from online self-disclosure

Criminal exploitation

The most obvious source of risk for adults is those with malicious intent. Crimes involving the abuse of trust in particular can be greatly facilitated by the misuse of information gleaned from self-disclosure on social networks. Not only might people reveal sensitive personal information about themselves directly – they also may unwittingly reveal sensitive personal information about others and very often they can reveal who their friends are (i.e. who they are inclined to trust). The most obvious example of this abuse is identity theft.

Identity theft and fraud

One in 14 US households reported falling victim to identity theft in 2010, up by a third since 2005 (Bureau of Justice Statistics, 2011). Although some argue that the scale of financial harm incurred by those whose identity has been appropriated by a third party is difficult to judge and may be exaggerated (Florencio & Herley, 2011), the upset and inconvenience associated with this crime cannot be reduced to financial losses alone.

It is not clear to what extent the rise in online self-disclosure has facilitated a rise in identity theft (and figures from the survey above show numbers affected broadly flat since 2007), but security firms (Webroot, 2009) and banks (Lloyds TSB, n.d.) have expressed concern that careless users of social networking services put themselves at risk. Frank Abagnale, a fraudster-turned-FBI security expert told a conference: 'If you tell me your date of birth and where you're born [on Facebook] I'm 98 per cent [of the way] to stealing your identity' (Sweney, 2013).

Once a criminal takes a victim's identity, it can be used not just to steal from or harm the victim themselves but also used as a means to gain others' trust if the victim's friendship links have been revealed. One study showed that while 16 per cent of university students were willing to go to a non-university website and enter their secure university credentials when contacted by a fictional stranger with a university address, the number willing to do so rose to 74 per cent when the email appeared to come from a friend – and the researchers derived the friendship information by '[simply harvesting] freely available acquaintance data by crawling social network Web sites' (Jagatic, Johnson, Jakobsson & Menczer, 2007, p. 96). Thus, even where personal information on a social network is only visible to 'friends', this may not protect users from a determined fraudster. In fact, the illusion of protection that social network services provide may itself be harmful insofar as it encourages openness within that setting. One study found that once a sample of Facebook users accepted an unknown stranger as a 'friend', 84 per cent revealed their full date of birth and 78 per cent listed their current address or location, among other details (Sophos, 2007).

Locational crime

Recent years have seen a phenomenal growth in ownership of 'smart phones' – 61 per cent of US adults (Smith, 2013) and 51 per cent of UK ones (Ofcom, 2013) now own such a phone, for example. As well as facilitating (and encouraging) instant self-disclosure anywhere at any time using their built-in cameras, these devices also continuously locate their users – directly, through GPS built in to many of them, and indirectly because of the use of Wi-Fi via known hotspots or via their mobile phone provider who can locate them by knowing which of their masts the phone is connecting to. This is, of course, convenient for users as they find their way around but it also enables information about users' locations to 'leak out'. Among adult US social media users, 30 per cent have at least one account set up to indicate their location when they post to it and 12 per cent of smartphone users use 'geosocial' services like Foursquare where indicating your location is the primary purpose (Zickhur, 2013). Services like Facebook's 'Nearby Friends' or Google's 'location sharing' and 'commute sharing' unveiled in recent years may make electing to reveal one's location increasingly expected (Facebook messenger already reveals your location by default when used) (Dzyre, 2014). Once this is activated, location information is also used by the providers of these services to provide geographically targeted advertising.

Moreover, when pictures are taken on smartphones and then uploaded, the location in which they were taken is often embedded in the files themselves and is either automatically displayed on picture-hosting sites like Flickr and Picasa or, worse, it is not immediately evident to viewer or poster but can be derived once the picture has been downloaded (Greenberg, 2010). As activists have pointed out using sites like http://pleaserobme.com/ and http://icanstalku.com/, indicating where you are over time can enable others to deduce where you live and work, predict where you will be and, as you post where you are, to know where you are not (e.g. at home guarding your possessions).

Stalking and cyberstalking

Stalking has been defined as 'conduct in which one individual inflicts on another repeated unwanted intrusions and communications, to such an extent that the victim fears for his or her safety' (Purcell, Pathé & Mullen, 2004) and cyberstalking is generally seen as occurring when these intrusions are digitally mediated in some way (Maple, Short, Brown, Bryden & Salter, 2012). This definition can overlap with definitions of cyberbullying – indeed, studies of 'cyberstalking' can use studies of cyberbullying as evidence (e.g. Sheridan & Grant, 2007), but while bullying implies malicious intent, stalking can be broader and include obsessional behaviour where harm is not intended to the victim (but is nonetheless experienced). While bullying can be experienced at any age (e.g. in the workplace), discussion of cyberbullying tends to focus on school-age and adolescent children.

The prevalence of cyberstalking is not clear – a meta-study covering all forms of stalking (Spitzberg & Cupach, 2007) found that 25 per cent of those sampled had been stalked in their lifetime, but the place of cyberstalking within that figure is unclear (and of course much of that stalking may have taken place before the ready availability of digital technologies to enable cyberstalking). There appears to be little survey data on cyberstalking covering adults who aren't college students. However, Sheridan and Grant (2007) concluded that even though their study was itself conducted online, only 7 per cent of their respondents who had been stalked were stalked online only, with a further 5 per cent graduating from online to offline stalking. They produced an online questionnaire about stalking on and offline linked to anti-stalking sites in the US, UK and Australia garnering 1261 responses, while Maple, Short and Brown (Maple, Short & Brown, 2011) received 353 responses from a survey attached to the website of Network for Surviving Stalking. Both found that stalking victims were in their early middle age – the former finding that the mean age was 30 and the latter finding that the largest proportion of respondents were 30–39 – suggesting that in this case a focus on young people as those most at risk from stalking would be misguided.

While a meta-study of all forms of stalking found 80 per cent of stalkers were known to the person they pursued and approximately half were associated with 'romantic entanglements' (Spitzberg & Cupach, 2007, p. 70), the Sheridan and Grant study (2007) found that 'pure cyberstalking [with no offline component] was perpetrated less often by ex-partners, and more often by acquaintances or strangers'. Maple et al. (2011) found more dramatic differences between those who had been cyberstalked (whether solely or alongside offline stalking) and the typical profile of a stalking victim, with 21.7 per cent of respondents being stalked by a stranger, 20.4 per cent by an acquaintance and 16.4 per cent not knowing who it was who had stalked them.

Social network sites, blogs and other places where online self-disclosure takes place can be conduits for cyberstalking themselves, but as well, the self-disclosure itself can also be a resource for the would-be stalker whether online or offline, and this is of particular relevance to strangers or acquaintances who may use details made available of habits, hobbies or locations as a means of tracking their victims. Once stalking begins, it is often recommended that the victim present a 'smaller physical and electronic footprint [making] pursuit more time-consuming and exhausting' (Spitzberg & Cupach, 2007, p. 73). As Mayer-Schönberger (2009) suggests, however, and as will be noted further in Chapter 5, it can be difficult to remove one's digital traces once they are published, there are significant social costs to withdrawal from the more popular online spaces and in any case, even if ongoing personal information is not broadcast, knowledge of the victim's behaviour patterns will have already been captured.

Employment harm

As noted in the introductory chapter, there are numerous anecdotal examples of people losing contracts or their jobs because their employers took exception to material they had posted online. The extent of this phenomenon has not yet been measured, but one UK survey found 7.8 per cent of employees admitting they had been 'very negative about their workplace' on a social network, and another 12.9 per cent 'implicitly' critical (myjobgroup.co.uk, 2010, p. 5). Yet according to one 2012 report, around 60 per cent of corporations expected to have a programme in place to monitor social media for security breaches (and other behaviour they may consider problematic) by 2015 (Gartner, 2012). While employees may be fired or disciplined for criticising their employers, such cases may only be the most visible and extreme examples of much more widespread employment-related harms to those who expose too much of their lives online. Social media usage is also being monitored by university admissions officers – in 2012, according to one survey, 26 per cent of them in the US had checked an applicant's social media profile, and 30 per cent found something that harmed an applicant's chances (Kaplan Test Prep, 2013). As with several of the other forms of online risk outlined below like reputation and relationship risk, social network users may be harmed entirely unbeknownst to themselves. In this case, they may not be hired, not be promoted or be otherwise passed over at work because of a negative reaction to their online profiles – without this factor being given as a reason.

The use of privacy-protecting settings as offered by many social network services as a technological 'solution' to the problem of inappropriate self-disclosure may not help in this case, since there is evidence that some potential employers demand the passwords to applicants' Facebook profiles so they can see material that would normally be hidden (Sullivan, 2012). Indeed, if privacy controls encourage more frank disclosure than would a more public profile – and there is evidence that suggests this (Brandimarte, Acquisti & Loewenstein, 2013) – they may actually further endanger social network users' employment chances. Many social network users – 43 per cent of Americans surveyed, for example (cross-tab, 2010) and 81 per cent of Britons (myjobgroup.co.uk, 2010) – believe recruiters should not look at their profiles. It is not clear whether the public believes that recruiters do not do so.

They may also underestimate the risks that their profiles, if seen, could influence employment decisions – 'while 70 per cent of US recruiters and HR professionals had rejected candidates based on information found online, only 7 per cent of US consumers thought that information about them had affected their job search' (cross-tab, 2010, p. 5), and 'a significant percentage of respondents (between 30 per cent and 35 per cent depending on nationality) don't feel their online reputation affects either their personal or professional life' (ibid., p. 3).

In fact, surveys find that potential employers say they have been influenced both negatively and positively by profiles they have seen (Careerbuilder, 2009; cross-tab, 2010; YouGov, 2007). At least one experimental study that used upper-level business studies students as hypothetical employers found that potential applicants whose (fictional) social network profiles showed them 'in an orange vest and hardhat with a beer in each hand with the caption, "Caution: Men drinking"' (Bohnert & Ross, 2010, p. 343) were viewed as less conscientious, were less likely to be hired and if hired would be paid less, though interestingly those with family- or professionally oriented social network profiles fared better than those who were represented by their CVs alone.

Anti-discrimination laws in many countries, including the US and UK, prohibit discrimination in hiring on the basis of 'protected characteristics' like age, disability and race, and forbid reference to such characteristics in interviews except where they may relate indirectly to job performance. These characteristics can be revealed in the process of a web search, however, and may lead to discrimination – in the US and UK at least this does not legally prevent employers from making such searches, it just prevents them from acting improperly on that knowledge.

Concerns have also been raised in industry about the potential for 'cyberbullying' in the workplace linked to social media (Broughton, Higgins, Hicks & Cox, 2012) – similar behaviours to those discussed in relation to schoolchildren and adolescents earlier, but between adults. Research suggests that between 10 per cent and 15 per cent of workers in the US and Europe are bullied in some fashion (Einarsen, 2011), but there is very little research into cyberbullying at present and none that relates directly to social network use, so it is difficult to assess the extent or nature of the associated risks in this context.

Commercial exploitation

All of the leading social media platforms are run by for-profit organisations which do not charge users and whose income is therefore derived primarily from online advertising. Social media companies in particular claim to deliver highly targeted advertising because of their ability to take advantage of their users' willingness to disclose personal characteristics and behaviour patterns as they interact on the site.

Of course, there may be consumer benefits to companies receiving more information about users in order to better target advertising at them, as the Network Advertising Initiative – http://www.networkadvertising.org/ – is keen to point out. Better targeted ads might be of more interest to viewers and may raise more money for sites hosting them, enabling them to produce more attractive content and services. However, even where advertising targeting is accurate it may not always be in the best interests of the recipients of such advertising. As suggested by Gangadharan (2012), for example, advertising of expensive and inappropriate mortgages before the sub-prime crisis was effectively targeted at ethnic minorities in the US, in part through online means. Wade Henderson, the head of the Leadership Conference on Civil and Human Rights in the US has said: 'while big data is revolutionizing commerce and government for the better, it is also supercharging the potential for discrimination' (Smith, 2014).

Social media data may be used to make people 'second-class citizens' – at least in financial terms – because of their perceived creditworthiness or membership of an undesirable group. When people in 'poor neighbourhoods' found it difficult to access credit this was known as 'redlining' – now companies have a much larger array of factors at their disposal by which they can discriminate between people, and thus a new term, 'weblining', has emerged (Andrews, 2012; Stepanek, 2000). As Stepanek points out, the bundling together of characteristics to group consumers may 'incorporate the biases and intellectual limitations of the software's designers and users. Not all lower- and middle-income consumers crave a steady diet of action films' (2000). But discrimination may not be on the basis of human-designed categories – increasingly, in the era of 'big data', groups are segmented using algorithmic correlations. In other words, you might find yourself denied a loan not because you are black but because, say, left-wing voters with pets tend to be a poor credit risk. It is increasingly hard under these circumstances to know just what information about yourself is likely to be significant and important to protect. And, of course, as with other forms of discrimination, victims may be unaware that it is taking place.

Under some circumstances even the delivery of accurately targeted and non-discriminatory advertising can itself result in harm. For example, Target, an American department store chain, used its knowledge of shoppers' purchasing patterns to identify whether or not they were likely to be pregnant. As a result, a teenage girl who had not told her parents she was pregnant was sent baby-related coupons and catalogues by the store, which were seen by her father (Duhigg, 2012). Indeed, as in this example such practices can be harmful whether or not the targeting that results is accurate if the company in question believes its data to be accurate and acts accordingly. In the US, data brokers who gather demographic profile information from a broad range of sources, including SNSes (with or sometimes without their cooperation), have been found to be selling lists of people whom those companies identify as 'rape sufferers', 'HIV/AIDs sufferers' and 'alcoholism sufferers' (Hill, 2013).

Government surveillance

It is not, of course, just the sites that enable and store online self-disclosures that may have privileged access to such texts, regardless of users' privacy settings – governments under certain circumstances can also collect data about their citizens (and others) that they reveal online. As with commercial exploitation of online data, there are potential benefits to this as well as drawbacks. Police and intelligence surveillance of social network services may help to catch criminals and terrorists (BBC News Online, 2009), or policymakers may collect citizens' online views on controversial policies in order to be more responsive to public opinion (Wandhofer, van Eeckhaute, Taylor & Fernandez, 2012). However, there is considerable scope for abuse of such powers, both by authoritarian regimes and by democratic governments.

In the case of authoritarian governments, the potential for abuse is clear. Although political organising and expression on social networks has been seen as an important enabler of the Arab Spring uprisings (Farrell, 2012; Howard & Hussain, 2011), even politically neutral data like friendship networks may be collected and misused by governments to suppress opponents. As Morozov points out, 'the more connections between activists it can identify, the better for the [autocratic] government' (Morozov, 2011, p. 83). Some services – Blogger, for example – do allow 'anonymous' use. However, as will be further discussed in Chapter 6, there is an increasing emphasis among social media sites on encouraging or even forcing users to identify themselves. Even where users are allowed to use services using a pseudonym, those who run those services can often identify them anyway – either because they have required users to give them personal information like a valid email address before they can register or because they collect the internet addresses of users as they log in. Governments can then request or force internet services to hand over such information – and there is evidence that such requests may be complied with even if the hosting organisation is not primarily based in an authoritarian country and does not share that country's values. Yahoo, for example, handed over the email records of Chinese dissidents to the Chinese government (MacAskill, 2007). This may be because of concern for employees based in authoritarian countries or simply because of a desire not to lose profitable business opportunities.

The secret services of democratic governments have also been accused of widespread monitoring of the internet including social network services. Particularly since 9/11, governments like those of the US and UK have been given sweeping powers to gather internet data for the prevention of serious crime and terrorism, but the scale of such surveillance has surprised many. In the US, concern was raised in 2002 when the *New York Times* uncovered a research project dubbed 'Total Information Awareness', designed to bring together personal data and look for patterns of suspicious behaviour (Markoff, 2002). After a wave of public concern, that programme was shut down the following year but subsequent leaks indicate that similar programmes remained in place. In 2013, a whistleblower at the US National Security Agency, Edward Snowden, discovered (among other things) a programme dubbed 'PRISM' that appeared to have collected data directly from the servers of leading SNSes including Facebook (Gellman & Poitras, 2013). Other intelligence agencies have been accused of doing similar work, and evidence suggests that many of them share surveillance data with one another (Nyst, 2013). Of course monitoring on such a scale has the capacity to capture a great deal of personal data through email messages and other common internet applications, but the social media undoubtedly add a great deal to the volume of available material of a personal character since they enable and encourage the circulation of this kind of information.

Interpersonal harms

Of all of the potential sources of harm that can result when personal information is shared across the internet using social media, the most prevalent is probably that of simple social misunderstandings and friction. Of course, misunderstandings can arise in all kinds of social interaction, but I will argue in the chapters that follow that there are important aspects of online self-disclosure that may tend to make such misunderstandings and frictions more frequent. Much of this may be of little consequence, easily brushed aside, forgotten or tackled and resolved without lasting harm, but some can undoubtedly have lasting consequences – leading for example to the break-up of relationships or friendship ties. In one five-country survey, the most frequently cited negative consequence of online activities was losing friendships – nearly half of those who reported problems cited this as one of them (Brackenbury & Wong, 2012, p. 54).

While there have been studies of how and why these relational problems occur in principle and in particular online situations, there is unfortunately little survey data available to measure the prevalence of such 'everyday' communicative problems and none that attempts to unravel the extent to which the overall incidence and severity of such problems may be exacerbated due to the increasing use of internet-mediated forms of communication. Such studies would be in any event difficult to perform due to the wide range of possible negative interactions and the profusion of online spaces in which they may occur.

Studies that look at potential harms from social media self-disclosure, aside from those associated with the release of personally identifiable information. tend to focus on 'potentially stigmatizing information' (Nosko et al., 2010). Goffman defines stigmatising as a process where a person who has an undesirable attribute is rejected as a result of that attribute, and suggests three sources of stigma – physical deformity, blemishes of individual character and tribal stigma of race, nation and religion (1963b, p. 4).

Because of the broad range of material that could conceivably be used to stigmatise individuals by identifying such attributes, the definition of qualifying material is also necessarily very broad. For example, Nosko et al. included 'religious views, political views, birth year, sexual orientation, photos, friends viewable, interests, activities, favorite music, favorite movies, favorite TV shows, favorite books, favorite quotes, and about me' (2010, p. 410). This very breadth demonstrates how difficult it can be to anticipate what aspects of one's online self might cause stigma when written, or subsequently.

As well as stigmatisation, other studies suggest different ways in which interpersonal harm can result from online self-disclosure. One suggests that Facebook 'may be responsible for creating jealousy and suspicion in romantic relationships' because 'using Facebook exposes people to often ambiguous information about their partner that they may not otherwise have access to' (Muise, Christofides & Desmarais, 2009, p. 441). Another small-scale survey (N = 205) suggests that Facebook use is linked to relationship break-up – particularly because of 'Facebook-related conflict' (Clayton, Nagurney & Smith, 2013). Gershon's interviews with students about their social media use when they break up with their partners found that they:

> insisted that Facebook gave them enough information to be curious, and keep searching, but not enough information to be satisfied, and never enough insight to know another's exact intentions or desires. Facebook allows you to know that there may be risk in your relationships, but the people I interviewed felt that Facebook does not give them enough information to evaluate it.
>
> (Gershon, 2011, p. 888)

Facebook use has also been linked to envy. In an online survey of German university students (Krasnova, Wenninger, Widjaja & Buxmann, 2013) (N = 357), very few (1.2 per cent) said they had felt envious after using Facebook, but when discussing 'others' ' feelings of frustration and exhaustion after Facebook use, 29.6 per cent attributed this to envy and 36.4 per cent of respondents said they felt frustrated or exhausted sometimes or more often after using Facebook. While 71 per cent of respondents said they last felt envious of someone because of a personal encounter, 21.3 per cent said it was because of something they had read on Facebook. A survey of 425 US undergraduates similarly found that those who spent more time on Facebook tended to believe others were happier and had better lives than they did (Chou & Edge, 2012). Chou and Edge suggest, drawing on Tidwell & Walther (2002), Walther, Van Der Heide, Kim, Westerman & Tong (2008) and others (who we will return to in the next chapter), that:

> Users of computer mediated communication can employ several techniques to optimize their self-presentation and promote desired relationships, such as spending more time with greater cognitive resources to edit the messages, carefully selecting photographs, highlighting their positive attributes, presenting an ideal self, having a

deeper self-disclosure, managing the styles of their language, or providing a set of links to other sites or associating themselves with certain people, symbols, and material objects.

(2012, p. 117)

They suggest that the frequent use of characteristics of computer-mediated communication to present lives in as positive as possible a light makes Facebook (and by implication other social media) particularly apt to induce envy. The quantification of relationships that Facebook and other social media enable is also blamed for encouraging envy: 'the Facebook interface encourages people to see their alliances in terms of quantity, and people can easily evaluate their and others' profiles in terms of how many friends they have' (Gershon, 2011, p. 874).

The authors' focus in these studies is generally on the negative implications for the envious readers' life satisfaction, but clearly there are also potential negative implications for those whose postings themselves cause envy if this harms their relationships with those who read their postings.

Envy, romantic suspicion and misunderstanding and revelation of stigmatising characteristics and behaviour are just some of the possible negative interpersonal consequences of social media use. Of course these negative emotions are inherently possible in all interpersonal interaction, however mediated (and face to face is just one form of mediation of communication, not an alternative to mediation), but I will argue in the chapters that follow that the ways in which online social media tend to be constructed and used are particularly apt to enable harmful interpersonal interactions, compared with face-to-face and other 'one-to-one' means of interaction.

The way in which social media spaces can be used to recirculate interpersonal disputes to involve much larger, often-unintended audiences can dramatically raise the stakes of such confrontations. This transformation of previously trivial and transient interpersonal friction into potentially life-changing public drama represents a new class of risky media practice poorly understood by both scholars and the individuals who fall victim to it. In the introductory chapter I have already mentioned the phenomenon of the 'human flesh search engine', where antisocial behaviour that might have passed unnoticed if not shared online – for example, joking after a catastrophic earthquake that you wished your school building would collapse so you didn't have to go to school (Tan, 2013) – can have major repercussions when it is picked up and recirculated.

What is particularly problematic is that the multiplicity of available interpretations of actions online – in particular the common tacit presumption that an online posting should be judged as a public, considered statement or action rather than an often ill-considered impulsive expression – can make it very difficult for individuals in practice to anticipate and therefore minimise the potential negative consequences of postings. Social media postings are often brief – Twitter posts, for example, are limited to 140 characters in length, but many other social media are also length-constrained either by technology or custom. This is not surprising, as non-professional typists type while composing at a rate of around 20 words per minute (Karat, Halverson, Horn & Karat, 1999) – mobile phone text entry may be slower still – while people generally talk eight or nine times faster. It is already difficult to communicate tones like sarcasm using typed text – hence the invention of the much-maligned 'emoticon' (Walther & Parks, 2002, pp. 536–537) – and research suggests we overestimate our ability to overcome these ambiguities (Kruger, Epley, Parker & Ng, 2005). The brevity of modern textual communication can but exacerbate it. At its extreme, this concision is exemplified by the retweet without comment or by the Facebook 'like' – these single-button actions take a fraction of a second to perform but are open to many interpretations. Does 'like'-ing or retweeting a controversial page or posting indicate interest? Approval? Disapproval? Any of these interpretations are possible – those who choose such brief expressions must rely on an assumed understanding by the audience of their reason based on prior knowledge of their likely attitude and disposition, but the atomisation of online discourse and activity into bite-sized chunks can cause such actions to become unmoored from their perceived context.

This is particularly problematic in the case of Facebook, which has its own algorithm that attempts to present to users only those posts that will be of most interest to them, and it provides users with a set of controls they can use to selectively view or ignore certain types of postings. As a result, the median Facebook posting is only read by 27 per cent of any given user's Facebook friends (M. S. Bernstein, Bakshy, Burke & Karrer, 2013). The precise formula used by Facebook to prioritise postings is not known. Although the broad outlines of the criteria are public – 'the number of comments, who posted the story, and what type of post it is (ex: photo, video, status update)' (Facebook, n.d.-b), it is not possible for any user to determine who will have read it and, as we will note in Chapter 4, users seem to have a poor understanding of the likely audience for their postings. One potential consequence of this is that users may intend their postings to be read in the context of other things they have said on Facebook, but there is no guarantee that their audience will have read (or attended to) those other postings. The Facebook newsfeed algorithm may also tend to highlight the most sensational or controversial postings a user makes, thus amplifying the potential for recirculation of decontextualised sensitive information.

Additionally, while one can attempt to police one's own online expressions, it is considerably more difficult to control what others online might share about you. The case of Adria Richards brings together some of these issues. She overheard sexist joking at a technology conference and tweeted a picture of those she felt had perpetrated it, saying: 'Not cool. Jokes about forking repo's in a sexual way and "big" dongles. Right behind me' (https://twitter.com/adriarichards/status/313417655879102464). She clearly intended to shame the perpetrators but she apparently did not anticipate the consequences both for her and them of the fact that her comment was recirculated widely (even though she had 90,000 Twitter followers). As a result, in the end, one of the men was recognised and fired from his job and a sympathetic backlash caused her to lose her job (Hudson, 2013). Although her reaction was understandable and in most contexts blameless, the manner in which the drama then unfolded on social media meant that entirely disproportionate negative consequences ensued. She later said: 'I don't think anyone... could possibly have imagined how this issue would have exploded into the public consciousness' (Hudson, 2013, p. 20). One might, of course, argue that she should have been aware of the potential power her statements had given the size of her known audience and the millions who represented her potential audience. However, as will be explored in Chapter 4, there appear to be many reasons people overlook the 'obvious' publicness of what they say.

Moreover, there are an increasing number of third parties who have taken upon themselves to highlight behaviour and attitudes that might have been envisioned as circulating only to a few, bringing them to much wider audiences. Their motivations may be not always be malicious but consider the consequences when, for example, Logan Smith uses his Twitter account @yesyoureracist to take Twitter postings he or his informants consider racist that were posted by those with perhaps 100 followers and he 'retweets' them to (at time of press) more than 46,000 followers.

A social media moral panic?

Although the focus of this chapter has been on the negative consequences of social media use, there are many persuasive arguments that social media use can be beneficial and, as will be further elaborated in Chapter 7, it can help people build and maintain their social capital, can provide a forum for creative activity and can be a new and potent means of circulation of political and cultural information. Moreover, I have attempted to show, particularly in relation to children and young people, that some of the more feared potential harms around 'stranger danger' (while certainly present) have been overstated.

On the other hand, while there has been much media coverage of social media-related employment and relationship harm, there has not been a proportionate amount of academic research into these less dramatic but more widespread harms and why they occur. However, earlier research into interpersonal interaction and mediated communication in general can provide us with some useful concepts and a theoretical vocabulary with which to describe what appears to be happening in this new online environment. In the next chapter I will briefly explore the theories of some key scholars and outline how their guiding concepts are relevant to examining risky social media use.

3
How and Why Social Media Interaction Is Different

In this chapter, I will outline two broad theoretical approaches to underpin and focus this book's examination of why people use social media in risky ways. The first, drawing on symbolic interactionism, is a micro-sociological set of tools looking at how individuals make sense of their interactions in a given space. The second, drawing on macro-level theories about the relationship between technologies and society, looks at how the nature of social media 'spaces' and the ways in which people are encouraged to interact with them are themselves influenced by legal, economic, technical and cultural contexts.

Social media as symbolic interaction

For as long as people have been communicating with one another they have also been miscommunicating. There are many ways in which inter-personal communication has been studied, but the school of symbolic interactionism provides particularly suitable tools for the examination of interpersonal communication misunderstandings and difficulties, as it focuses on how meanings are jointly created through interactions between individuals rather than being created in isolation by the speaker and passed on to the listener. This approach had its intellectual roots principally in the work of the American pragmatist school and was developed at the University of Chicago from the 1930s (Plummer, 1996). The best known representative of this school and the one who will be drawn on most in this book is Erving Goffman.[1] Most of his work relates to face-to-face interaction – indeed one of his key works, *Interaction Ritual* (1967), is subtitled 'essays in face-to-face behaviour' – but his close examination of such interactions is valuable as a point of comparison with other communication forms – in particular computer-mediated communications (CMC). Goffman's work has also been used, as we will see, as a starting point for further exploration by subsequent communication scholars – notably, Meyrowitz (1985) (in relation to television), John B. Thompson (1995) (in relation to media more broadly) and Joseph Walther (1996) (in relation to CMC).

Goffman and interpersonal interaction

It is important at this point to differentiate between self-*presentation* – the central concern of Goffman and many of those who have used his theories – and self-*disclosure*, which is the term that will predominantly be used to describe, for example, self-related postings on social media in this book. Psychologists have defined self-disclosure as the 'process of making the self known to others' (Jourard & Lasakow, 1958, p. 91). This is a purposeful act, but not necessarily aimed at creating a particular impression on the person or people to whom you reveal yourself. Ruffner and Burgoon (1981) talk of 'consummatory' communication in which the act of communication is its own 'reward'. Relatedly, Langer, Blank and Chanowitz have suggested that routine interpersonal interactions can be 'mindless' – based on habit and custom rather than conscious calculation (Langer, Blank & Chanowitz, 1978).

Self-presentation, by contrast, has been defined as 'the processes by which individuals attempt to control the impressions others form of them in social interaction' (DeLamater & Myers, 2010, p. 89). The conflict between the two ways of seeing statements that reveal (or appear to reveal) something about the self is, I will argue, crucial to the examination of social media. It appears from studying those who disclose online that much self-disclosure online is not deliberate self-presentation, with creation or maintenance of a persona as its object, but of course whether intended or not it potentially becomes a self-presentation in the minds of those who view or read it. There is also an underlying set of assumptions governing each way of viewing statements about the self. Self-disclosure tends to assume there is a central 'self' which is disclosed, while self-presentation tends to imply a set of roles which are acted out in different contexts without necessarily a central 'self' behind them – but this deep argument about the nature of identity goes beyond the scope of this text – see, for example, Gergen (1985) and Grodin & Lindlof (1996) for further reading.

Branaman (1997) divides Goffman's work into four themes, two of which will be discussed below.[2] One of these themes is 'the nature of social life', which he describes variously as a series of interactions in the form of games, rituals or dramatic performances. Of key importance here is how he describes how interactional spaces are divided into 'regions' both physically and by social agreement and how access to these regions is generally carefully controlled.

The second major theme is 'frames and the organization of experience', where a 'frame' is a 'definition of a situation built up in accordance with principles of organization which govern events' (Goffman, 1986 [1974], p. 10). Crucially these can be vulnerable to misconstruction and thereby lead to miscommunication.

In *Frame Analysis* (1986 [1974]), Goffman maintains that in general 'our interpretive frameworks [governing interpersonal interaction] are more-or-less adequate' (p. 440) because the context of an interaction 'rules out wrong interpretations and rules in the right one... and when the context might not suffice, participants take care to act out requisite evidence, here, as it were, helping nature to be herself'. While he catalogues a number of ways in which frames may be temporarily misunderstood, he notes that:

> Ambiguities have to be resolved, lest the individual remain in doubt about the entire nature of the happenings around him. Ambiguities in regard to primary frameworks typically seem very short-lived and for a good reason: because these frameworks are fundamental to the organization of activity.
>
> (ibid., p. 304)

Likewise, he says that errors in interpretation are short-lived because 'the action the individual introduces on false assumptions is likely in itself to create contradictions and add to the likelihood of his detecting that (and how) he has gone wrong' (p. 321). If, for example, your boss approached you as you sat with your family in a restaurant, there might be some initial uncertainty about whether in the interaction you would be talking as employer and employee in a work context or as mutual acquaintances, but both sides would feel pressure quickly to establish which form of conversation should be taking place.

As we will see later, one of the factors that can cause problems in online interaction is precisely the possibility that the assumptions of writers online about the kind of interaction they are having may be mistaken. In some social media contexts the purpose of participation is meant to be relatively unambiguous – LinkedIn, for example, both through its branding and in the forms of interaction like 'endorsement' that it enables, is designed to be a space primarily for businesslike interaction – instead of 'friends' you are encouraged to link to 'connections' and to grow your 'professional network' on the site.[3] The social context of content contributions on some other social media sites, however, like Facebook, Twitter and Tumblr is not always clear as these sites are used for multiple purposes. Moreover, individual users may be trying to reach multiple audiences with multiple contexts in the same interaction. When the contexts of interaction conflict, this can cause what has been dubbed 'context collapse' (Hogan, 2010; A. Marwick & boyd, 2011; Vitak, 2012).

As Goffman observes, in order to organise experience, participants in interactions generally 'bracket' activities they perceive to separate relevant from irrelevant and appropriate from inappropriate observations – for example by deliberately 'disattending' distractions (Goffman, 1986 [1974], pp. 202–210) or onlookers (p. 225). A social media user who comes across material about another that they might sense is something that they would not have learned in ordinary social interaction might therefore 'disattend' that material or at least attempt to do so. However, discreditable information once learned is difficult to set aside entirely. Moreover, as will be examined in subsequent chapters, the expectation that others will exercise this disattention can give those who post on social media a false sense of security. Moreover, the sense that readers of sensitive material may have that they should not be reading or at least should not admit to reading it may cause them not to respond explicitly or warn the author of such material that what they had posted could cause offence or embarrassment, because in doing so they would be admitting that they had paid attention to it.

In the absence of feedback from readers (for whatever reason), users of such sites may not become aware of the contradictions that can be created when the context they imagine for their self-presentation does not match that of other users who encounter it. As a result, they may continue to present themselves inappropriately or in a manner that is only appropriate to a part of their actual audience. In addition, as I will note in Chapter 4, it appears on occasion that social media users can be so invested in their practices of self-disclosure that even when they receive negative feedback they disattend that feedback in order to maintain in their own minds the framing of the interaction that they desire.

In Goffman's best known work, *The Presentation of Self in Everyday Life* (1959), he discusses in some detail the contexts for interpersonal interaction, their roles and maintenance using a dramaturgical metaphor and suggests that we deliberately perform different personas when in different social situations.

In his Chapter 4 on Regions and Region Behaviour (1959, pp. 106–140), Goffman describes three principal spaces of interaction – 'front stage' areas where social actors are engaged in formal interactions with their intended audiences, suppressing all facts about themselves that might contradict the performance; 'backstage' areas where individuals and, particularly, teams, can 'let down their guard' to themselves or each other; and lastly 'outside' where individuals not presumed to be involved in the performance are expected to remain. As Giddens points out in his discussion of Goffman's work, divisions between these areas may be 'real' (in the sense that a physical barrier may completely prevent interaction) but may also be co-constructed by social convention: 'Walls are socially respected communication barriers as much as they are purely material divisions' (Giddens, 1987, p. 125).

Goffman points out that people who are co-present will generally collude to maintain normal relations and avoid potential loss of face:

> Just as the member of any group is expected to have self-respect, so also he is expected to sustain a standard of considerateness; he is expected to go to certain lengths to save the feelings and the face of others present, and he is expected to do this willingly and spontaneously because of emotional identification with the others and with their feelings. In consequence he is disinclined to witness the defacement of others.
>
> (Goffman, 1967, p. 10)

For example, individuals show tact by staying away from regions to which they have not been invited (ibid., pp. 229–237). The concept of 'civil inattention' (Goffman, 1963a, pp. 83–88) is a useful illustration of the complexity of tact in action. As he describes it,

> One gives to another enough visual notice to demonstrate that one appreciates that the other is present (and that one admits openly to having seen him), while at the next moment withdrawing one's attention from him so as to express that he does not constitute a target of special curiosity or design.
>
> (Goffman, 1963a, p. 84)

With a momentary movement of the eyes, co-present individuals imply to one another, that he has no reason to suspect the intentions of the others present and no reason to fear the others, be hostile to them, or wish to avoid them (at the same time, in extending this courtesy he automatically opens himself up to a like treatment from others present.) This demonstrates that he has nothing to fear or avoid in being seen and being seen seeing, and that he is not ashamed of himself or of the place and company in which he finds himself.

(ibid., p. 84)

Thus even a momentary glance is not just about the practical business of seeing or being seen, but is freighted with social meanings which each party assumes the other will understand.

The tact exercised by others is one of the ways that what Goffman calls the Umwelt is preserved. The Umwelt is 'the sphere around the individual within which potential sources of alarm are found' (Goffman, 1971a, p. 252). Of particular interest in Goffman's discussion of the Umwelt is one of his few references to media technologies – in this case as a potential threat:

A working assumption in everyday life is that one's surround will be 'dead' – that is, contain no recording and transmission devices. The subject therefore assumes that he can scan his Umwelt and correctly determine how he is being witnessed and by whom, for at worst there will only be a hearsay link between what happens inside the frame and allegations made about this outside the frame. Orientation segregation is thus taken for granted and otherwise vulnerable activity predicated on it.

(ibid., p. 286)

Separately, Goffman developed a related pair of concepts – the informational and conversational preserve (Goffman, 1971b). The former describes 'the set of facts about himself to which an individual expects to control access while in the presence of others' (ibid., pp. 38–39) and the latter 'the right of an individual to exert some control over who can summon him into talk and when he can be summoned; and the right of a set of individuals once engaged in talk to have their circle protected from entrance and overhearing by others' (ibid., p. 40).

Social media are inherently a means of recording and transmission. Many social media sites provide their users with controls over who can read what they write, providing some control over these preserves, but the default controls can in practice be permissive – likely more so than users may perceive. For example, in discussions about online privacy, survey respondents who restrict access to their writings to 'friends only' are often classed as having made their profiles 'private'. However, as noted in the introductory chapter, if a user's setting for accessing post-ings is 'show only to my friends' and – like 71 per cent of American teenage Facebook users (Madden et al., 2013) – they have more than 150 Facebook friends, this privacy may be limited. Crucially, interactions are regulated in part by users' *imagined* audiences (as we will return to), but there is often little feedback available when using social media to reveal who has read a posting or who might in future read it, so this mental picture may be based on little or no evidence.

Since (unlike in most face-to-face situations) social media users tend to be unaware of exactly who (among a group of friends and acquain-tances) is party to any particular interaction, they might be expected to write with due attention to the threat that might be posed to themselves in doing so. This implies continual mindfulness of undesired witnesses, but our habits of everyday face-to-face interaction often assume and take for granted that unintended witnesses are not of concern.

Goffman observes, for example, that strangers who are not the focus of an interaction tend not to be perceived as a threat in everyday interactions:

> Just as the individual assumes that the apparently incidental contacts he is now having with others in his Umwelt have not come about because of nefarious design, so he also assumes that the minor deal-ings that he is now having with persons passing on their separate ways will not be used by them to provide the bases for unanticipated costs to him later. In brief, he assumes that many of the involve-ments he sustains with those in his Umwelt will give way shortly to no connectedness at all.
>
> (Goffman, 1971a, p. 320)

This habit of treating 'incidental contacts' with 'persons passing on their separate ways' as transitory may be reasonable when dealing with face-to-face activities, but more problematic to the extent that interac-tions in online spaces may be permanently recorded and searchable. It also may have an influence over users' propensity to use privacy set-tings to restrict access to what they write in the first place using social media – why bother to keep passing strangers from reading one's post-ings if once having read them they will shortly no longer be connected to you?

It is not just those who are present but do not interact who are given the benefit of the doubt. As I will discuss further in a later section, a CMC theorist influenced by Goffman – Walther (1996) – suggests in his 'hyperpersonal' model that when CMC users interact with people online (who they only know online) in a primarily textual way they tend to exaggerate the others' positive characteristics.

Having explored the relevance of Goffman's work itself, let us pass now first to the use of Goffman to analyse the mass media by other theorists and then to other theories of CMC.

Using Goffman to examine mediated communication

Meyrowitz and the 'middle region'

In *No Sense of Place* (1985), Meyrowitz took some of the dramaturgical concepts developed in Goffman (1959) primarily to study face-to-face communications, and adapted and modified them to theorise how the growth of television might change a variety of social relations.

Meyrowitz suggests a focus on mediation in communication primarily as a means of enabling new communicative situations, which, in turn, foster new behaviours. In particular, he suggests that, through television, viewers increasingly gain access to areas once thought of as backstage, bringing into existence a new communicative region he terms 'sidestage' or 'middle region' (1985, p. 47). He notes that 'the competent performer adjusts his or her social role so that it is consistent with the new information available to the audience' (1985, p. 47) but maintains that while 'in once sense middle region behaviours are simply *new* front region behaviours ... if we think of them merely as front region behaviours we lose the ability to see the nature and direction of the behavioural change' (1985, p. 48).

He argues that while people can adjust in the short term to the ways in which television reveals the backstage behaviour of themselves and others, over the longer term it becomes impossible to maintain one's 'front stage' in the same fashion:

For a brief period, a revealed back region can be converted into a relatively traditional front region performance. The less performers can control and restrict others' access to themselves, however, the more back region behavior must come to light. A normally sloppy teenager, for example, may clean his room when his aunt comes to dinner on Easter Sunday. But if Aunt Mary stays for six months, she will undoubtedly witness a different drama ... The longer and more

closely people are observed, either in person or by camera and micro-
phone, the more their behaviour is stripped of its social symbols and
posturing.

(1985, p. 48)

This shift in behaviour takes place, he suggests, in a 'largely invisible'
way because 'people very quickly adapt to the new definitions of situations' (1985, p. 48). In his study, only those few who are on television
develop 'middle region' behaviours – his concern is mainly about the
effect on others of seeing this increased self-disclosure among those they
see on television. But as I will suggest in rest of this book, we often act on
social media as our own 'camera crews', so middle-region behaviour is
much more prevalent and Meyrowitz appears to be right – under conditions of near-continuous self-surveillance it is difficult if not impossible
to continually monitor our self-disclosures to make them appropriate
self-presentations.

No Sense of Place is subtitled 'the impact of electronic media on social
behaviour', but Meyrowitz' discussion of media is centred largely on the
role of television. He does mention computers in passing, but only as an
alternative form of information retrieval tool that may be more effective
than television but which is also less accessible (1985, pp. 324–328).
Because of the state of development of computers at this time he did
not envisage them as interpersonal communication tools, nor did he
examine the ways in which CMC might differ fundamentally in kind
from televisual communication. Indeed he did not focus his attention
on the nature of the interactions that are mediated through television
at all – his focus was on the presumed cumulative effect of the exposure
to new social information that is enabled via this new communicative
situation. As a result he did not fully take into consideration the way
in which individuals and organisations can reflexively adapt to such
situations. To provide a framework for a focus on the way specific characteristics of particular media forms can shape interactions, and on the
ways in which individuals can adapt to these pressures let us to turn
now to John B Thompson.

Thompson: New forms of interaction and the role of the imagination

In *The Media and Modernity* (1995), Thompson outlines a typology of
interaction. In it he contrasts face-to-face interaction with a variety of
forms of mediated interaction. His definition of mediated interaction
is broad: 'Mediated interaction involves the use of a technical medium

(paper, electrical wires, electromagnetic waves etc) which enables information or symbolic content to be transmitted to individuals who are remote in space, in time, or in both' (ibid., p. 83). Thompson then splits the communication enabled by media into two types. Communication aimed at 'specific others' and 'dialogical' in character he terms 'mediated interaction' (which, for clarity's sake I will style as mediated interpersonal interaction), while those aimed at 'an indefinite range of potential recipients' and which are predominantly monological in character, being disseminated via the mass media he terms 'mediated quasi-interaction' (ibid., p. 85).

Thompson here differentiates mediated quasi-interaction from mediated interpersonal interaction using three distinct criteria I have labelled *the intended audience* (specific or indefinite), the imagined or desired *direction of flow of interaction* (whether the communication is monological or dialogical) and the *nature of the medium* (mass media or interpersonal media) used for communication (ibid., pp. 84–85). All three criteria are implicitly linked. Although Thompson does not spell this out, his argument might be that because they reach a large audience, mass mediated messages cannot be intended solely for specific others, that the consumers of such messages recognise that they are not specifically targeted and, therefore, do not generally attempt to enter into a dialogue with the creator of such messages, and that both sides of the communicative process understand and anticipate the other's expectations. While Thompson characterises the intended audience of mass mediated communication as 'indefinite', this is only true in the sense that specific individuals are not addressed – in general, whether in the interests of advertisers, for technical reasons of distribution or to simplify the creation of content, specific *categories* (geographic and sociodemographic) of reader, listener or viewer *are* generally envisaged. Such communication generally has a significant cost to create and distribute and, therefore, an intended audience can be assumed in order to justify incurring such costs: 'producers in turn depend on recipients for their willingness to watch and for the support afforded by their spectatorship' (ibid., p. 99).

Thompson goes on to problematise his division of media into dialogic and monologic. He points out that 'many of the interactions which develop in the flow of day-to-day life may involve a mixture of different forms of interaction – they have, in other words, a hybrid character' (ibid., p. 85). Individuals can adjust to and compensate for technical limitations of communication flows in one medium by supplementing it with another. For example a television show (normally monological – those broadcasting cannot directly hear or see their viewers) may encourage viewers to engage in a dialogue using mediated interaction via telephone (e.g. a 'call-in' talk show). He also suggests that 'new forms of interaction might be created by, for example, the development of new communication technologies which allow for a greater degree of input from recipients' (ibid., p. 86). Unfortunately, because the technologies he refers to were only just beginning to attain widespread adoption he did not develop this theme further. The advent of CMC has enabled a fourth 'ideal type' of communication (distinct from face-to-face, mediated interpersonal and mediated quasi-interaction) that follows the 'logic' of this new medium and which scholars have called 'telelogic' (Ball-Rokeach & Reardon, 1988; Voiskounsky, 1997).[4] This will be described in more detail later in this chapter.

While Thompson's typology of mediation may be useful in itself when extended to include telelogic communication, it is also useful insofar as it focuses our attention not on how the technical properties of particular communicative tools influence interactions, but on how important the imagination is in visualising the context of mediated interactions. As Thompson puts it,

> In face-to-face situations, the interlocutors are able (and are generally obliged) to take account of the ways in which others respond to what they say, and to modify their subsequent actions and utterances in the light of these responses... In so far as mediated interaction (such as a telephone conversation) is dialogical, it too involves the reflexive monitoring of others' responses, although the symbolic mechanisms and cues which are available to participants for this purposes are generally more restricted.
>
> (J. B. Thompson, 1995, p. 96)

By contrast, producers in situations of mediated quasi-interaction are 'deprived of the kinds of continuous and immediate feedback which would enable them to determine whether and how their messages are being received and understood'. This, he claims, 'enables them to determine the course and content of the quasi-interaction without having to take account of recipient response' but 'is also a potential source of uncertainty and trouble' (ibid., p. 97). The producer's message is not the only relevant element in a mediated quasi-interaction – knowledge of a recipient's response (whether 'given' – explicit – or 'given off' – revealed – in Goffman's terms [1959]) is also important.

Thompson's focus is primarily on the receiver of mass mediated communications rather than the producer, so he does not develop an in-depth analysis of how producers respond to this situation of uncertainty. However, if audience reactions are not directly perceived, yet must be taken into account, this clearly provides a role for the producer's imagination. Two of the three principal differentiating criteria I identified above with which Thompson divides mediated interpersonal interaction from mediated quasi-interaction are, in some fashion, activities of the imagination – that is, it is the *intended* not the actual audience and the *anticipated* level of interactivity that are important in the framing of mediated interaction. While the particular communication medium chosen can affect the *likelihood* of interaction (given technological constraints) or the actual size and composition of the audience and in that way affect producer's expectations, there is always an element of uncertainty about the audience in mediated communications which must be taken into account. In Chapter 4, the way in which this is negotiated in the case of the personal webloggers I interviewed will demonstrate the importance of the distinction between reacting to imagined, potential and actual audiences.

Thompson: Mediation and space–time

Thompson's work on mediation also touches on the re-ordering of time and space that mediation can entail. In *The Media and Modernity* he outlines some of the implications. While face-to-face exchange of symbolic content requires both parties to be in the same place at the same time, mediation uncouples communication. With electronic communication, symbolic content can cross great distances in almost no time, and with this 'the experience of simultaneity was detached from the spatial condition of common locality. It became possible to experience events as simultaneous despite the face that they occurred in locales that were spatially remote' (J. B. Thompson, 1995, p. 32). As a result, 'the spatial horizons of our understanding are no longer restricted by the need to be physically present at the places where the observed events etc. occur' (J. B. Thompson, 1995, p. 34).

His analysis of the implications of the uncoupling of time and space in television production and consumption is of particular interest. As he notes, the space–time coordinates of the contexts of production, the message itself and of reception are separate and are spliced together by the viewer in a process he calls 'space-time interpolation':

In receiving televisual messages, individuals routinely orient themselves towards space-time coordinates which differ from those characteristic of their contexts of reception, and interpolate mediated space-time coordinates into the spatial-temporal frameworks of their everyday lives.

(J. B. Thompson, 1995, p. 93)

He adds that television requires recipients to 'negotiate effectively the different space-time frameworks which are in play' (ibid., p. 94) and if they are unsure about these they can be bewildered or disoriented:

['Competent' viewers'] experience of space and time becomes increasingly discontinuous, as they are able to move between worlds, both real and imaginary, at the flick of a switch. And yet, despite this increased mobility, the space-time framework of the context of reception remains the 'anchor frame' for most viewers, since their life projects are rooted primarily in the practical contexts of their day-to-day lives.

(ibid., p. 95)

Thompson mentions but does not analyse the fact that mediated communication generally results in 'extended availability [of the communication] in time and space' (ibid., pp. 84–85). Goffman also touches obliquely on the importance of this aspect of time in *Frame Analysis*, with particular reference to the potential risks of loss of face that may occur when an interaction occurs outside of its original temporal context:

Howsoever the individual presents himself on any occasion before any audience, there will be other places, times and audiences when he quite properly conducts himself in a manner that would discredit this first performance were his other conduct to be vividly brought to light. Barriers to communications such as walls and distance, along with audience segregation, ensure that such discrediting will not occur. Any monitoring of any individual's behavior that he does not know about will then have a discrediting power; all forms of secret surveillance function to undermine later activity, transforming it into a discreditable performance.

(Goffman, 1986 [1974], pp. 168–169)

While the greater geographical reach that mediation provides for messages is widely understood and analysed in relation to social media and other media forms, the implications of more extended temporal availability are less often considered. Viktor Mayer-Schönberger (2009) vividly illustrates the importance of both factors using two case studies. Stacey Snyder is a would-be teacher whose picture of herself drinking reached an unintended audience (university administrators) and prevented her from receiving her qualification. Andrew Feldmar wrote about having taken LSD in the 1960s and, nearly four decades later, found he was barred from entry to the United States as a result:

> If in hindsight Stacey should have self censored after considering who, in addition to her friends, might access her website, Andrew should have constrained his writing based on an unforeseeable future. That makes Andrew's case even more troubling. If we have to imagine how somebody years – perhaps decades into the future – we interpret and weigh our words, we would be even more careful in formulating them. If Stacey's case is part of a *spatial* version of Bentham's panopticon, in which she does not know who watches her but must assume she is watched by everybody, Andrew's story exemplifies an even more constraining *temporal* panopticon.
>
> (Mayer-Schönberger, 2009, p. 111)

As I will discuss in Chapter 5, the degree to which particular social media utterances can be made available at different times or in different (online or offline) places, can vary. When analysing this it will be useful to distinguish between two different potential 'space–time coordinates' of reception – what I will call 'primary reception', which takes place at something approximating the time that a posting is first made, and 'secondary reception', which takes place at a greater temporal distance. Among other issues, secondary reception may be more likely to discredit current performances, and I will argue that some of the problems people encounter when using social media stem from their focus on the primary reception of their messages and overlooking their secondary reception.

The next section discusses theories that relate specifically to CMC, and introduces a new conception of CMC particularly associated with social media – what I have dubbed 'interlinked telelogic communication'.

CMC theories

Computers enable 'telelogic' communication

As noted earlier in the discussion of Thompson's typology of mediated communication, the advent of computer networking has necessitated the recognition of a new form or class of 'telelogic' communication.

This form reflects the ease with which individuals using computers can reach and be reached by many others at low cost. To the extent that CMC can reach a large audience it resembles (monologic) mass media, but because it enables those reached to respond it is in some respects dialogic. Ball-Rokeach and Reardon argue that 'the telelogic communication form exhibits some characteristics of the interpersonal form and some of the characteristics of the mass form; but the idea that telelogic communication is simply a blend of interpersonal and mass forms cannot account for the total pattern of differences' (Ball-Rokeach & Reardon, 1988, p. 147). One of the key novel characteristics of telelogic communication and the one that sets it apart from the other forms is its ability to enable an interactive communication with an audience consisting partially or wholly of people previously unknown to the communicator – what is sometimes called a 'multilogue' (Kitzmann, 2003; Serfaty, 2004; Shank, 1993).

The internet enables many kinds of communication, not all of them telelogic. A web page that does not provide contact information for its author is monologic, and email (with the exception of mailing lists) is predominantly dialogic, since it generally involves communication with known and specified others. Social media in general vary in their characteristics depending on the particular site and settings. At one extreme the technical features of weblogs appear to favour telelogic communication, as by default a weblog posting is available to an unspecified and unlimited audience, and (again by default) they invite a response from readers – either through the 'comments' section to each posting or through email and other contact details that may be provided on a blog's 'profile' page. On the other hand, it is possible to set up most social media sites to distribute only to a small group of friends, and there is a growing number of niche social media sites designed around more intimate sharing with just the family (http://notabli.com/) or even just a 'significant other' (http://couple.me/), making it unambiguously dialogic.

Again, it is important to differentiate between what a given social media application does or has been designed to do and how its users use and perceive it. Those attempting to define weblogs and weblogging, for example, frequently stress the importance of interaction with bloggers' audiences in those definitions, positioning weblogging as an essentially telelogic practice (Conniff, 2005; Halavais, 2005; Nardi, Schiano & Gumbrecht, 2004; Rettberg, 2008; Walker, 2005), since most implementations of blogging allow for and appear to encourage interaction. Nardi, for example, asserts that 'Blogs then, are a studied minuet between blogger and audience. Bloggers consider audience attention, feedback, and feelings as they write' (Nardi et al., 2004). While Halavais acknowledges that 'a large number of bloggers might be classified as "mumblers"... who seem to post weblogs to a void, without obvious comments or reader', and goes on to say that 'Even in this case, though, it is clear that one of the motivations for blogging is feedback through comments, links, and other channels' (Halavais, 2005). As Halavais' choice of term reveals, there is some stigma attached in both media and academic accounts to people who do not appear to use blogs in a telelogic fashion – just one example of how, as we will explore in the second half of this chapter, the wider social context for a particular communicative form can influence how people take it up and use it.

This is consistent with a tendency among media scholars to associate particular media forms exclusively with whatever relationship between communicator and audience appears best suited to that medium. Thus face-to-face interaction is predominantly framed as a dialogical situation while radio- and television-mediated practices tend to be framed as broadcast or monological situations. In practice, as many scholars in the social constructivism school have pointed out in other contexts, technologies can be adopted in a variety of ways which do not necessarily follow what later appear to be its 'natural' potentials. Radio was once seen as a 'one-to-one' medium while telephones were initially seen by some as a broadcasting medium (Pool, 1977, p. 19) – precisely reversing the way in which they are used now, which seems inevitable or technologically determined (Marvin, 1988; Winston, 1998); and the ARPANET, the precursor to the internet, was designed to give remote users access to data and processing power, not to facilitate interpersonal communication (Hafner & Lyon, 1996, p. 189). Moreover, as interactive digital technologies are increasingly incorporated into existing practices (as with interactive television), the boundaries that seemed to be distinct between broadcast and interpersonal communication have begun to blur.

CMC is increasingly interlinked

It is a commonplace of textual analysis that any piece of text is explicitly or implicitly linked to a variety of other texts – what Genette calls 'paratexts' (Genette, 1997). As CMC has moved increasingly to a web-based hyperlinked platform, however, and as SNS providers in particular seek to chart and maximise the connections between their users, the interlinking of messages with other messages and data, whether intentional or automated, has become easier and more prevalent. This has important implications for risk and disclosure on social media in particular. If I used Facebook to communicate with friends about a party I have held that you were at, I might include a picture showing some of the other people who were there, including you. Facebook intentionally fosters extensive interlinking of messages and would encourage me to 'tag' the people in that picture and their names if they are mentioned in my textual description of the event. Should I comply, not only might news of this event go to my friends, but it might circulate to your friends and the friends of all of the people mentioned or photographed. Although it is possible to opt out from being implicated in other people's narratives in this way on Facebook, that is not the default setting.

Facebook is the service that appears to have refined the provision and encouragement of interlinking of postings most effectively, although largely within its own semi-private ecosystem. Even before Facebook, however, one of the defining characteristics of what was dubbed 'Web 2.0' (O'Reilly, 2006) is that online entities have ways to interconnect with one another and become interdependent – through APIs (application program interfaces) for example or using protocols like RSS (Rich Site Summary). These let individual users or programs automatically pull information from one site and insert it or manipulate it in another. One contentious example of this in practice was the 'Girls Around Me' iPhone application. This used the API provided by the Foursquare location-based 'check-in' application to find women (or men) near its users' current location and display their profile pictures (BBC News Online, 2012). Thus, by using profile pictures intended by Foursquare's users to help their friends identify them and overlaying them on a dating-based application, they changed the context and thus the meaning of that publicly available information completely.

In addition to these direct interlinking effects, the fact that social media communications are being read using devices capable of, at any point, performing searches for supplementary information means that effectively any message is tacitly interlinked with a vast array of other messages and information easily retrievable at the point of reception. Genette in the context of printed literary texts refers to two different paratexts – peritextual elements and epitextual ones, where the latter is not 'materially appended to the text' (Genette, 1997, p. 344). This distinction in the case of online texts is increasingly arbitrary. To return to my party example, not only might the fact of your attendance at my party be revealed directly by Facebook but once your name or some other searchable piece of information was mentioned, a profile of you which might reveal reasons you should not have been there could be constructed through online search with a few clicks.

Of key importance looking to the future is the potential for *automatic* interlinking of increasing amounts of 'given off' metadata with each message shared online. In mentioning my party online, I might incidentally provide information about its exact location (frequently derivable from the data shared when you take a picture on a smartphone), its time, who was there (thanks to facial recognition) and even whether some or all of them were unclothed (using software that scans images for skin tones). All of that information could be cross-linked automatically by search engines or SNSes themselves to tell a story about the party and those attending, without any human intervention. We will discuss this further in Chapter 6.

The difficulties posed by the interlinking of telelogic communication expose the weaknesses in the conventional neoliberal defence of social media – that privacy controls are available for those who wish to use them so that each social media user is responsible for monitoring their own self-presentation and, if they aren't happy, they can just withdraw from the service(s). Thanks to interlinking and, increasingly, the automated nature of social network disclosure, it is not sufficient to carefully control your own social media postings – you must also be aware of the possibility that others will post evidence that undermines your self-presentation and that that evidence will in turn be interlinked with your original self-presentation.

Those who do such posting may not have malicious intent. For example, Litt et al. in their study of third-party 'face threat' on Facebook (2014) found, broadly, that less than a third of people reporting harm caused by others felt that it had been intentional (Litt & Birnholtz, 2014). Instead, the problems seem often to arise because third parties do not understand the risks of harm when they share information from one context into another. They found that only 6 per cent of the harmful or uncomfortable examples given by survey respondents involved others revealing unambiguously counter-normative public behaviour. Instead, 'the overwhelming majority of norm violation stories submitted (39.3 per cent) showcased others exposing the target engaged in behaviour that was normatively acceptable to one sub-audience on Facebook, but counter-normative to another' (Litt et al., 2014, p. 5).

It is also possible that because not just what you say but your connections with or affinity towards friends, celebrities, news articles and cultural products are now articulated, you will be judged by those connections – whether accurately or inaccurately. One (deliberately) provocative study found that it could predict with a high degree of accuracy whether a given Facebook user was likely to be homosexual by counting the number of their Facebook 'friends' who had publicly stated a homosexual orientation – and this could be calculated even when a target user's privacy settings meant that their profile could not be seen by the researchers (Carter & Behram, 2009). A subsequent study found that when researchers had access to enough data about what US Facebook users had 'liked' using the service's Like feature (which is currently public by default), they could predict a man's sexual orientation 88 per cent of the time, whether they were Caucasian or African American 95 per cent of the time and whether a person was a Democrat or Republican 85 per cent of the time (Kosinski, Stillwell & Graepel, 2013).

CMC: Imagining the anonymous other

CMC empirical research from the 1980s and 1990s relied on experiments that isolated online communication from offline communication and studied situations in which communicators had never met – often focusing on situations where both parties were using pseudonyms. It focused primarily on the manner in which the other party to communication is perceived and the effect of such perceptions on what is communicated.

Early research has been categorised as the 'Cues Filtered Out' school (Culnan & Markus, 1987), which suggested (consistent with Goffman's logic) that the lack of visual and audible feedback available to communicators would make it difficult for CMC users to get a clear sense of the person with whom they were communicating, and that this would therefore make it difficult to use CMC for anything but impersonal, task-oriented communication. Social presence theory (Short, Williams & Christie, 1976) was developed prior to CMC but was influential in early CMC studies – it focused attention on 'the degree to which a medium is perceived as conveying the presence of the communicating participants' (Rice, 1993, p. 452) but, as Rice's study suggested, there is often no clear connection between the affordances offered by a particular medium and its being selected as a communicative tool.

These researchers also noted that in their experiments CMC frequently resulted in anti-social behaviour ('flaming'). However, it became evident subsequently that CMC was frequently used for personal, emotionally charged messages and that flaming was less prevalent in workplaces than it had been in experimental conditions. Further research, culminating in what was called the SIDE model,[5] questioned the initial technologically determinist interpretation of the likely effects of CMC in this context and took into account that CMC users would attempt to fill in missing social cues, relying on whatever information was available (and possibly exaggerating the few cues that were available) – particularly where communication took place over a sustained period (Postmes, Spears & Lea, 1998). Walther noted that CMC often resulted in 'idealized perception' of the other and explained this with his model of hyperpersonal interaction. It draws on Goffman's theories of self-presentation (1959) and suggests that idealised perceptions frequently arise in asynchronous CMC because message senders take advantage of the time available to 'concentrate on message construction to satisfy multiple or single concerns at their own pace' (Walther, 1996, p. 26).

What these researches tended not to consider in detail is the *imagined social context* of communication. In most of the experimental studies, the social context is a completely artificial one. Naturalistic studies in this tradition have tended to study more-or-less *bounded* internet spaces – in studies of 'virtual communities', for example, researchers have looked at message boards on particular themes, mailing lists inside particular organisations and multi-user dungeons among other spaces (Hiltz, Johnson & Turoff, 1986; Kiesler, 1997; Postmes et al., 1998; Sproull & Kiesler, 1986). Participants in these spaces may not have met any of those with whom they are communicating and may not know their number or identities, but they normally can assume that the context of the communication is mutually understood (or, importantly, they *believe* that they can) and in case of disagreement they may be able to appeal to other members of the group, including leaders (whether formal or self-appointed). Certainly the lack of visual cues to communication may have an impact in such cases, but perception of others is likely also to be shaped by the nature of the online space itself, as noted above in the discussion of Thompson and new forms of interaction and as Hogan (2010) argues later. Participants in an online disease discussion group, for example, might reasonably expect the other participants to be supportive and eager to hear about their experiences, while participants in an open political discussion group on a contentious issue may envisage a much more critical set of potential readers.

In the case of general-purpose social media sites whose contents are normally intended to be private (at least rhetorically so), as with Facebook or Google+, the imagined audience may be sympathetic but there is no explicit frame dictating subject matter under discussion. Where responses are received, however, they are normally identifiable, not anonymous and respondents are normally at least minimally known to the writer (89 per cent of US respondents' Facebook friends are people they had met, according to one survey [Hampton, Goulet & Purcell, 2011, p. 27]).

In the case of the personal weblogger, the imagined social context is brought into even sharper relief. As with SNSes like Facebook, the personal weblog unusually lacks the explicit subject or organisational boundaries that would provide a ready-made social context. In its place the writers in this case may be expected to construct an *imagined* social context that gives subjective purpose and psychological security to their activity. Related to this, the relevance of anonymity in interaction – often treated as an important influence on online behaviour – is difficult to gauge in relation to blogging. Even when bloggers do not use their real names or provide pictures of themselves, they often reveal information which would allow others to identify them and, over time, they might reveal enough personal information such that they might come to expect readers to treat them as if their readers knew them. Likewise, commenters to weblogs can be pseudonymous but it is not clear to what extent such pseudonymous users might be identifiable to those whose blogs they post on. Lastly, it is unclear how or whether those readers who do not choose to reveal anything of themselves by posting comments might be perceived as a group by those who post. Might they be grouped mentally in an idealised way alongside the others who do respond? As Walther suggests, 'it is well accepted that, offline, we respond to others based largely on our expectations despite what their actual behaviour may present' (Walther, 1996, p. 28).

Boyd: Becoming 'hyperpublic' and Hogan: Performance or exhibition?

Several of these considerations were brought together concisely by danah boyd and applied directly to social media (2008a, 2008b). She identified four key properties of communications in what she termed 'networked public spaces': 'persistence' (through time), searchability, replicability and invisible audiences. She saw these characteristics leading interactions to become 'hyperpublic' (d. boyd, 2008b, p. 128). Not all of these four properties are common to all social media, however. Certainly, almost any digitally mediated communication is replicable because of the way digital devices normally make copies of what they receive in order to display them – even services like Snapchat which were intended to facilitate the exchange of pictures that only remain on a receiver's screen for 10 seconds can be easily subverted (Ludwig, 2013). The other properties boyd identified are more variably present in social media, however. To take Twitter as an example, the searchability and persistence of tweets is variable. Twitter itself and companies with which it is in partnership can search any tweet and search backward through time to the beginning of the service. Members of the public without the funds to pay a Twitter partner company and who attempt to search the entirety of Twitter's archive by keyword will only get a limited number of 'matches' – typically going back a week. This variability in both capabilities and practices on specific platforms points to a need for detailed consideration of the specific contexts surrounding online interactions, as I will explore theoretically in the next section and will elaborate upon with case studies of specific social media services in the next two chapters.

The characteristics boyd identifies are, nonetheless, useful as a summary of the principal 'risk characteristics' of social media that can lead to interactional trouble.

Hogan (2010) draws a distinction between 'performances' and 'exhibitions' online. The former he characterises as happening synchronously and 'subject to continual observation and self-monitoring as the means for impression management' (ibid., p. 384). To him, much social media use is the creation and maintenance of artefacts (pictures, postings, etc.) which are curated as if in an exhibition, and since 'it is simply impractical to have a human curator pore over one's social information and devise a unique and relevant exhibit for each person, on demand [so] computers have taken on this role' (ibid., p. 381).

In the article he makes a useful distinction between 'that which requires the present in order to be understood and that which makes no such demand' – calling our attention once again to the importance of time as a context for message reception. In calling attention to the existence of a (generally algorithmic) 'curator', he also implicitly highlights the often hidden power of code to shape an interaction online, a subject to which we will turn next. He also implicitly references what I will refer to as 'local norms' of particular internet services (as distinct from what I term the wider 'societal norms' which individuals may share, for example, as a result of their socio-economic status or cultural background). He suggests (echoing boyd) that participants in social media are mindful of the unintended audiences for their material:

One might not be posting for one's parents (or children or students) on Facebook, but again, one is posting in light of the fact that these individuals may have access; these individuals define the lowest common denominator of what is normatively acceptable.

(ibid., p. 383)

The explanation he gives for 'how in an age of profound surveillance (both from authorities and peers), individuals still submit content that is unambiguously questionable' is that different sites imply different expectations and therefore 'one may have a clean profile on Facebook but a series of lewd pictures on Xtube.com' (ibid., p. 383). Crucially, he suggests that (when making 'exhibitions') 'it is likely that people do not create sophisticated projections of their social network, nor need they. Instead, their behavior is in reference to specific salient individuals, who are small enough in number to be coherent'. In subsequent chapters I will provide some evidence to support this characterisation of many social media users. In one sense, it is true that people do not 'need' to create sophisticated projections of their social network – they are psychologically able to exhibit themselves precisely because they do not create them. However, the consequences of this lack can be damaging if, as he notes in his conclusion, 'misunderstandings about the basic ontological structure of data, its curation, and exhibition give rise to new unintended problems: social information overload, collapsed contexts, accidental disclosures, and "identity" theft' (ibid., p. 384).

Wider contexts of social media use

So far we have been treating social media's spaces of interaction as given, and users' understanding of them and framing of their use as individual decisions taken at the time of a given interaction. However, there are many relevant prior contexts for each interaction, which shape the form that interaction takes. We have already discussed whether an interaction is understood to take place in a backstage, side stage or front stage region, whether it is addressed to a specific or indefinite audience, whether that audience can respond or is expected to, and the extent to which the interaction is understood to have both a primary and a subsequent secondary reception. To these 'micro' interactional considerations, one can add a number of overarching macro-level forces, which may also influence how interactions take place online. Lessig (2006b) provides a convenient outline of the potential categories into which these forces can be grouped – legal, market, norms and what he terms 'code' – the ways in which technological forms (like the design or capabilities of a particular piece of software) can encourage or constrain certain forms of interaction.

Legal

In their everyday interactions on social media, most users are unlikely to have to consider the legal environment or environments that govern their activity. This is reflected by, for example their documented reluctance to read, for example, written privacy policies (Milne & Culnan, 2004) as noted in Chapter 2. Early on in the history of the development of the internet, a number of prominent pundits and activists – most famously John Perry Barlow (Barlow, 1996) asserted that governments could not and should not attempt to control speech online. Western governments have generally at least paid lip service to the notion that internet-based communication should be regulated as little as possible (Clinton, 2013). Nonetheless, in practice what users do and the risks taken by them take place within a web of governmental and corporate regulations. International and national governmental regulation may govern the extent to which what users produce online may be accessible by their fellow citizens, government agencies or companies seeking to use it for marketing purposes and whether their employers or potential employers may be entitled to read it. And as Lessig notes, 'Copyright law, defamation law, and obscenity laws all continue to threaten ex post sanction for the violation of legal rights' (Lessig, 2006b, p. 124).

A large proportion of the governance of internet-mediated interaction has been left to (largely unaccountable) companies and industry groups. Facebook, for example (in common most likely with other major social media companies), has largely 'outsourced' the regulation of content posted by users to ill-paid contractors across the world (Gillespie, 2012). In authoritarian regimes like China, a substantial amount of the policing of social media content for dissenting views is also done by companies (Dong, 2012). Facebook's numerous changes in its privacy policies and default settings (Waugh, 2011) have arguably not been the result primarily of direct regulatory pressure, but are rather the result of conflict between what advertisers would like (which has tended to push Facebook towards more permissive privacy settings) and public opinion as expressed by Facebook users and in the media, which is only secondarily reacted to by politicians.

Market

As noted above in the case of Facebook, markets also represent an important constraint on and shaper of the operation of the spaces in which people interact on social media. The vast majority of online social media spaces are run by for-profit organisations. For the most part, their primary source of revenue is advertising, whose value depends firstly on the number of users they can attract, secondly on the value of each user linked to their propensity to spend, and thirdly (and most appropriately to the social media) on the ability to target such users with precision based on the information about themselves they give or 'give off'.

The form that these online spaces take must be appealing to potential users or they will either fail to adopt it or desert the space and move to another more congenial one. However, as the majority of these spaces do not get the majority of their money directly from users but indirectly from advertisers and others, there is no necessary connection between the needs or interests of the users of such services and what they will be offered (which in the end must provide what the market demands).

As Lessig remarked, 'advertisers reward popular sites; online services drop low-population forums' (2006b, p. 124) – this may take place even if less popular sites or online forums are fulfilling a public service role. Conversely, although clearly there are still opportunities for new websites to emerge and thrive, there are several reasons why good ideas or socially useful ones may not thrive in the face of market power or the inherent advantages in existing social media organisations. Services that do not have the resources to buy brand recognition can struggle to gain attention, and while at a small scale they may not cost a great deal to maintain, those costs can rise dramatically if a small-scale experiment takes off. Once users have committed to a popular social network and their friends have done so too, it can be difficult for new social network-based services in particular to take on an existing contender. The value of a network to its users increases greatly – some suggest exponentially – as the number of users increases – what has been dubbed 'Metcalfe's Law' (Shapiro & Varian, 1999, p. 184). To reach the mass market, social media organisations are increasingly dependent on a web of hardware and software support from third parties. This support may arise organically through user demand or it may arise through direct and indirect investment and subsidy by financially powerful institutions.

To give an example, a high-profile social media service like Twitter does not benefit only from the value that users attach to being able to reach a potential audience of millions, it also benefits from the existence of an ecosystem of third-party websites. These use its APIs and freely available data streams to provide a number of complementary services (e.g. reputation quantification through services like Klout.com, brand monitoring through recon.io). It also benefits from the bundling of Twitter tools with smartphones and in desktop operating systems, and from the increasing propensity of the media itself to use Twitter and to publicise Twitter events. Likewise these factors, as much as the technical capabilities that Facebook offers, may explain how it is that that company can claim 1.15 billion users (Facebook, 2013a) while the principal non-profit alternative, Diaspora – an open-source attempt to build a social network without advertising – can claim fewer than half a million members after three years of operation (diasp.eu, 2013) despite considerable journalistic coverage.

Norms

This deceptively simple term encompasses a potentially huge variety of different macro-level social influences on behaviour in social media – too large a number to be exhaustively covered in this volume. Lessig in his book and other researchers of CMC like Hogan (2010), above, have tended to concentrate on local norms. Lessig suggests, for example, that if you talk about politics in an online discussion forum devoted to knitting you may be criticised for being off topic (Lessig, 2006b, p. 124). These norms may be explicit (e.g. in 'Frequently Asked Questions' files and 'community guidelines') or may be tacitly understood and policed informally within online spaces.

In addition to these local norms there may be a range of 'societal norms' which vary between national cultures and between different social groups or generations. As noted in Chapter 2, it has been suggested by some scholars that young 'digital natives' have a different, more permissive attitude towards online privacy than older people (Palfrey & Gasser, 2008; Solove, 2008). National cultural norms have also been cited, suggesting that Germans are more concerned about privacy on Facebook than Americans because culturally the former are more risk averse (Krasnova, Veltri & Gunther, 2012), or that Chinese people and policymakers see the value of privacy differently to people in the West (Lu, 2005).

Code

As the title of Lessig's book – *Code: and other laws of cyberspace: version 2.0* (2006) – suggests, he was primarily interested in exploring the way in which online spaces are 'regulated' by the programming 'code' or 'architecture' used to create and maintain them:

The software and hardware that make cyberspace what it is constitute a set of constraints on how you can behave... In some places the transactions you engage in produce traces that link the transactions (the 'mouse droppings') back to you; in other places this link is achieved only if you want it to be. In some places you can choose to speak a language that only the recipient can hear (through encryption); in other places encryption is not an option. The code or software or architecture or protocols set these features, which are selected by code writers. They constrain some behaviour by making other behaviour possible or impossible. The code embeds certain values or makes certain values impossible.

(Lessig, 2006b, pp. 124–125)

His chief concern was to make these constraints visible in order to contest and debate them. As he notes, 'architectural constraints work whether or not the subject knows they are working, while law and norms work only if the subject knows something about them. If the subject has internalized them, they can constrain whether or not the expected cost of complying exceeds the benefit of deviating' (Lessig, 2006b, p. 345).

Like him, I would wish to call attention to the ways in which software architecture (in this case of social media sites) can influence behaviour. Lessig, however, whose background is in law, tends to see code primarily as a constraint to action and does not clearly address how this 'code' can both shape and be shaped by the market, laws and norms that operate alongside it. To provide a richer, more nuanced theoretical vocabulary to analyse the interaction between code and society, let us turn to Feenberg.

Feenberg's critical theory of technology (Feenberg, 1999) provides a sociologically informed framework that recognises the reciprocal interplay between a technology's development, its eventual technical features and its social adoption. He recognises that 'technology is not merely a means to an end; technical design standards define major portions of the social environment' (Feenberg, 1999, p. 78) but adds that 'differences in the way social groups interpret and use technical objects are not merely extrinsic but make a difference in the nature of the objects themselves' (Feenberg, 2002a, p. 6).

He describes the process of the design of a technological artefact as involving two analytically separate but intertwined processes – primary and secondary instrumentalisation. In primary instrumentalisation, a set of 'primitive decontextualized and simplified elements' (Feenberg, 2008, p. 15) with certain technical features are assembled to achieve a particular goal. These have to be 'systematisable' – that is, the artefact as designed has to be linked to its technical and natural environment – social networking services, for example, rely on the widespread availability of internet access among potential users. There are, however, inevitably a number of different ways in which elements can be combined to accomplish such goals. The process he calls secondary instrumentalisation describes the ways in which a variety of social pressures work to define the goal of an artefact in a particular way and to favour some potential implementations while excluding others. These 'valuative enactions' include

Legal, moral, and aesthetic constraints [which] intervene in the design and production process, determining an artefact capable of entering a specific social world.

(Feenberg, 2008, p. 17)

As the above implies, a variety of social actors are involved in this process. Feenberg mentions 'businessmen, technicians, customers, politicians and bureaucrats' (Feenberg, 1999, p. 11) but he does not attempt a comprehensive outline of relevant actors – he focuses on the roles of the market, legislators and designers on the one hand – the 'technical context of development and production' and the user's 'lifeworld context of disclosure and use' on the other (Feenberg, 2008, p. 23).

An example of the secondary instrumentalisation process that Feenberg uses is the widening of the definition of the internet from a data transmission mechanism to include interpersonal communication, spurred, he says, by 'a cultural shift that occurred unexpectedly among the user community' (Feenberg, 1999, p. 126). Although during the invention, design and initial adoption processes the nature of the emerging artefact is somewhat malleable (at least given the limitations of technical implementation inherent in primary instrumentalisation), Feenberg suggests that artefacts over time acquire 'technical codes':

Standard ways of understanding individual devices and classes of devices emerge, called 'black boxing' in constructivist studies of technology. Many of these standards reflect specific social demands shaping design. These social standards impose the technical code. Technical codes are durable, but they can be revised in response to changes in public opinion.

(Feenberg, 2008, p. 23)

In influencing how artefacts are perceived, these codes, he implies, also influence (to a greater or lesser extent) the ways in which a given artefact is used. They emerge through iterations of design and in response to the generation of further secondary instrumentalisations by the lifeworlds of those who adopt them. Such codes, says Feenberg, are 'similar to law in a democratic state' and 'establish stable regularities in social life' (Feenberg, 2008, p. 24). Unlike such laws, however, he argues that 'these codes are usually invisible because, like culture itself, they appear self-evident' (Feenberg, 1999, p. 88) (this echoes Lessig's point made earlier).

Feenberg is particularly interested in these codes when they result in what he calls 'formal bias' – systems or artefacts that favour a particular social group (Feenberg, 2008, p. 10) – because his approach is rooted in the political economy tradition. One can nonetheless usefully employ his framework in a more interactionist mode, as I will do in Chapter 6 in particular, extending the notion of bias to encompass systems and artefacts which favour particular forms of interaction, without attempting to assess the extent to which any changes to the patterns of interaction that result might favour particular groups.

He identifies two forms of bias, depending on the source of such bias.[6] Biases that emerge because of the nature or design of the artefact itself he terms 'constitutive bias'. These include the bias against disabled people inherent in a sidewalk designed without ramps. The second form of bias he calls 'implementation bias' – biases which stem from the way in which a particular artefact has been adopted and integrated into society. An example of the latter he suggests is the digital divide – 'it strengthens the rich at the expense of the poor, but only because the artefacts are distributed in a specific context of wealth and poverty, not because computers are inherently hostile to the poor' (Feenberg, 2008, p. 11).

This second form of bias, and the example chosen to illustrate it, help to expose an underlying ambiguity in Feenberg's work – is the object of his analysis particular artefacts as designed objects or is it a set of practices centred around such artefacts? He often appears to be discussing the former but it is apparent in his introduction of the notion of 'implementation bias' that his primary focus is on the latter, since he suggests that artefacts that are problematically biased in one implementation (i.e. biased when made part of particular practices) may be blameless or even beneficial when in a different context.

The focus of Feenberg's work is on the necessity to tackle harmful biases through more democratic forms of technological design. He argues (counter to what he describes as the technological essentialism of Heidegger & Lovitt (1977) and Habermas (1970)) that while under capitalism the biases of technology tend to buttress the interests of the powerful in society, this is not an inherent weakness of technology itself. He concludes:

A socialist technical code would be oriented toward the reintegration of the contexts and secondary qualities of both the subjects and objects of capitalist technique. These include ecological, medical, aesthetic, urbanistic, and work-democratic considerations that capitalist and communist societies encounter as 'problems,' 'externalities' and 'crises.'

(Feenberg, 2002b, p. 184)

While the term 'bias' as used by Feenberg tends to imply a harmful influence, it is more useful than other terms used to describe how technology influences practice like 'affordances', 'limitations' or 'regulation'. A technical code does not merely either enable or prevent certain behaviours – it can also *encourage* certain forms of behaviour – presumably a socialist technical code in Feenberg's model would encourage the practices it enables to be done in a more ecological fashion, for example.

In the case of social media, I will argue that the technical codes may often enable the limitation of circulation of sensitive personal information (through the provision of privacy tools) while at the same time in practice encouraging the release of such information through 'constitutive biases', as in the manner in which postings may be openly visible by default.

Clashes, compromises and co-creation

For the most part in this chapter, these micro- and macro-level influences on behaviour have been discussed independently but of course each of these individual factors can interrelate with the others in complex ways. Code and societal norms can reinforce each other – it has been suggested, for example, that the Cyworld internet service in Korea takes the particular technical form it does 'as an extension of pre-existing modalities of communication in to-day's Korean youth culture' but that in turn its structure encourages and intensifies the need to maintain existing social links in this new space, 'placing on the user a social obligation to stay constantly signed-in' (Choi, 2006, p. 184). Local norms may clash with societal norms – for example, as Livingstone observes, 'teenagers may disclose personal information with up to several hundred people known only casually. This is in part because social networking sites typically display as standard precisely the personal information that previous generations often have regarded as private (notably age, politics, income, religion, sexual preference)' (2008, p. 404). Here also, as Livingstone implies, the code of a service – what is 'displayed as standard' – can further reinforce local norms.

This is consistent with Feenberg's analysis of the interaction between society and the technologies it invents and adopts. In his model, technologies do not emerge in natural, pre-ordained forms and dictate human behaviour in predictable fashions. Conversely, they are not infinitely socially shaped – they may have to take certain forms because of their primary instrumentalisation. While their secondary instrumentalisation (the social shaping of that technology through time) can bend a technology and associated practices in a certain direction, once a code emerges – a blend of technical implementation and social standards and interpretations – it can durably (though not irreversibly) influence practices.

A conceptual framework for studying risky social media self-disclosure

In summary, this review of theory in the areas of interpersonal communication and the sociology of technology suggests the following conceptual framework to analyse risky self-disclosure using social media.

Macro-level influences

Social media services have emerged and flourished globally thanks to the widespread availability of internet access, of hardware – particularly mobile phones – that enables ubiquitous sharing of text, pictures and video, and the emerging ability of internet sites and users to share and recombine content and functions – what has been dubbed 'Web 2.0'. This 'primary instrumentalization' (Feenberg, 2008) has subsequently developed and is being shaped (the 'secondary instrumentalization' process) in response to a variety of forces. This results in a set of 'technical codes' that are still emerging for different social media platforms that tend to regularise the user practices based on those platforms by providing a consensus view of what each technology can and should be used for. Alongside these codes, Lessig (2006a) outlines some other key influences on the way technologies are used – markets, law and norms (a mixture of what I have called local norms – Feenberg's 'implementation biases' (Feenberg, 2008) – and wider societal norms of behaviour). While there appear to be some core similarities in the way macro-level forces influence the forms and practices of social media worldwide, in the remainder of this book the sheer variety of social media platforms and national and regional markets, laws and societal norms worldwide means that it is inevitably impossible to generalise with confidence about social media in all contexts, but I will draw on my own research and those of others to analyse some key services and contexts in the chapters that follow.

Micro-level influences

The apparent emergence of 'implementation biases' in social media sites towards an unselfconscious sharing of potentially risky information about the self can only be partially explained by reference to the macro-level forces outlined above. Each instance of such sharing can be also envisioned at a micro level as a social interaction, and as such analysed in more detail to understand how social media practices are understood and framed by their users and why and under what circumstances the risks of self-disclosure are overlooked or minimised by users.

Goffman suggests that people generally attempt to control who they are interacting with – the conversational preserve – and what people know about them – the informational preserve (Goffman, 1971b). A key determinant of the kinds of social interactions people have and what they reveal in them, according to Goffman, is therefore whether such interactions are considered by those taking part to be public (or 'front stage') or private – (or 'backstage') (Goffman, 1959). When communication is mediated, this complicates matters. As boyd suggests, social media present particular potential problems for those who participate – what they say is persistent through time, searchable, replicable and its audience is invisible (d. boyd, 2008b). Why then does this not substantially constrain participation?

Meyrowitz (1985) suggests that under conditions of continuous mediated exposure, people may lose the self-consciousness required to maintain 'front stage' behaviour. Thompson's analysis of mediated communication (J. B. Thompson, 1995) highlights that communications are shaped by the intended or perceived audiences for communications and that these perceptions are not always accurate – moreover, mediated communications take place not just between a given set of actors at a single time (what I have called 'primary reception') but can also persist and be read in a different context at a time in the future – 'secondary reception'.

Implicitly, given that social media audiences are often partially or completely unperceived by people posting their information online, the number and kind of people who are imagined as the audience will be important in establishing the level of risk involved in such postings. According to Walther (1996), where there is an interaction between people who are not known to one another, they tend to make flattering constructions of each other. Even if the unknown audience is not seen in a positive light, Goffman suggests that in face-to-face situations unintended audiences of strangers are often ignored because it is assumed they will not use such knowledge of the poster against the participants of an interaction later (1971a).

In light of this, the next chapter looks at how much information social media users have about the people who read or view their postings and to what extent they seek such knowledge.

4
Imagining the Reader

As noted in Chapter 3, Thompson suggests that in mediated interpersonal interaction, if you are aware that your message is going to an indeterminate audience this might be a source of 'uncertainty and trouble' (J. B. Thompson, 1995, p. 97). A sense of the size, composition and attitude of the audience for what you write online would help you determine whether the online space in which they can be found should be considered 'front stage' or 'backstage', for example (Goffman, 1959) – of particular importance when communicating material about yourself that is potentially sensitive and therefore not normally delivered 'front stage'. On the other hand, Goffman also suggests there are a number of ways in which the perception of 'threat' in an environment where inappropriate audiences may overhear conversations can be defused – either by the overhearers exercising 'civil inattention' (Goffman, 1963a, pp. 83–88) or by the overheard assuming that the overhearers will not use what they hear to cause harm (Goffman, 1971a). As this illustrates (and as was discussed in more detail in Chapter 3) the nature of interactions is not influenced directly by the nature of the communicative space but indirectly by the awareness of and attitude towards that space that communicators have. This can also be influenced by broader forms of what Feenberg terms either 'constitutive' (inherent) or 'implementation' (socially shaped) bias (2008) in the way a given social media site is used.

What this chapter will therefore examine is the extent to which social media services enable their users to gauge their audiences, to what extent those users seek to do so, who they think of as their audience and the connection between their imagined and actual audiences. Interviews I have conducted with personal webloggers will help to illustrate some of the points raised. This chapter focuses on what in Chapter 3 I dubbed 'primary reception' – the period immediately following the publication of a message when it is generally expected to be heard or read. The next chapter focuses on 'secondary reception' – how social media messages may linger through time and how this is (or is not) perceived.

Websites (social media sites and others) have many ways in which they can (and do) track readers and gather information about them in order to more effectively tailor content or sell advertising to them. At the most basic level of what is known as web analytics, organisations can use information that visitors' web browsing software provides automatically. This is stored in a web server's 'weblogs' and records readers' location, the link they followed to get to a page or the kind of web browsing software and hardware they are using. Using more sophisticated tools like internet 'cookies', organisations can spot returning web users and track individuals from site to site – even collecting information on what they type into forms or looking at what parts of a web page they move their mouse over (Angwin, 2010; Froomkin, 2000). And of course social media services in particular gather a great deal of personal information, voluntarily provided by users in the course of their profile building, maintenance and use of these services, all of which is visible to the owners of such services and often shared with advertisers (and potentially others with legal authority).

However, it is not just large organisations that can in principle take advantage of these technologies to gain a better awareness of their audiences. Depending on the social media they are using, 'ordinary' users may be able to get at least an imperfect view of who reads their work – sometimes using the same tools that are used by professional website producers. Before analysing what is and is not possible for users to find out depending on which service they use, it is important to recognise and account for a common characteristic of nearly all computer-mediated communication – a poverty of physical cues indicating the nature of the interaction when compared with face-to-face interaction.

Mehrabian's claim that only 7 per cent of a message's impact is in the text of that message itself (1977), compared with 55 per cent in the speaker's body language and 38 per cent in non-verbal aspects of speech, is contentious but the broad importance of extratextual communicative elements, both deliberate and 'given off', has long been recognised by scholars. Such elements need not be consciously attended to in order to be important. Indeed, as Hargie and Dickson point out, we are actively involved in the perceptions that we make rather than being merely passive recipients. Furthermore, we seldom attend to all that we might in any situation but tend to filter out the less conspicuous, less interesting or less personally involving elements. As such perception is inherently personal and ultimately subjective.

(Hargie & Dickson, 2004, p. 40)

Some of the relevant extratextual elements that come into play when self-disclosing and which are not readily available online include 'kinesic' and 'vocalic' aspects of interaction. Kinesic elements refer to facial expressions and gestures both of the speaker and the listener (Birdwhistell, 2011), while the 'vocalic' elements include tone of voice, volume and other auditory cues which 'sometimes contain a metamessage that lets the listener know how the verbal content is to be taken (e.g. "tongue in cheek", soberly, respectfully, etc.)' (Hargie & Dickson, 2004, p. 79). Together, these help participants in face-to-face conversations to observe how their message is being received and adjust both the message itself and its manner of delivery.

The physical context of online sharing

However large the potential audience for a given online posting might be, generally, the physical experience of making it feels private. This problem was noted in early discussions of the ethics of internet research:

On-line interaction allows users to 'publicly' interact from the 'privacy' of their home or workplace. As King (1996) notes, such a situation promotes a perceived sense of privacy. The ability to interact with others from the 'privacy' of one's home or workplace shapes the resulting definition of the online situation. Alone at one's computer, one may extend this situation into interactions on-line, making it easy for participants to define the situation as 'private' and interact accordingly.

(King, 1996; Waskul, 1996, p. 132)

Bratteteig, analysing digital storytelling, makes a similar observation:

To the user, the fact that the production tool is also a distribution tool is potentially confusing... Even when I know that I publish my text on the Internet, it is difficult for me as a non-journalist to imagine the potential number of readers that will have access to my text the minute I publish it. The text is still a text on my pc – the blurring of consumption, production and distribution tools into one tool (or tool box) makes it conceptually difficult to maintain these distinctions.

(Bratteteig, 2008)

Historically, the communicative modes envisaged by communicators have been strongly linked to the medium they are using or to the communicative situation in which they find themselves. If one speaks quietly in an empty room to another person, one does not expect others to know what one says. Conversely, someone addressing a television camera generally expects a wide potential audience. The presence of a television camera does not itself make the eyes of thousands or millions apparent to those appearing on the screen, but even when those televised are not in a studio, there are usually a sufficient number of other cues (additional participants like sound and lighting crew, the necessity to rehearse and possibly repeat what is said) to impart a sense of heightened occasion (and risk) in the production of any televised communication. Of course communicative 'leakage' could always occur – private diaries can be unearthed and published, private utterances can be caught on microphones – but such leakages are generally deemed exceptional and are not normally anticipated.

With social media-based sharing, however, the communicative context is blurred, both experientially and technologically. Changes in the hardware used for capture of audio and video may also contribute to this – recording the self or others using a handheld or tripod-mounted video camera is more obtrusively a moment of mediation than the same recording using a mobile phone or a camera built into eyeglasses.

As I will discuss in Chapter 7, it may be that if physical cues were more evident, social media use would be significantly less popular (or more often privacy protected). If typical social media practices were transposed to an analogous environment offline (perhaps writing a series of notes to your friends while in a pub and leaving them there, permanently), the risks and uncertainties that Goffman suggests we would try to minimise in most interactions would become more apparent.

The typical physical experience of posting to social media – sitting in front of a computer or phone and typing onto a screen not visible to others – does not change whether the poster is writing for him- or herself, for friends or for thousands. Each of these possibilities is open for any posting and unless the poster knows and is mindful of the typical size of their audience, there is no way for them to judge at the moment of production whether he or she is engaging in the online equivalent of writing a diary, conducting a chat in a pub or making an appearance on a televised chat show. As Charles, one of the personal webloggers I studied, remarked,

> Because I don't know who the people are who are looking at it and because I can't see them in a way they are not there and in a way it is anonymous and it is just like writing a diary in a bedroom and keeping a lock on it – you're not really aware of the fact that people are reading it.

As will be discussed further in the concluding chapter, it would be possible for social media software designers to provide intrusive cues and reminders to users about their potential or actual audiences as they post but they do not generally do so – possibly because this would not be in social media companies' financial interest if it reduced usage.

Not being able to see the audience means not having the instantaneous ability to shape and reshape one's communications based on expressions of approval or disapproval 'given off' by the audience 'kinesic' feedback (Birdwhistell, 2011). Any tailoring of the message has to be done in response to explicit written feedback which is less likely and, in any case, potentially too late to avoid harm.

In the case of written or photographic communication, shadings of meaning that can be delivered through particular tones of voice or postures are inevitably lost.[1] However, it seems likely that in many cases this lack is not felt at the moment of writing – the writer hears the tone of voice they intend to communicate in their own head as they write, unless they are particularly self-conscious. When writers do reflect and attempt to fill this gap, emoticons – graphical smiling faces like this one :-) – have been employed as a substitute for non-textual cues but the few studies available (Walther & D'Addario, 2001) suggest they have limited effectiveness in modifying reception of messages that contain them. They also cannot perceive the kinesic feedback (e.g. frowns or stares) that they might receive if delivering an unwelcome revelation face to face.

Lastly, as I will explore further in the next chapter, the rhythm of social media postings and responses may also have a misleading effect on how users perceive such exchanges. Generally, postings tend to receive the most responses (insofar as they receive any response) immediately after their appearance. The more rapid the responses, the more this might tend to give social media posting the rhythm and therefore the *feeling* of an (ephemeral) oral conversation rather than a (more or less permanently inscribed) written exchange. This contradiction may be most marked in conversations that take place using instant message services (which are now often embedded in other social media tools like Facebook). As a result, Voida et al. suggest that 'the majority of tensions in instant messaging stem from conflicts and ambiguity among the multiple, overlapping conventions of verbal and written communication' (Voida, Newstetter & Mynatt, 2002).

Digital literacy and audience perception

It requires no special expertise to correctly perceive the audience for a face-to-face interaction (or indeed for one-to-one-mediated communication), but attempting to define audiences and control them using software can be a complex process and the more fine-grained control one attempts to introduce, the harder such controls are to use and maintain. As a result, although Facebook for example allows multiple ways to subdivide one's readership from post to post, a representative survey of American teenage Facebook users found that 'the vast majority (81 per cent) say that all of their friends see the same thing on their profile' (Madden et al., 2013, p. 5).

The way Twitter's privacy controls operate is particularly interesting, as in addition to allowing users to make their tweets available only to followers who have been given permission by the tweeter, there are an array of other ways in which even 'public' tweets can have their audiences specified depending on how such tweets are written. However, while the way the syntax operates is documented on Twitter's site in the help documentation (Twitter, n.d.-a), it is not explained to new users when they create accounts, and as I will outline later there are aspects of the way Twitter operates which tend to bias users towards more disclosure than they might wish – something I also note below in the discussion of LinkedIn.

Compounding these problems, there appears to be a continual tug-of-war within social media companies like Facebook between commercial and apparently ideological imperatives driving them to change defaults and the architecture of the software to encourage greater openness and concerns raised by the public, media and government about the potential for unintended information release. A side effect of this, whichever way this battle is resolved, is that social media users have to learn to navigate and use privacy tools which change frequently and rapidly. For example, over 18 months in the period 2010–2011 Facebook changed its privacy policies eight times (Waugh, 2011), and it also frequently changes the way in which the privacy controls are presented to users – although always ostensibly to make them easier to use or more effective. With services as popular as Facebook there are always guides available to the management of one's privacy provided by third parties, but the rapidity of these changes means that such guides are often out of date and therefore not just unhelpful but potentially misleading and even harmful.

Surveys suggest that notwithstanding this, young people are fairly confident in their understanding of these controls while older people are more concerned. One US survey (covering all internet use, not just social media) found that 24 per cent of adults felt they had 'little or no' control over the personal information they shared online, but there's a significant split between those 55 and older, 30 per cent of whom felt this vulnerability, and 18–34 year olds, only 17 per cent of whom felt this way (Microsoft, 2013, p. 2). Another five-nation study found that 30 per cent of adults and 23 per cent of children aged 8–17 felt they had 'little or no' control over their online reputations (Brackenbury & Wong, 2012, p. 15). A study of US teenagers found that only 8 per cent said that managing Facebook privacy controls was 'somewhat difficult' and 1 per cent 'very difficult' (Madden et al., 2013, p. 8).

Surprisingly little work appears to have been done to measure the extent to which confidence or lack of confidence is actually warranted – for example, the extent to which users have used the privacy controls at their disposal correctly. Such studies as do exist (Acquisti & Gross, 2006; M. S. Bernstein, Bakshy, Burke & Karrer, 2013; Brandtzaeg, Luders & Skjetne, 2010; Livingstone, 2008) are outlined in the sections on Facebook and Twitter that follow. They tend to suggest that when tested, social media users are not as aware and capable as they sometimes believe themselves to be.

Social media services and what they reveal to users about audiences

Thus far, I have discussed characteristics social media have in common, but social media applications vary widely in what information they offer their users about how many and what kind of others read what they say. To the extent that awareness of audience can in turn influence interactions, each social media application can be considered to exhibit different forms of 'constitutive bias' (Feenberg, 2008, p. 10) towards different online sharing practices. There are hundreds of such services – each with different biases – but for illustrative purposes I will briefly analyse the audience monitoring and/or limiting tools offered by four leading social media services – LinkedIn, Twitter, Tumblr and Facebook, and (where studies illuminate this), how and to what extent users appear to employ such tools.

LinkedIn

LinkedIn is built around the sharing of business-relevant personal information. It therefore has a different – even inverted – relationship to privacy than many other social media sites. While most social media sites allow users to control who has access to their profiles and postings on the presumption that unanticipated visitors might be unwelcome, LinkedIn only lets users limit access to certain parts of their profiles like their photographs, and implicit in the structure and business model of the site, unanticipated viewers are not just accepted but sought after as potential employers or customers. Any time a user views another's profile – even without choosing to say anything – the person viewed is notified. Moreover, unless the visiting user elects to do so anonymously, their name and job title will be shared with the person whose profile they visited. Users are discouraged from browsing anonymously because (unless they have bought a premium membership) if they do so they cannot collect information about visitors to their own profiles. This collection of visitor data is clearly understood to be one of the more valued LinkedIn features, as at the top of the list of 'premium' (paid-for) features is the ability to gather further information about visitors, including the country they came from and what they were searching for when they found you.

Twitter

Like most social media services, Twitter can be configured to circulate only to a set of pre-defined 'followers', but this is not the default setting for Twitter users and according to one survey, fewer than one in eight people have elected to protect their tweets (Beevolve, 2012). Unlike with LinkedIn, you cannot discover who has read any particular posting. Your 'followers' will automatically have your tweets sent to them but they might not read them, and conversely, your tweets if public may be read by anyone searching for words or 'hashtags' that you used in a posting. People can also read your recent postings by going to your page without signing up as one of your followers.

There are a large number of actions related to a user or their profile that Twitter users may take that are automatically tracked and shared with those that they are reading. These are grouped under the prominent 'connect' button – at least if they follow standard Twitter protocols when sharing your information. Categories of interaction that are tracked include when a user decides to follow you, when you are added by them to a grouping of users they have created (a 'list'), when they make a posting a 'favourite' – for example for later reference – or (most commonly) when they 'retweet' – recirculate one of your postings – or when in a posting they refer to you by your Twitter or 'handle'. When you look at your profile page you are presented with a current count of the number of followers you have.

As noted earlier, there are a number of ways that the audience for a tweet can be directed or limited even when a twitter account is public. On the Twitter website, the interface to send a private 'direct message' or to send a public tweet is the same text box – although the way in which tweeting is presented to the user depends on the device they use and whether they use third-party software (and as with other social media sites) can change frequently. If you typed 'd drbrake keep this just between us' into this box, that message would be a 'direct message' visible just to me (and Twitter), while if you typed '@drbrake keep this just between us', the same message would be visible to anyone who visited your Twitter profile on the web, would be distributed automatically to anyone who was a 'follower' of both of us, and could be found by anyone searching for the words it contains. 'Hey, @drbrake keep this just between us' would be visible to anyone who followed you as well as to people who visited your Twitter profile (and again, anyone who searched for any of the words in the message).

There is evidence that this complex syntax can be poorly understood and that accidents can easily occur. A former US Congressman, Anthony Weiner, for example, accidentally sent a suggestive picture of himself publicly instead of directly to a fellow twitter user (Weiner, 2011), and there have been several other high-profile examples of 'mis-tweeting' (Kinder, 2013).

Twitter protects its users from unwanted messages by insisting that private messages can only be sent to people who 'follow' the sender, but as a consequence in order to carry on a conversation with another Twitter user about something they have tweeted, users are often forced to start that conversation by addressing a public message to the target individual and unless at that point the conversers elect to mutually follow one another, that conversation will continue in a semi-public fashion (visible to followers of both or to visitors of their web profiles). Because of what Goffman termed 'civil inattention' (Goffman, 1967, pp. 83–88), the audience for such interchanges may feel it would be inappropriate to join such conversations, thus maintaining the illusion of their privacy.

There is a large ecosystem of services, such as http://www.twitonomy. com/ and http://twtrland.com/, with which users themselves (or those interested in particular users) can track almost anything quantifiable about Twitter users and their postings and profiles – for example you can easily discover which of your tweets has been 'retweeted' (quoted by others) the most, who among those who have retweeted you has the most followers, and where your followers say they come from (by city and country). These services, however, are designed primarily to serve 'power users' like businesses or celebrities who use Twitter strategically – it is not clear how much they are used by the broader Twitter-using public. Moreover, there is a great deal about the nature of the audience which is either not tracked (postings that are pasted instead of being retweeted) or indeed which is not trackable – the attitude and attentiveness of those people who have been sent any given posting, for example.

Despite the apparent constitutive and implementation biases in Twitter that encourage users to treat their postings as public and track their reception, Marwick and boyd in a study of Twitter users found that some users resisted this framing and, implicitly, even the awareness of their audiences. They remarked:

Respondents with relatively few followers typically spoke about friends, but some focused on themselves [...]

'I think I write to the people I follow and have twittered something recently. And I also tweet to myself. Is that wrong?'

'I guess I'm tweeting to my friends, fans ... and talking to myself.'

Emphasizing 'me' may also be a self-conscious, public rejection of audience: 'Myself. It is MY Twitter account so, it's mostly about me.'

'< Who do you tweet *to*?> No one & I love that. Or maybe myself five min. ago: I write the tweets I want to read. I don't tweet to anybody; I just do it to do it.'

Although these individuals may not direct tweets to others, they are not tweeting into a void; they all have followers and follow others. Their emphasis on 'me' implies that for them, Twitter is personal space where other people's reactions do not matter.

(A. Marwick & boyd, 2011, pp. 118–119)

Tumblr

In several respects, Tumblr's facilities for audience awareness are similar to Twitter's. The practice of 'following' other Tumblr blogs is an important part of the norms of the service – indeed, you cannot register without following some blogs and you can 'reblog' (retweet) or 'like' (favourite) postings, for example. As with Twitter you can also indicate desired audiences for particular postings by 'tagging' a posting to indicate its topic. Some tools to explicitly control the audience for postings are available but they are primitive – your 'primary' Tumblr blog has to be public but you can create additional 'secondary' blogs that can only be accessed by users with a password. You cannot set different explicit levels of security for each posting on a blog as you can with items of content on Facebook, for example.

Unlike Twitter, it does not have a large 'ecosystem' of services to track and quantify audience response and a user's influence. On the other hand, in one particular aspect it offers its users more knowledge of readers than Twitter. With Tumblr (and with most blogging services), it is possible to install external services to enable you to roughly track the number of readers of any individual posting and their locations,[2] whether or not those readers do anything public with your text. This feature is not provided by default, however – to do this users have to register separately for a service like Google Analytics and follow instructions that Tumblr provides but does not highlight when setting up accounts: http://www.tumblr.com/docs/en/google_analytics.

Facebook

In certain respects, Facebook appears to provide a great deal of information about the audience – in others very little. The maximum potential audience for any posting is defined by the user. Each posting and each element of content on a user's profile has its own defined potential audience – either the default audience – normally user-defined 'friends' – or one of several possible sub-audiences the user can set up using Facebook's privacy settings. As with most other services, Facebook does not provide you with any way to ascertain who among the potential readers of a message has actually read it. Assessing one's audience on Facebook is even more difficult than it is on other SNSes as, in addition to controlling who is allowed to see particular postings according to users' settings, Facebook uses an algorithm that selectively passes on or conceals any given posting to others depending on its likely 'interestingness'. This is necessary because of the astonishing volume of postings that its users are producing – the company estimates that 'every time someone visits News Feed there are on average 1,500 potential stories from friends, people they follow and Pages for them to see' (Facebook, 2013b). A group of researchers from Facebook (M. S. Bernstein et al., 2013) were able to compare the number of readers Facebook users said they felt they had for a post to the number of potential readers they actually had. The median post reaches 24 per cent of a user's friends, but Facebook users consistently underestimate the audience size for their posts, guessing that their audience is just 27 per cent of its true size. Their survey found that the most popular ways users gave to estimate the readership of a post was simply to guess (23 per cent), or to extrapolate from the number of 'likes' and comments a posting received (15 per cent). Unfortunately, the latter cue is not a good indicator – particularly where a message gets no feedback:

> the median audience [for such a post] was 28.9 per cent of the user's friends, but the 90 per cent range was from 1.9 per cent to 55.2 per cent of the user's friends. So, while users may be disappointed in posts that receive no feedback, the lack of feedback says little about the number of people it has reached.
>
> (M. S. Bernstein et al., 2013, p. 6)

An early study of Facebook users at a US university (Acquisti & Gross, 2006) illustrated strikingly the problems many users appear to have in understanding their privacy settings. It studied how expressed attitudes towards privacy were consistent with observed behaviour and found:

> Around 16 per cent of respondents who expressed the highest concern for the scenario in which someone 5 years from now could know their current sexual orientation, partner's name, and political orientation, provide nevertheless all three types of information – although we can observe a descending share of members that provide that information as their reported concerns increase. Still, more than 48 per cent of those with the highest concern for that scenario reveal at least their current sexual orientation; 21 per cent provide at least their partner's name (although we did not control for the share of respondents who are currently in relationships); and almost 47 per cent provide at least their political orientation.
>
> (Acquisti & Gross, 2006, p. 11)

A follow-up study of Facebook users at the same university (most of them undergraduates) found that between 2005 and 2011 they had significantly reduced the amount of profile information about themselves that they shared – however, there were some notable exceptions to this trend. 'High school, hometown, address, interests, and their favourite movies, books, and music' were all more likely to be made public in 2010 and 2011, a fact the researchers linked directly to changes in Facebook's privacy default settings (Stutzman, Gross & Acquisti, 2012, p. 25). Moreover, as they point out, compared with 2005 there are many more opportunities for Facebook users to share data 'privately' – that is, to potentially very large groups (including Facebook itself and third-party 'apps') but not to the whole internet. They noted four drivers towards increased 'private' disclosure:

> The number of profile fields available to Facebook members to share information expanded over time ... certain fields started being used dynamically, for repeated sharing: for instance, status updates in 2006 and the Timeline in 2011 ... more diverse user data started being generated by third-party apps (which were introduced in 2007) ... [and] friends connected to a Facebook user started being able to add information about that user for instance, by tagging individuals in photos in 2006, and by tagging their location in 2010.
> (Stutzman et al., 2012, pp. 26–27)

A smaller-scale study of 65 university students found that not one had been completely successful in using Facebook's privacy controls the way they intended, and 93.8 per cent of participants revealed some information that they did not want disclosed (Madjeski, Johnson & Bellovin, 2011).

Face-to-face research into people's ability to control their audiences online provides revealing detail. Livingstone's study of teenage users of social network software (Facebook, but also MySpace and others) found:

> When asked, a fair proportion of those interviewed hesitated to show how to change their privacy settings, often clicking on the wrong options before managing this task, and showing some nervousness about the unintended consequences of changing settings (both the risk of 'stranger danger' and parental approbation were referred to here, although they also told stories of viruses, crashed computers, unwanted advertising and unpleasant chain messages).
> (Livingstone, 2008, p. 406)

Brantzaeg, who studied Norwegian Facebook users across a wide age range, found similar hesitancy and confusion when interviewees were asked to perform privacy-related tasks:

> Several users seemed to have difficulties finding their way around Facebook's privacy settings. In many cases (particularly in the older adult sample), the participants gave up and sought help from the interviewer. Two of the older adults had never seen the privacy settings before and could not find their way around at all – indicating a generational gap in awareness of and ability to handle privacy settings. [...] Several of the participants, three young people and four older adults, did not realise that their profiles were visible to all members of the network Norway. Many confused the wording of My Networks with My Friends, and by doing so, their profiles were accessible to all people in the 'Norway network,' which contains nearly 1 million people.[3]
>
> (Brandtzaeg et al., 2010, pp. 1024–1025)

As with Twitter and Tumblr, Facebook enables users to track the recirculation of their postings to elsewhere in Facebook as long as the people who do this recirculation follow Facebook's own conventions for this (i.e. using the 'share' button rather than copying and pasting text). Because of Facebook's greater emphasis on privacy, it also allows users to formally limit others' ability to recirculate their content and even to retrospectively remove metadata others may have added (e.g. tags identifying a user on a picture shared by another). Again, these controls only operate where other users have used the 'conventional' means of sharing instead of, for example copying and pasting.

Compared with the other services mentioned, it is often difficult in practice to use tagging or other cues to provide a specific context to a particular Facebook posting in a way that would segregate it from other postings aimed at other contexts – at least in the case of the 'status update' which is the most prevalent kind of Facebook posting. In the case of LinkedIn, all postings are broadly presumed to be business-related. With Twitter and Tumblr as noted above, each posting can be given one or more 'hashtags' designed to draw the attention of a particular audience to the material discussed in that post. Facebook also provides a hashtag function but it does not appear to be widely used. A profusion of Facebook groups also exist into which users can elect to post on focused topics, but a Facebook status update does not have an explicit categorisation and although the Facebook poster can see and adjust the size of a posting's intended audience, the Facebook reader can only infer that information from the content of the post. Moreover, unlike LinkedIn, Facebook allows and encourages a multiplicity of different audience relationships.

Categories of reader knowledge

There are three kinds of knowledge about the readers and their response to social media that emerge from this analysis. Some is directly 'given' – when particular readers choose to respond directly to the author of a posting. Some is 'given off' (Goffman, 1959, p. 7) – for example, numbers of visitors to a particular weblog page and their country of origin can be estimated with the appropriate software because visitors' web browsers provide this information, and with Twitter and Tumblr, when others react publicly by either repeating or repeating and commenting on ('retweeting' and 'reblogging') something that has been said, the original poster is (normally) notified.

Much information about readers, however, is inferred, either because an audience is explicitly limited (e.g. a message can only be seen by Facebook 'friends') or because a user explicitly targets a specific audience by attaching metadata like a hashtag or placing the posting on a particular kind of service (a posting about genetics on the message board of white supremacist site stormfront.org has a different anticipated audience than one on the same subject on the BBC's news site, even though both may have in principle the same potential audience as they are visible to any passing browser and archived by search engines).

Much that might be visible in face-to-face communication is often unknown and unknowable when using social media to communicate in a 'telelogic' fashion – see (Ball-Rokeach & Reardon, 1988) and Chapter 3. If you use a site with privacy controls like Facebook or Twitter, you have a list available to you of the people who might be allowed to read something you have written using that particular service but you cannot know who among them has specifically chosen to read any one particular posting (with the exception of postings on certain specialist sites like LinkedIn). You do not have access to the emotional reaction of those who read a posting that might be 'given off' in face-to-face communication. As will be discussed in Chapter 5, you also cannot know when a particular posting might be read (though some sites like Twitter and Facebook make it difficult for readers to search back in time beyond a certain point).

Case study: How much do personal webloggers know and seek to know about their readers?

Some of them I don't even know what they look like. I don't even know that the gender they are is the gender they actually are.

– Donald[4]

My own research into UK-based personal webloggers suggests that they were unconcerned about the paucity of information that they had about those who were able to read what they posted, even though some of it could be potentially sensitive.[5] They seemed contented with the information about their readers that they inferred and, while some were curious, most did not seek confirmation of their actual audience through 'given off' data that they could have chosen to gather.

Though weblog analysis tools are available free of charge through a number of websites, there is only limited evidence that bloggers use such tools to track the number of visitors who read their pages. Of those who do use these tools, it appears few check their results regularly. A US survey found that nearly half of webloggers surveyed had no idea how many people read their sites (Lenhart & Fox, 2006). Similarly, a survey I conducted of personal webloggers based in London prior to interviewing them ($N = 150$) found only a third said they used traffic analysis tools and a third of these said they used them to check their traffic monthly or less often. It is possible that some of those without tracking tools would want them but were not aware that such tools exists or did not know how to make them work. In the case of the 23 bloggers I interviewed, however, there was little evidence that they were interested in tracking tools. Most interviewees were asked whether there were things they would like to be able to do with their weblogs that they had not done, but only two (Betty and Renia) evinced a desire to be able to better identify or track their readers.

Three of the six people interviewed who said they had used tracking tools were unenthusiastic about using them. Charles said at interview that he had stopped looking at his: 'I did actually sort of have a hit counter because I was intrigued to see whether anyone was reading and I was you know horrified to find that pretty much nobody was'. Nancy, similarly, said: 'I think I used to have one but... I don't know... it's not that interesting. It's just numbers'. And Frances was hard-pressed during her interview to guess how many people viewed her site:

Um... I don't know. I know there are a lot of bloggers who are really crazy about traffic and who really go by what their stats say. It's not something I check all the time but I think that's about ... and it goes ... looking at it weekly I think maybe there are about ... I don't know there must be ... I don't know there's about maybe 30.

Harriet, by contrast, said she was 'always checking my stats' but said she was doing it less often now because 'I don't quite have the same time to doss at work', and Annie was also a regular user of such tools. Betty's weblogging software was basic but she said: 'I'd love to have a tracker that told me everything about everybody. Because I'm really nosey. It just fascinates me'. She said she would not be willing to pay $6 a month to the weblogging software company to have more detailed information though, and for most of those interviewed the audience data when sought at all remain, in Nancy's words, 'just numbers'.

A few of the bloggers that were interviewed – Annie, Donald and Harriet – did use or contemplate using their internet skills and available tools to track individual readers as well as aggregate numbers. Of these only Annie (who has now ceased blogging) could have been described as a committed user, even though she does not have a technical background. She said she did not just count the number of visitors she got, daily, she also looked at 'where they are coming from and I can break it down and see how much time they are spending and what keywords they use to find my site and stuff'. She used the information available in an attempt to find whether the people who visited her site had weblogs themselves, 'just because it's interesting'.

While Donald did not track his user numbers – 'I wouldn't ever bother with that' – he did use his understanding of internet tracking once because a friend posted a comment anonymously that angered him and he traced the anonymous comment back to its source. In this case it seems to have been done as much as a display of expertise as anything, however: 'He seriously didn't realise that he could be traced through the internet which is quite funny. I just sat at work and traced his IP'. In Harriet's case she said she tracks the number of readers she has daily, but she worked in technology-related advertising and might therefore have come to see the use of reader-monitoring tools as normal, even though she was not exploiting this information for commercial gain. She did threaten to track down specific readers, but only after they had written a number of offensive and abusive comments on her site:

I said 'you know what – I have IP addresses for you guys. If you guys keep on continuing I can get it traced and you people will be ... ' He said 'oh you can't take threats from us ... ' funny enough this guy who I know as well from the blog he said 'I'm going to speak to a friend of mine'. And it all stopped.

There was little evidence in interviewees' blog text itself of direct appeals to the readers to identify themselves or state why they were reading or what they felt about the blogger him- or herself, although some bloggers asked their readers for help on a factual matter, for advice on what they should do in a given situation, or for feedback on the quality of their writing itself.

This apparent absence of concern about the audience is to some extent an artefact of the sampling method used to find interviewees – those who were seriously concerned about their potential audience and took care to control who might read them by managing the privacy settings for their weblog to exclude the uninvited would have been excluded from my study, which was focused on people who disclosed about themselves publicly online.

The mixed picture of concern and lack of concern about unknown readers accessing the interviewees' weblogs could also be attributable to a perception by the authors that their identities would not be discernable, thus insulating them from any non-virtual repercussions of what they wrote – consistent with other research into anonymity and blog disclosure (Hollenbaugh & Everett, 2013). However, the evidence from the blogs of those interviewed suggests this was not always the case. Although 14 of the 23 interviewees used some form of pseudonym instead of their names on their weblogs, of these, eight were more or less easily associable with their owners by the reader without any further contextual information.[6] In addition, the degree of self-disclosure evinced in the weblogs of the interviewees for this study themselves did not appear to bear any strong relation to the degree of perceived or desired anonymity. Two of the bloggers most open about their personal lives in their weblogs were also open about their identities – Annie gave her name and profession in order to promote her business, and Frances gave her (unusual) first name and (small) country of origin on her weblog.

Case study: How do personal webloggers picture their readers?

Although as noted above, the personal bloggers interviewed did not generally have much information about their readers either 'given' or 'given off', the lack of 'hard' information about their readers did not appear to worry most of them, even those who acknowledged that they could face embarrassment or worse if some of what they wrote was read by the 'wrong' people. While some of the bloggers expressed concern about this potential harm – and those who did normally said they took care not to reveal material that could harm them – there appears to be a strong tendency for bloggers to concentrate attention on the readers they *do* know about (the ones who comment, for example – who tend to comment sympathetically) and to ignore the rest. Frances, for example, was asked about those readers who found her by accident:

> Whether there's 50 of them or 500 of them is neither here nor there for you?
>
> No I'm pretty nonplussed. There could be 500 people reading for all I know but they don't comment. Lurkers – that's what we call them.

Most intriguingly, some of the bloggers interviewed appear to selectively disattend the fact that they have an audience at all. One of the interviewees referred to this as a 'slight form of insanity':

> I put things on my blog but I don't think of anybody reading it. Someone will say, 'what the hell did you write that for?' and I'll say 'oh yeah – sorry'. I just don't put two and two together – it's a slight form of insanity I suppose.
>
> – Elaine

This is all the more surprising as Elaine was not a blogger who set up her blog without telling anyone and had few readers – in fact, she was a journalist and wrote about her having set up a blog in a technology magazine. As a result she had (and knew she had) hundreds of readers.

However much or little the bloggers I interviewed actually reported that they know about their readers, it appeared that when they were writing their imagined communicative space was seldom primarily constructed based on that knowledge – as had already been noted implicitly in A. Marwick & boyd (2011). Most often they imagine themselves to be writing in a safe space occupied by well-disposed readers (whether strangers or close friends or a mixture). As Lenhart remarked in her own blogger study, 'Even with all the other sources of information, there are still audience members not captured or unknown, and the blogger fills in these "real" or "hoped for" readers through his or her imagination' (Lenhart, 2006, p. 83).

The presumption of sympathy is clear in Colin's reflections on why he moved from writing a private diary to writing a weblog:

mainly because there was nobody to read it [the diary]. There was no one to say, 'hey that's really good'. Um, just very difficult question to answer. It suddenly became an attractive proposition. 'Wow, I'm writing my diary. People are reading the bits I want them to read...' And I think in some cases they know what I feel. This is very nice.

Donald likewise referred to his readers as 'like-minded people':

In order to be able to write about things and not get into pointless arguments about them... Having the journal I thought 'I'll be linked to people I know – friends – and it'll be a much easier space to have discussions'.

Those who are not sympathetic are often assumed not to want to continue reading. Phillippa remarked, for example:

I think most people are pretty polite and if they don't like it they just move away. If they don't like it who's going to waste time writing a... why would you do that?

And Frances elaborates:

there seems to be this kind of unwritten code of ethics with blogging and commenting on other people's blogs and that's basically if you don't... if you really strongly disagree with what someone says then go ahead and comment and say that you disagree but don't ever be rude about it. If you don't like what you're reading then go to the next blog but don't waste your time here insulting me. I suppose it's kind of like if you walked into my house and you said, 'you know your curtains really fucking suck' then I would say 'get the hell out if you don't like looking at them'. So that's part of it. But I think most people who read blogs know that and I've had very few negative comments as well.

A few echoed Elaine (above) in saying they felt initially as if they had no readers at all, though unlike her they said this perception changed as they began to receive comments:

It started as a diary... it very quickly became, 'I'm writing a diary but people are reading it'. The moment you start to have comments on it, it actually shifts – or for me it shifted the way that I approached it. Suddenly I'm not writing something for me to read.

– Colin

When I first started I think I was writing it to myself.

– Isobel

Others recognised that they must have readers but appeared to find it difficult to admit to themselves:

There was the idea that one day it *might* be found... with blogs you seem to get... you seem to be online on a different format and there's always the *possibility* that someone was reading it.

– George (emphasis mine)

I won't permit myself to think 'oh yeah there will be thousands of people reading my blog' it just seems a bit self-important to think that really. Why would they read my blog when they can go and read the BBC News website instead?

– Elaine

This echoes the findings of Lenhart's study of webloggers. While maintaining that 'bloggers blog simultaneously for an audience and in apprehension of them' (2006, p. 102), she also found that 'bloggers sometimes forget exactly how public their blog really is' (2006, p. 138). This is in marked contrast to the results from Kendall's interviews with users of the LiveJournal blog service, who 'were conscious of their use of the filtering feature of LiveJournal to manage their appearance to different elements of their blended audiences. For instance, many were careful to keep their personal and work lives separate' (Kendall, 2007). To some extent this may be a sampling issue – those who maintained highly filtered LiveJournals would not have been included in the sample for this research – but may also reflect the nature of Kendall's snowball sample of mostly 'savvy computer users' which, as she acknowledged, 'do not represent typical LiveJournal users' and which she interviewed in 2003, early in blogging's development. More experienced weblog users or more experienced internet users in general may be more aware of the likely readership of what they post. Linda, for example, remarked:

They [her more experienced friends] were more aware than I was that other people can just click on [her journal] and see it. I still don't understand how the internet works so I have the idea that 'oh I'm just writing this to you guys so only you guys will get that'.

The perceived safe space that enables those I interviewed to write freely is often maintained in the face of experiences that one might expect to challenge that perception. For example, Annie, Elaine and George, in particular, were all aware that what they wrote might be read by a large audience but when interviewed they reported that they acted as if their audience is small – or even non-existent. Annie, as remarked earlier, claimed to check her site statistics daily and according to these she was getting around 100 visitors a week – at least a third of them new. Yet when asked whom she visualised when writing, she said: 'I usually write it for my friends, and I write it for myself'. Elaine as noted earlier created a weblog initially just to show magazine readers how to do one but said: 'I didn't expect anyone to read it you see – it was just a means to an end' – an attitude that persisted even though she used site-tracking tools and indicated that she was getting 250–1000 readers per week. George was fired from his job because of his weblog, but did not appear to believe his employers could really have found it:

> My social life was very fortunately separate from my working life. There was not much chance of work discovering it really I think. The official line is that a client typed their name into Google and my thing popped up. I don't know.

These are just a few of the most extreme examples of what appears to be a consistent pattern in the interview data. Whether bloggers wanted to be read only by strangers, only by their friends and family or by a mixture, they perceived their readership as being generally supportive and made up of the kind of people for whom they were intending to write. George remarked that, in his previous writing (for a music zine), 'people used to always really like it and they used to compliment my writing' and said 'most people seemed to like' his blog as well. Harriet suggested that her audience were 'people who buy into my ethos and values', and Donald spoke of his internet use as a way to find 'like minded people'. Conversely, they appeared to assume that people who did not like them or their blog would not find it or bother to read it. As Annie put it, 'I wouldn't go and spend time on blogs I don't like – so if they don't like my blog they don't have to spend time there', though in fact she subsequently closed her blog after being stalked through it.

Moreover, there is some evidence that if the desired audience changed, the perception of the audience would change to match it. At first Charles reported that he used his weblog for political postings, then he used it to allow friends and acquaintances to keep up with his life and feelings while abroad. When he returned, the purpose of the blog changed again, becoming less personal. As he put it,

I felt like what I was doing in America was pretty much honesty about my emotional states without any particular sort of editing – except the general that you do when you're emailing a bunch of friends some of whom you haven't seen for a long time. It wasn't pouring my heart out but I was fairly sort of honest. Whereas I think when I am doing the political stuff and more generally when I am just doing 'here is a [post?], here's a this here's a that' it's a bit more of sort of a public face if you know what I mean.

He refers here to the need for levels of disclosure to be appropriate to the intended communication recipients but the changing context in this case appears to be subjective – as his motivations for writing changed so too did his reported imagined readership.

Justifications were frequently given by the interviewees for their differing views of their likely readers and, since the desired audiences for these sites are different, the accounts of who would be likely to read the blogs and why also differ, often being diametrically opposite. For example, George said: 'blogs don't register much on Google do they? ... on the whole it's proper websites'. Harriet said at one point in the interview that she felt nobody read it. However, towards the end of the interview when she was explaining that she saw her blog as a potential tool for self-promotion: 'because Google now owns Blogger all the blogspot.com domains Google likes them so they get ... so it's easy for people to find you'. In other words, it is possible Harriet thought Google helped one to be found because she wanted to be found while George, who wanted not to be found, assumed that Google tended to avoid weblogs.

What is important to note here is not whether these interviewees were right or wrong about Google's interest in weblogs – in fact Google's search preferences are a closely guarded trade secret and also change over time so it would be difficult to be sure – but that each blogger appeared to interpret whether he or she would be found in the way that was most convenient to their prevailing vision of their communicative space.

The assumption of a sympathetic reader and its consequences

While the majority of the bloggers I interviewed saw their blogging as a means of staying in touch with known others, whose potential attitude towards what they had written might be known and adjusted for, there were substantial minorities who appeared to wish to communicate largely with or to strangers rather than friends or family or, intriguingly, who appeared to have a very distant and abstract vision of an audience 'in principle' or even no audience at all.

Five of the 23 interviewed appeared to be using what they wrote in their personal weblogs as a means to feel better about issues and feelings in their lives – as a form of what Harriet described as 'therapy'. Rather than using the weblog to invite comment or, through writing, to enable self-reflection, their dominant use appeared to be purgative. That is, by writing down thoughts or feelings – particularly those that bothered them – the authors could then put these feelings behind them. It appears that those who practised this 'quasi-therapy' felt it worked more as a palliative than as a cure for what was troubling them. As George put it, 'if someone pissed me off or annoyed me – generally if I put it down it didn't annoy me any more'.

To the extent the interviewees in this study appeared to be conducting quasi-therapeutic practices, they did not generally appear to be seeking responses to their writing from their readers, whether as judge/confessor or interpreter. Some did say they sought advice – perhaps to legitimate the fact that they were using a communicative medium – but generally it emerged that they tended to disregard it unless it suited them, as seen in this testimony from Harriet:

> You've still got to remain true to yourself and follow your gut. Just because you are putting your heart out to people doesn't mean you've got to do as they say. I'm not beholden to my commenters.

In any case, consistent with earlier quantitative studies (Mishne & Glance, 2006), comments on the sites of those interviewed tended to be brief and superficial, so it seems unlikely that the bloggers could have gained much insight from them.

This form of blogging practice would seem to be potentially the most problematic in its consequences for those who were motivated by it. Of course there is a long history of people from all walks of life keeping self-reflexive diaries in which they may write about matters that could harm themselves or others if made public, but because this form of practice involves by its nature sharing the most sensitive social information it exposes practitioners to greater risks than other forms of personal blogging.

If the writing itself serves as a quasi–therapeutic process, however, why not simply write a paper diary or keep it on your hard disk? George seems to suggest an answer:

> For years I tried to type a journal as opposed to write it – just in Word – but there was something really unfulfilling about it...I guess it's because it wasn't tangible perhaps – it was just on the screen...whereas with blogs you seem to get...you seem to be online on a different format and there's always the possibility that someone was reading it.

This response suggests that the possibility of readership in the abstract – as with the idea that a paper notebook might be read by a vague 'posterity' – prevents the practice from feeling meaningless and self-indulgent.

Others appear to blog as a means of creative expression, and as such appeared to put to one side the question of audience reaction or assume a positive one, as authors through the centuries have done.[7] If they kept the audience's reaction too much in mind, these interviewees appeared to feel it would stifle their creativity. They sometimes also referred to a norm of openness and truthfulness in writing, something I will return to in Chapter 6.

Conclusion

It appears that in overlooking or purposely ignoring the possibility that what they write will be read by those they are not addressing, social media users may be attempting to maintain an imagined informational or conversational preserve, in Goffman's terms (1971b) – see Chapter 3 for more on this theory. The bloggers I interviewed also appear to assume that those who are reading will be broadly sympathetic to what they express and interested in what they wish to say, even if they do not have a clear sense of who they are – an assumption which enables them to satisfy a desire to reveal facets of themselves that they would find difficult to express face to face.

As will be discussed in Chapter 6, there are a variety of 'implementation biases' (Feenberg, 2008, p. 10) which also come into play, encouraging social media users to see social media tools as being appropriate for certain goals – the evidence in this chapter suggests that these perceptions of what social media should be used for might feed back into selective perception by users of what they are used for and by whom.

5
Time and Memory in Social Media

As I briefly outlined in the section 'Thomson: mediation and space time' in Chapter 3, the ways in which mediated messages can persist through time and the consequences of this have received less attention than the way that mediation enables such messages to travel through space. This is of particular concern because as Mayer-Schönberger suggests (2009), in some respects it may be more difficult to craft messages appropriately to address *future* audiences than it is to address *geographically disparate* ones. While you can develop some understanding of present audiences anywhere, the future is generally to a large extent unknowable.

There are three major ways that viewing a message out of its original temporal context may cause interactional difficulties. Firstly, behaviour that was normal at a given life stage can become problematic when it re-emerges associated with the same individual at a different life stage. Typically, for example, a parent might not wish their own unenthusiastic attitude towards homework when they were a student to be known to their own student-age children. Secondly, and relatedly, past crimes and misbehaviour that might have been forgiven or forgotten due to the passage of time may cause renewed censure if they are re-presented on social networks. Lastly, as alluded to in Chapter 2, broader social norms can also change over time. Just as we now may disapprove of the unthinking sexism and racism of previous generations, it is possible that future generations looking back at our social media postings from a world further damaged by climate change may find our use of long-distance air travel for holidays disturbing.

In this chapter, I will first briefly outline how the workings of the 'memory' of the internet may differ from the workings of our own memories. In the next section I will analyse four social media services to illustrate the diversity of ways in which they 'remember' and enable retrieval while highlighting areas of common concern – as noted in Chapter 4, social media differ widely in the way that they 'bias' usage (Feenberg, 2008). I will then focus on blogging in more detail – one of the social media practices whose content is most 'memorable' (because it is most extensively and publicly indexed). I will summarise how academics studying blogging have debated the perception that personal bloggers have of the 'secondary reception' of their postings (see Chapter 3) and what it is they believe that bloggers want from such secondary reception. Lastly, I will outline the complex and conflicted relationship that the bloggers I have studied appear to have with the way in which what they write may be remembered digitally, and discuss the potential implications of this for the study of other social media usage. Throughout, I stress the importance of differentiating between what *in principle* digital memory could allow us to remember (i.e. what is stored), how the vagaries of differences in power, ease-of-use of services, legality, etc. shape *practices* of digital remembering, and – particularly in the last section – how differing motivations and levels of digital literacy shape *awareness of and attitudes towards* these practices.

Social media memory

Scholars, journalists and members of the public tend to describe digital 'memory' as perfect while our own is imperfect (Kessler, 2013; Mayer-Schönberger, 2009) but, as I will describe, both retrieval systems have their strengths and weaknesses. Because we are at some level aware of the practical weaknesses of the internet's memory, I argue that we tend to perceive that what we write is protected from perfect and indefinite retrieval just as we perceive that most of our day-to-day interactions with people will gradually be forgotten. While this practical approximation may be correct in most circumstances, a better understanding of the detail of the way that the internet's memory works might help users avoid communication problems.

Mayer-Schönberger (2009) describes three key characteristics of digital remembering – accessibility (by which he means sharability of data with others out of its original context), durability and comprehensiveness (by which he means the extent of one's data now captured digitally and thereby 'memorable').[1] In each case, we must distinguish between what is possible in principle and how digital remembering is presently implemented. To his three characteristics I will add two more – digital remembering is unequal and is evolving.

Accessibility

It is undeniable that the ease with which material once retrieved can be circulated has been greatly increased thanks to digital technology. However, barriers remain to total accessibility. Particularly in the case of social media, much content is stored in an increasingly Balkanised ecosystem of services (Wu, 2010) whose content is not necessarily accessible to search engines and therefore may be harder to gather and spread. You may have profiles on Facebook, LinkedIn and match.com but a single search using a conventional search engine would not find and combine matches for certain keywords across your social media presences.

Durability

Regarding durability, it is true that there are many ways in which data can now be stored and are now routinely stored which would, in the predigital era, have been discarded. However, it is as easy to discard huge volumes of data as it is to collect them and nearly all social media organisations are commercial operations which only collect and keep what is of value to them. The time you spend on social media services, what you share about yourself as a consumer while using social media and the relationships you articulate with others may be of considerable commercial value today. However, it is worth noting that the content itself produced by social media users appears to have little intrinsic commercial value and those who store such content appear to have little compunction about discarding it when it suits them. As Matt Schwartz notes, 'GeoCities, once the third-most-trafficked site on the web, lost 38 million homemade pages when its owner, Yahoo, shuttered the site in 2009 rather than continue to bear the cost of hosting it' (2012). As a result, one study found that 27 per cent of social media content found in June 2009 appeared to have been completely lost by March 2012 and a further 14 per cent was only available through internet archives (SalahEldeen & Nelson, 2012). Another study of 300 sites indexed by the Open Directory Project http://www.dmoz.org/ found that if a typical site from that collection (itself consisting of more high-profile than average sites) disappeared tomorrow one could only expect to recover 61 per cent of its resources using internet archives (McCown, Diawara & Nelson, 2007).

The durability of human memory varies depending on, amongst other things, the perceived importance of that memory to current circumstances (Schacter, 2003). Similarly, all social media utterances are not equally digitally memorable. Unsurprisingly, it appears that sites that are more popular (as measured by the number of links from other sites to that site, for example) are more likely to be archived (McCown et al., 2007). Also, as noted earlier, many search engines do not have access to the content inside social media services so the durability of memory of those services depends entirely on the capabilities and preferences of those individual services. For example, as will be discussed below, you might only be able to see a tweet from 2006 if you paid one of Twitter's search partners for the privilege. If Facebook were to go bankrupt, there is no guarantee that the terabytes of content therein, most of it not indexed elsewhere, would be preserved. On the other hand, some appear to have noted that it can be the very material that people choose to delete that is the most interesting to others, and have attempted to preserve it. Researchers have analysed deleted tweets (Almuhimedi, Wilson, Liu, Sadeh & Acquisti, 2013) and Facebook status updates (Das & Kramer, 2013) and, as a means to illustrate peoples' vulnerability, Dean Terry produced a public site – http://undetweetable.com/ – publicly archiving people's deleted tweets. Twitter then objected and although it has now stopped him from adding new ones, a sizeable database of earlier ones is still available (Hughes, 2011), and http://politwoops.sunlightfoundation. com/ continues to archive politicians' removed tweets with Twitter's blessing.

Comprehensiveness

The comprehensiveness and scale of digital remembering – in social media and across modern society more broadly – is clearly huge and growing, a subject to which we will return in Chapter 6. While in some ways this is dangerous, it also indirectly provides what many people tacitly rely on for the protection of their personal information – 'security through obscurity'.

If you have a common name, for example, you may find it difficult to find yourself in a web search and thereby suppose that unintended others might similarly be unlikely to find you. A low level of 'search engine literacy' among the general public may compound this misperception – one study found, for example, that 20–35 per cent of all search engine queries were only a single word (Jansen & Spink, 2006). More generally, as I found in my interviews with personal webloggers, people sometimes believe that there are so many social media profiles and personal websites out there that only those they know well or those who they have shown the site to would come across their profiles.

The sheer scale of what a given search could provide because of the comprehensiveness of digital memory means increasingly that in searching we are at the mercy of algorithms designed to help us by prioritising results or, in some cases, filtering information out altogether. It is well understood that people have a marked tendency to click on only the first few results of a given search (Granka, Joachims & Gay, 2004) even when there may be many potentially matching responses – the ranking of responses by search engines may be considered a form of 'implementation bias' in information retrieval (Feenberg, 2008). Similarly, Facebook's 'top stories' algorithm governs by default which of a user's friends' postings they will be presented with in their newsfeed, filtering out altogether those that it deems insufficiently interesting.

Inequality

What much of the public appears to fail fully to appreciate is that both in terms of what can be retrieved and how easily, digital remembering varies greatly among different people and organisations. Importantly, this variance is not primarily because of random variations in capability as with human memory but can be linked to two key factors: differences in motivation to seek and master digital remembering tools, and differences in availability of social media data for privileged actors.

In everyday consumption of social media, both readers and producers of postings appear to be focused on 'primary reception' – reading of material as they are alerted to it or as it is presented to them when they visit the appropriate website or application. Under normal circumstances they would not search back through time to find something they themselves or somebody else wrote earlier, although they might read something that was produced in the past if it were circulated anew in the present.[2] As a result, they may not be motivated to seek out social media search tools or learn to use them effectively (particularly those that are not presented by default by social media services but which are provided by third-party websites that index them). Nonetheless, depending on context, social media postings can be seen not as more or less ephemeral or phatic exchanges (Miller, 2008) but as something more valuable – evidence of character or creditworthiness, for example. Once material from the past becomes more valuable, it becomes worthwhile to invest the time necessary to retrieve it effectively. Sometimes this desire to retrieve can be triggered in everyday life situations – for example, when a partner in a relationship becomes suspicious (Muise, Christofides & Desmarais, 2009). There are also a number of professionals whose daily concern is to retrieve this evidence from social media,

whether related to specific individuals (in the case of private investi-
gators and HR managers, for example) or in relation to individuals as
members of particular target groups (in the case of insurance companies and government agencies). Not only do they have an incentive to
learn how to use the social media tools that are available (in principle)
to all – they are also able and willing to spend money to use paid-for
social media search services like http://www.discovertext.com/ or to get
'pro'- or 'premium'-level access to additional features from free services
like http://topsy.com/.

Moreover, there is a third, deeper level of access to social media data,
which cannot be bought but is nonetheless available to privileged actors.
Most obviously, the companies on whose servers the user's social media
resides generally retain those data indefinitely and could search for them
themselves. In some cases, of course, companies and their employees
either choose to limit or are legally obliged to limit their ability to perform such searches. Social media companies themselves are not the only
ones with privileged access to social media data, though. As we will
examine further in Chapter 6, there are a number of others both covertly
and covertly able to gain access to data that are not disclosed to most
other social media users – principally advertisers, employers, parents and
law enforcement agencies.

Advertisers who work with social media services can generally target their users using a variety of criteria – not just the demographic
characteristics listed on their profiles (whether public or private) but
also based on interests they express or that can be inferred from their
postings – past and present. It is this greater access to information
about consumers that social media companies generally present as their
key business advantage when attracting advertisers. This information
is generally 'anonymised' (the advertiser does not know which specific individuals they have targeted), but the targeting can nonetheless
be (or appear) very precise. In 2005, early in the evolution of social
media-targeted promotion, Facebook helped Interscope Records find
college cheerleaders and those who mentioned cheerleading in their
profiles (Kirkpatrick, 2010, p. 141). It appears that by using https://www.
facebook.com/advertising I could now target a message at (for example)
42-year-old Spanish-speaking single parents in a long-distance relationship, living within 10 miles of Bangor, MI, with kids 13–15 years old,
interested in higher education, with self-described liberal political views.

Employers may also have privileged access to what their employees
write and have written online – not through a special relationship with
social media services but through more direct monitoring of what an
employee does when they are on a machine provided by their employer.

The legality of such monitoring varies by country but in the UK, for example, employers can generally collect a broad range of data about, for example, social media use as long as employees are aware that such collection might take place (Information Commissioner's Office, 2011; Tokc-Wilde, 2011). Similarly, in most countries parents have the right to monitor their children's internet communications and often do so (d. boyd, 2014; Clark, 2013).

The degree to which law enforcement agencies around the world are granted access to the vast amount of social media data that are held by social media companies and the length of time that they store such data are difficult to assess and vary from country to country depending on both formal regulation and, it would seem, the desires and capabilities of increasingly powerful secret surveillance organisations like the US National Security agency or the UK's GCHQ, who have been accused of gathering information about tens of thousands of users of Facebook (Ullyot, 2013) and other social network services without effective legal scrutiny. Authoritarian regimes have even fewer controls over their activities. In China, providers of internet services must provide the authorities with data records up to 60 days prior to the date of a request (Dong, 2012), and as storage capabilities continue to advance there are fears that 'enormous databases of captured information will create what amounts to a surveillance time machine, enabling state security services to retroactively eavesdrop on people in the months and years before they were designated as surveillance targets' (Villasenor, 2011).

Evolution

The fundamental capabilities of human memory have changed little but the tools we use to help us recall are growing in sophistication. With the continual increase in computing power at our disposal and science's focus on making the most of the 'big data' now being made available by ubiquitous computing devices and sensors, feats of 'memory' that were inconceivable may become commonplace in the space of a few years. To return to a case outlined in this book's introduction, in 1986 people who posted messages on the USENET newsgroup 'net.motss' about gay-related issues generally did so under their own names (it was then both technologically difficult and outside social norms to have anonymous e-mail addresses). They might have been aware that the newsgroup could be archived and searchable but they surely could not have anticipated that, thanks to the World Wide Web and vastly increased storage and processing power, everything they posted has been digitally 'remembered' from 1986 to the present day at https://groups.google.com/forum/#!forum/net.motss.

When the World Wide Web began, it could only be navigated through manually curated lists of links until the advent of continuously updated search engines capable of finding web pages using keywords. Even these were of limited utility because of computers' difficulty in prioritising pages until the technical improvements popularised by Google. Nonetheless, at present the retrieval of computer 'memory' generally relies on people typing a few keywords and this information being supplemented by a limited amount of contextual information about the location and prior interests of the search user.

With the passage of time, however, we may find ways to pose and answer search queries more effectively. Take the shift towards a better visual 'memory', for example. Until recently, one could generally only find pictures of a person that had been explicitly labelled as such by the picture taker. Now, on Facebook or Google+ for example, a picture with you in it taken years before might be identified by yourself, a friend or algorithmically thanks to facial recognition software. Increasingly, the location at which a picture was taken is automatically captured by the smartphone taking it and is uploaded alongside the picture itself – as image recognition improves, location information may also be retrospectively added. What we say on video clips that we upload today is generally not indexed or searchable, but the technology to do so is being researched (see, e.g., http://research.microsoft.com/en-us/projects/mavis/). As we will see in Chapter 6, the steady growth of small, cheap and more convenient data-gathering devices in the future will digitally document an ever larger proportion of the world and, in doing so, may indirectly bring ever larger parts of our past lives to light.

It is not just improvements in technology that may in future make what seemed digitally unmemorable memorable – social norms and regulation of what we look for and why may change too. It is possible, of course, that in future we will be more cautious about how and why we look back at what others have written in social media, but so far the evidence suggests a move in the direction towards greater openness, encouraged as we will see in Chapter 6 by a variety of commercial imperatives. This may make living in a future social media-saturated world more comfortable for some, but what of those who wish to retain earlier norms of privacy and discretion?

Social media services and primary and secondary reception

Above, I have examined some of the overall trends shaping digital memory making and recall but it is important to bear in mind that social media services (and digital technologies in general) may share similarities but are implemented in different ways, which can influence the ease and extent of secondary reception of messages they circulate. In this section I will examine the relationship of four different popular social media services to secondary reception and archiving. At one extreme we have Snapchat, which is designed to minimise secondary reception, then Twitter, Facebook and Tumblr, which at the other extreme, like other blogging services, enable a lengthy period of secondary reception.

The key factors that will be assessed are the length of time any postings remain visible on each social media service and the degree to which these are public and therefore potentially archived and searchable on other online services – two 'constitutive biases' of these services – and the ease with which older postings can be either browsed or searched – this could be conceived of as 'implementation bias' (Feenberg, 2008).

Snapchat

This photo-sharing service appears to have been designed precisely to avoid problems of secondary reception and lack of control over redistribution encountered in other social media. Snapchat's premise is that it enables smartphone users to exchange, with their friends, photos that will only be visible by default for a few seconds (up to ten). If recipients wish to save them for longer they can, but if they choose to do so within the application the original sender of the photo is notified. As soon as the last designated recipient has viewed the picture, it is deleted from the company's server as well.[3] Although the images travel across the internet (and as a result are technically potentially subject to interception), they never appear on the web and are thus un-indexable by search engines.

The service quickly developed a reputation for enabling the kind of risky sharing that in other social media can be problematic – most notoriously, sexual pictures (Bilton, 2012). Moreover, as soon as the application became popular, ways to circumvent limitations on picture circulation began to be found (Ludwig, 2013). These ways highlight a more general issue – whatever the formal limitations placed on distribution of text by social media services, the highly digitally-mediated nature of social media makes limitations on copying and redistribution problematic. Almost any tool used for viewing social media is programmable and multifunction, whether it's obviously a computer or whether like most smartphones it's a multifunction computing device masquerading as an appliance. These devices can take texts (or images or video) received in one context and distribute it in other ways. Ironically, the more 'backstage' an area appears, the more tempting it is for some to attempt to breach the barriers in place. Such breaches are not limited to broader distribution among friends but can end up open to all and in an entirely different context, as with sites like http://snapchatleaked.com/.

Twitter

Unlike Snapchat, although Twitter does not remove old tweets, the way in which the service presents itself emphasises primary reception – a continual presentation of what has just been written. This emphasis starts with the way in which new tweets are framed – the user is invited to answer the question, 'what's happening?' While as noted in Chapter 4 there are numerous different ways in which different software applications may implement Twitter's features, the default interface presented on the website generally displays the tweets which those you follow have sent in reverse chronological order, and searches display this way as well – although the company continues to experiment with different features to pull chronologically distant conversations together visually.

The length of time that tweets are available is not easy to assess, even for researchers let alone users. In one important sense, the answer is 'indefinitely' – Twitter claims to have retained all tweets, has licensed the ability to search the entire archive of public tweets to third-party organisations who charge clients to access this information and has given the same archive to the US Library of Congress (though researchers will not have access to tweets less than six months old). Several more sophisticated free Twitter search tools are also available from third parties (http://snapbird.org/, http://socialmention.com/ and http://topsy.com/ among others) but, as alluded to in Chapter 4, it does not appear likely that Twitter users who are not using it professionally would be aware of or engage with such tools regularly. Thus, Twitter highlights particularly strongly the inequalities in remembering noted earlier.

For most users the duration of availability of tweets for web searchers using the free search tools provided by Twitter itself and by Google is most relevant. On Twitter itself, users can search through or scroll back through only the last 3200 of their own tweets and the default search only shows the last 10 days' worth of matches to a search term, according to http://snapbird.org. The extent to which Google or other free-to-use search engines index tweets is not clear – Google does not appear to index every public tweet but it certainly could do so, now or starting in some point in the future and, as Twitter points out, once a tweet has been made and indexed, there is no guarantee that it will be removed promptly (or at all) from third-party indexes even if the original author deletes it from Twitter's own visible data stream (Twitter, n.d.-b).[4] In practice, users who do not take a professional interest in tracking Twitter are seldom presented – whether searching or browsing – with tweets more than a few days old, but this is an artefact of how Twitter presents its search results and how extensively Google appears to index the service, and not a reflection of how easily historical Twitter results might be searchable in future.

Facebook

Facebook's contents appear to be divided between relatively 'static' elements – one's profile including picture and biographical details like marital status – and elements that are more transitory – for example, status updates. For much of the early history of Facebook, while it was possible to scroll back through a user's updates, the site privileged primary reception. Gradually, however, opportunities for secondary reception of personal information published on Facebook have increased. The first change was the introduction of the news feed in September 2006 and, in particular, the addition to the feed of notifications of changes to profile information. Henceforth – by default at least – whenever users change their profiles – changing their relationship status, for example, or political affiliation – the fact of that change has been recorded and becomes itself an update that is instantaneously broadcast. Thanks to a further change in March 2012, Facebook actions are also added to a much more visible and easily navigable 'Timeline'. Prior to that, if you were interested in what a friend had said or done in the past it was possible to scroll back through postings and activities via their profile page, sorted in reverse chronological order, but this was an inconvenient way to browse back more than a short time for people who used Facebook regularly. A study (Harper, Whitworth & Page, 2012) that appears to have been done before the new 'Timeline' feature emphasises this, both through an analysis of the interface itself and through semistructured interviews with 12 users. It concluded:

> users almost naturally come to focus on generating new content rather than reconfiguring the old; the system encourages them to (though of course the users are willing and compliant in this). Though some of their comments and responses to 'What is on your mind' prompts might allude to past events – to other's postings particularly – the experiential theme is the present.
>
> (ibid., p. 12)

The new 'Timeline' feature, however, makes it easy to scroll through 'key' events (as defined by Facebook, though potentially editable by each user) going back months or years. The timeline also stretches back past when the user first joined Facebook, adding key dates like school graduation or joining workplaces where they have been provided. As Van Dijck notes, this cues members to 'post pictures from the pre-Facebook days of their youth – a baby picture, family snapshots, school classes, old friends, college years, wedding pictures, honeymoon – and thus experience content in terms of their life's story' (2013, p. 55).

While Facebook is increasingly making secondary reception of its users content accessible while browsing its site, in at least two key ways it remains focused on primary reception. Firstly, much of what users post (anything that is not fully public) is not indexed by search engines and thereby it is not open to ongoing circulation and archiving outside of Facebook. Secondly, Facebook's own internal search engine (revamped in 2013) does not appear to be intended as a fully featured tool to find arbitrary text in the past or present, whether written by an individual user or across users. Instead, 'Graph Search' appears designed primarily to enable certain kinds of 'structured' queries – searches for friends or people or events in a given location, for example. It is possible to search for given terms written by friends or by anyone who has a public account, but this aspect does not work well or support sophisticated search queries. Of course, just as Facebook changed its user interface to make it easier for people to browse back through time on other people's timelines, it may in future make it easier to search as well.

Tumblr

While the other services mentioned fit users' data into rigid visual templates, Tumblr blogs can be presented in a variety of ways depending on what 'theme' users choose to format their content. Broadly, though, Tumblr blogs, like Facebook, contain some fixed elements but the materials of primary importance (and normally positioned centrally on the page) are 'posts' which are placed in reverse chronological order as they are made. These posts are also automatically archived for later reference – by date and by 'tag', though the relative prominence of such archives varies depending on the theme. As a result, all of these postings are generally given their own pages and are individually indexable by search engines (unless they have been set to be 'private').

Tumblr blogs like other blogs on different services are among the most 'memorable' forms of social media. As a result, temporal aspects of blogging practice have received more academic attention than the temporal aspects of other social media practices. The following section examines prior research evidence and debates about the role of time in blogging practice.

Blogging and time: Debates in the literature

There are three key themes that emerge from the discussion of bloggers and time – the (disputed) importance of blog archives to bloggers and readers, the significance of the rhythm of blogging to its perception, and changes in individuals' blogging practices over time.

Killoran, in his examination of blogs, suggested that despite the *technical* persistence of blog entries noted earlier, this feature has little *social* significance:

> Like newspapers, blog entries are normally dated and thereby highlight both their currency with the day's events and also their much shorter shelf life. Unlike the permanence posited by the personal homepage, which preserves the past in the form of old photos, genealogical trees, and résumés, the past in a blog, exemplified by older postings that get pushed down the page with each new update and that eventually get archived, quickly fades from view and from relevance.
>
> (Killoran, 2002)

Sorapure appears to agree that earlier postings are viewed as being of lesser importance: 'past entries are relegated to the archives' (Sorapure, 2003, p. 15). Hevern, on the other hand, implies that weblog archives are central to blogging practices: 'Bloggers travel along connected paths through their lives... they look back on what has happened to them and forward to what might occur' (Hevern, 2004, p. 332) and Van Dijck suggests that blogging is 'about revising one's experience over time, allowing to adjust one's former observations and reflection – even the ones stored in the "archive" – as time goes by and as personality evolves' (Van Dijck, 2004). In a later piece, Van Dijck also stresses the importance of the archive for bloggers:

> The fact that almost every software program contains an archive holding selected entries that go back to the very beginning of a person's blog signals a desire to build up a personal repository of memories. Although this hypothesis has never been empirically tested, it would be no surprise to find that bloggers, like teenagers

using SMS or cellphones, value their lifelog's archival function as much as its communicative function.

(Van Dijck, 2007, p. 72)

The divergence in the perceived importance of blogging archives is understandable since these scholars base their analyses almost entirely on textual and technical interpretation of blogs rather than on discussion with blog authors.

Little systematic discussion of the importance of archives can be found in interview or ethnographic studies of blogging. Hodkinson does note in passing that the conversations on the LiveJournals of those he interviewed had a 'short overall time-span' because posts that were commented upon were 'buried' by later posts (Hodkinson, 2007, p. 638). Reed, on the other hand, suggests that the bloggers he studied 'view the weblog as a form of chronicle; they post entries with their own future reception in mind' (Reed, 2005, p. 231).

One temporal aspect which does emerge in some studies relates to an intriguing ambiguity about the perceived rhythm of blogging practice – whether blogging interaction is perceived as oral (synchronous, unarchived) or as writing – as also alluded to in Chapter 4. To the extent that blogging feels like oral communication in the mind of the blogger, this would appear to contradict the emphasis put by some blogging theorists on the importance of the archive.

In a study of Persian-language bloggers, Doostdar remarks that blogging draws on a 'rich reservoir of speech genres, including many primary oral genres... blogging may be closer to an oral mode of communication than to a written one' (Doostdar, 2004, pp. 20–21). Mortensen, in an auto-ethnographic piece, likewise reflects that for her the weblog is 'a confusing medium' because of the manner in which it straddles oral and written communication:

You have the speed, the immediacy, the two-way turntaking dialogue, you look away... and the message is still there... It appears to invite and promise oral immediacy, but it allows for written distance and delay.

(Mortensen, 2004, p. 4)

She notes that this contradiction not only causes difficulties for the writer, it can also result in differences between the writer and their readers if their framing of blogging practices conflict, citing public arguments about the blog postings of David Winer. He was accused of criticising others on his blog then removing the criticism from his blog's archives (Jogin, 2003). 'People expected communication and notifications from Winer with the long-term vision and the formality of the written language. Winer delivered it with the expediency and the informality of the spoken language' (Mortensen, 2004, p. 5).

A last potential theme of interest relating to time is the changing framing and purpose of blogging practices through time. One study that raises the issue notes:

> People have more than one motivation for blogging, and these change throughout the blogger's lifecycle... A primary motivation was always supplemented by additional and often different motivations for continuing to blog as knowledge is acquired.
>
> (Brady, 2006, p. 10)

This is potentially important because the presence of archives in blogs means that this changing framing of one's blog is visible through time. Thus, unless personal bloggers elect to remove or edit their archives, any contradictions in the way they have presented themselves through time on their blog are available to readers, who may enter the blog's narrative at any point via links to the archived material or a search engine. Mortensen remarks that a blog 'exists within a certain context, living in dialogue with a certain group of writers and readers, and to understand it reading one post is not enough' (Mortensen, 2004, p. 7). However, Himmer notes: 'multiple entry points are not only dynamic, but entirely beyond the constraint or control of the original author and the original text' (Himmer, 2004). One of Reed's interviewees provides an example of what can occur when the framing of a blog changes:

> Peter... told me that when he started his weblog he didn't want anyone he knew to be aware of its existence. This was because he wished the text to be a full and complete account of his thoughts and feelings, including the day-to-day impressions he had of people around him. But one night, in a drunken state, Peter let his boyfriend know about the weblog. As a consequence of this indiscretion, he felt he needed to go back through the archives and edit large extracts from his old entries, anything that he didn't want his partner to read.
>
> (Reed, 2005, p. 232)

It is noteworthy that while old paper notebooks, photographs or video recordings often provide a number of subtle visual and/or aural cues that place them in the past, weblog postings may provide very little in the way of such cues aside from the posting date generally printed at the top. While an old web page may reveal its age through a dated layout, when a blog's layout is updated, all of the earlier postings are generally retrospectively updated with the same visual style. Though in some cases archived blog postings will be accessed via links on the home page to the blog's archives sorted by date, thus placing what is read in a temporal context, old blog postings can also be found via search engines or linked to directly via their 'permalinks', thus minimising contextual cues to the age of the posting encountered (and potentially presenting a single posting from the past as representative of the author's current attitudes or behaviour if read in isolation from other subsequent postings).

Blogging and time: Evidence from the field

In this section, based on interviews with personal webloggers, I provide new empirical insights firstly into the ways in which their social media practices change over time and secondly into the attitudes those interviewed have towards the secondary reception of their postings.

While personal blogs can have a natural beginning and end and they can be focused on a single aspect of a blogger's life or personal issue (as with a pregnancy-centric blog, for example, or one related to a journey), the blogs of the bloggers I interviewed were much more loosely structured – even when they began with a particular topic in mind. They generally appeared to have begun without a strong motivating impulse or clearly articulated purpose, drifted from topic to topic and even from one central framing to another, and finished without a conclusion – often without warning – in response to changes in the author's motivation, in their life stage or, in some cases, due to concerns raised by a change in their perception of their readers. As a result blogs can record in their archives different blogging practices as well as different life stages, with potential consequences for the perceived consistency of bloggers' online self-presentation.

While home pages and social network profiles to a large extent allow users to continually update what they have written so that it presents a self consistent with what is desired at the present moment, doing so on a blog site would be significantly more difficult because of the way weblog archiving operates, as will be discussed later.

Interviewees were invited to reflect on how their blogging practices changed as their life circumstances changed and as their experiences of blogging – continuous and discontinuous – matured. Although based on self-reports, and therefore subject to the varied processes of recall about their imagined communicative environments online, there were often clear distinctions between early and later periods evident in the interview data. In addition, after the initial interviews, some changes in the way bloggers framed their practices appeared to have occurred that were reflected through changes in the blogs themselves, and the reasons behind these apparent changes were probed via follow-up emails to selected interviewees.

While 12 of 23 of those interviewed expressed a purpose for their blog at the start and continued more or less down that path, the remainder either claimed to have had no clear purpose to begin with and to have discovered one along the way, or said that they had found their practice developing in directions they had not anticipated. Three principal reasons for changes in blogging practice over time were identified – changes in bloggers' imagined relations with their readers, changes in bloggers' motivations and changes in their circumstances.

Changed relation to readers

A common way in which a blogging practice can change over time is a shift in the perceived nature of the relationship of the bloggers to their readers. Four of those interviewed appear to have shifted the focus of their blogging to recognise the existence of audiences they had not anticipated. At first Colin, Elaine and Isobel claimed that they had blogged as if nobody was reading what they wrote. Colin recalled changing his blogging practice twice in response to shifting conceptions of his readership:

> It started as a diary. It was a, 'this is what I have done.' And it very quickly became, 'I'm writing a diary but people are reading it.' The moment you start to have comments on it, it actually shifts – or for me it shifted the way that I approached it. Suddenly I'm not writing something for me to read. I'm writing for my friends. And I think it was about six months in I started seeing people there I didn't know. And I'm writing for an audience. And there is a paradigm shift during that period
>
> – Colin

He then discovered that some work colleagues also had LiveJournals, causing him to be more cautious about commenting about his work. Similarly, Isobel started by viewing her blog as akin to a personal diary but came to feel 'pressurised to write for the people actually reading it'. As she put it,

When I first started posting it was very much an online diary to myself. And then as it kind of grew and as more people started reading it I think I started writing it for them.

Elaine said she started her blog as a purely personal writing exercise and, although she quickly gained readers, she continued to treat it as if it were only being read by herself until two factors intervened – she went freelance and was approached by a professional blogger who encouraged her to see her weblog as something she could market to potential clients. Annie's blog at the time of interview was conversational in tone and included content (notably about her drinking) which she acknowledged could cause her family or an employer concern. Several months after the interview, she removed all her archives and began blogging exclusively about her work, and then removed her blog entirely. When asked what had happened she explained:

Initially I stopped blogging as it was being used against me, and I was being 'e-stalked' by various people – I was putting too much information out on the internet. Then since I had some success with visibility on the internet, I thought I would use the blog to further my career – this didn't work. So I just retired the idea altogether.

Changed motivations

The interviewees also reported changes in their practice because their initial motivation was not satisfied or was overtaken by another. Charles reported that he began his blog with political links, then changed to a more personal diary format when he moved temporarily to the US because he felt he needed a way to keep in touch with those he left behind and wanted to chronicle what happened there. In the period post-interview he returned to predominantly political blogging but with intermittent personal posts. Donald said that it took him too much time to write stories:

Originally it was just up there to post stories. That's why I started it. But slowly but surely the stories have dropped off and the opinions come through although the odd story does go up.

His move away from stories could also have been a reaction to his own evaluation that his stories were not getting commented on while more opinionated pieces were: 'People don't go to blogs necessarily to read two or three thousand word epic poems or something – they go there to get snapshots of people's lives and I think I maybe misunderstood what the point of my blog was going to be at that point'. That said, in his weblogging practice after the interview he returned to posting short stories, interspersed with occasional personal comments. Quentin claimed that he had started his blog thinking he could build a readership and perhaps emulate the success of other bloggers in attracting an audience and building a journalistic brand on which he could capitalise. He came to realise early on that attracting an audience big enough to make a living from or to interest a mass media outlet was not a realistic target. Instead, he adjusted his expectations. He said he no longer sought a 'huge' audience – instead, he looked for an audience large enough to provide him with good feedback on his ideas and his writing style. He addressed his blog to 'maybe 15 or so friends who are other bloggers' and a sufficient number of other readers to ensure 'about five to ten comments [per blog entry] which is ideal for me'. After the interview he abandoned the blog altogether, however.

Phillippa began her blog with practical, work-related aims in view, but while 'I was trying to be quite serious about it in the beginning... it started to relax pretty quickly – within a month I would say' – led in part by the example of another artist whose blog she found – Ivan Pope (http://www.ivanpope.com/):

> He's quite open on his blog – he just puts it out there and says this is what I'm doing and this is what stage it's at, this is what I'm thinking and these are the things that annoy me or whatever it is and I love that – I love his transparency and I thought 'OK – why not? What have I got to lose?'

She appeared to find that the purely practical benefits she sought originally – archiving and promoting her artworks – were overtaken by the pleasures of interaction with others from across the world. In fact, even before the interview, her artwork very seldom appeared on her LiveJournal at all.

Changed circumstances

There is also evidence in the interview data that changes in life circumstances can lead to changes in blog content. Almost anything can, it seems, be used as the basis of a personal weblog entry, but four of the bloggers (all of them women) tacitly or explicitly made discussion of their relationships – particularly their unsatisfactory relationships – a central feature of their blogging practice and, when those relationships changed, it caused the owners to dramatically shift their blogging practice, or to abandon it altogether.

For example, Isobel had recently formed a steady relationship at the time of interview and it was clear in the context of the interview that it was this fact that meant 'things were becoming stable' in her life, just as she noted earlier in the interview that she increased her blogging as she reached her early 20s because there 'was more personal stuff going on like there was "him" or whoever else I happened to be madly in love with at the time'. As she said,

> A couple of weeks ago – a month ago. I thought, 'is there actually any point in carrying on because things are quite stable now. I don't have exciting and thrilling new things to write about because I am very settled. Is there any point in continuing?'... I can see it petering out – it's just a question of when. I am not sure when it will but I am sure it will at some stage – probably in the next year....
> – Isobel (who abandoned her blog shortly after the interview but started another at a different address but with similar content a year later)

Harriet's blog was the only one among the interviewees with a stated theme – her dissatisfaction with men. In practice, this was not by any means the only theme explored on the blog, but when she found a man and then had a child, she eventually elected to put a formal end to her original blog in favour of a blog of relationship advice and a motherhood-related blog that continued the previous blog in style and content but with a different framing more suited to her new circumstances (though she later also restarted her original blog).

Frances also said that she had considered stopping her blog during a period when she found herself happy in a relationship because she felt less need to write to vent her worries and frustrations. She was also uncomfortable in talking about how happy she was (because others might be more sceptical) and in discussing problems (because the reactions of others might magnify her perception of these problems). She foreshadowed this when she was interviewed:

> I suppose if I suddenly found a boyfriend or got married or won the lottery and decided to travel around the world then maybe it might get scaled back... because then there'd be no drama and nothing to write about if everything was smooth sailing.

Phillippa started a new weblog at a new address (and on a new platform – Blogger instead of LiveJournal) because she did not wish her estranged partner to be able to continue to read it.

Surveys find that propensity to blog appears to decrease with age (Dutton & Blank, 2011, p. 27; USC Annenberg School Center for the Digital Future, 2013). There are several possible explanations for this. Firstly, to the extent that blogging is an attempt to communicate with imagined peers, the lower internet penetration and use of older people may cause older people to assume their peers are not potential readers. Secondly, it has been suggested that generations who have grown up with the internet are more comfortable with online revelation (see Chapter 2). The interview data suggest a third possibility – that the desire to tell stories about one's self may be related to one's life stage (and people earlier in their lives without family responsibilities may have more free time available for such activities).

Although this was not mentioned as a factor by interviewees, it would appear reasonable that blogging practices may change over time as the features of the enabling technologies change. For example, Betty remarked that she considered it rude to put up several pictures on a single blog posting because it would make the page slow to download, but added that, in the context of increasing broadband adoption, this might change. Indeed, as broadband-connected smartphones have become increasingly prevalent, the physical context of much social media activity is also changing, from being predominantly a computer-based, stationary activity to a mobile one.

In summary, many of the bloggers interviewed appeared to change their blogging practice over time because of changes in the way they perceived their audiences, changes in the motivations to blog, changes in their circumstances and potentially because of changes in the underlying technologies. Even when blogging practice changed significantly these changes often did not result in a change of 'venue', nor was there often a formal demarcation between different practices.

The place of archiving in blogging practice

The fact that blogs incorporate a visible archive of all postings is one of the key defining features of blogging technology. However, just as academics' framings of the importance of blog archives vary, the attitudes towards such archives varied among those interviewed. Six of 23 said that they valued the existence of these archives and reread them from time to time – the rest seldom mentioned them. Two interviewees whose attachments to their archives appeared to be particularly strong are Frances and Phillippa. Frances said that she reread old entries 'just because I'm stuck in a really really boring job' and that 'I like to go back and read it and think, "that was really well written and I really expressed what I was feeling at the time"'. And Phillippa, an artist, said that she valued being able to look back at her creative thought process – 'it's a huge asset to my work, I think', but this perceived benefit was not entirely practical or work-related – it appeared tied to a more personal appreciation of the value of memory. She compared the archiving function of the blog to the 'stacks of sketchbooks' she had in her studio and said: 'they're lovely and I do love them. The feel of them and looking at the pages and everything but if you're on the road or something like that you can't just carry them all with you'.

Two others also spoke of the practical benefits of the recording and archiving of more personal material – the use of a blog as a form of 'outboard memory' (Doctorow, 2002). George said: 'you can go through your life and have 101 stories but what's the point if you don't document them – they might as well not exist'. And Simon spoke of his blog as an 'experiment' to 'help me keep track of the changing world. New attitudes to things or new ways of doing things' – a form of permanent record 'lest the world forget', or to himself, even of trivial things like 'an account of my trip to WH Smith'.

Doug, by contrast, said looking back was 'very rare' – in part, because finding a particular post in the past was 'a real effort' – you would have to 'dig and dig and dig'. Whatever these bloggers said about their attachment to their archives, it was not clear whether they actually revisited their archives often or whether it was largely the knowledge that they would be available to them that they felt was important.

A further six of the interviewees claimed that their archives contained material that they were ashamed of. Betty, for example, said that she does not like to look back at hers because of this:

> I would curl up with embarrassment if I were to go back. . . . I did revise the one I had way back originally. And it was horrifying. I sounded like an over excited five year old. . . . It's like hearing one's self recorded.

Marie had a weblog she wrote when she was 13, which was abandoned and then disappeared, and she said it was 'sad' but 'it's like reading things which you've written and you think to yourself "oh my God how could I have written that?" so I wasn't particularly upset to have lost all that'.

Whatever their embarrassed feelings about old postings, however, six of those interviewed said that they should stand by what they had said and were reluctant either to edit or delete old postings. Charles was concerned that some of his earlier postings did not reflect his current political views but said he would not edit them:

> because I think it would be somehow dishonest. I mean something that's on there from two years ago is what I was thinking at the time and it would seem meaningless to go back and change it and then publish it as still being then and it would also seem meaningless to go back and post it now given that most of the time the issue has moved on or whatever and is no longer relevant.

As we have seen, George, who was fired after his weblog was discovered by his employers, nonetheless said he could not bear to remove it. Harriet noted that although what she had posted about previous relationships might endanger future ones: 'I think my fingers don't post if I can't stand by it. I may live to regret that sometime'. And Renia – who was 17 at the time of first interview and whose blog mentions a suicide attempt and episodes of self-harm among other issues, said nonetheless: 'I tend to try to leave it as much as I can because I think it might be wrong to alter it just because I am a bit embarrassed'. Annie said she did sometimes take down postings she regretted making but 'it doesn't happen very often – usually I leave it up. I hate it when people don't leave their posts up. I like to go back and read'. She did remove her weblog a few months after being interviewed, however.

Some simply suggested that the task of editing would be too onerous – Bruce said that after he heard of someone else having been fired for blogging he became more cautious about postings that would breach his work contract, but he hoped that people would not read back and find his more contentious writing and he 'never actually got around' to editing his older postings. In 2008, he was approached by his employer about his journal and at that point he was able to use a 'mass editing' tool in LiveJournal to make it friends only. This tool was not available for the majority of LiveJournal users who did not pay a subscription to the service, however (LiveJournal, 2008) – and having maintained a journal since 2003 he had produced approximately 500 postings. Betty considered trying to delete the old postings that she found embarrassing but 'realized it would be an enormous job' and abandoned the task. The only person who mentioned large-scale retrospective editing of his archives was Doug, who did it at the request of a now-estranged LiveJournal 'friend' who asked him to remove links between her journal and his.

Consistent with the observation in Chapter 4 that those interviewed ranged widely in their perceptions of the likelihood that others were reading, their perception of the likelihood that others would read their archived postings also varied.

Simon appeared to hope that, in future, historians might read blogs like his to learn about life today (though he is 'quite ashamed' of some of the postings he has made which are 'very trivial and of no value to anyone, probably'):

> One thing about weblogs is that they might be an interesting reflection of our society in the future. Maybe for a social historian. Um. And there are people who are archiving websites before they disappear. So the sites like The Way Back Machine, yeah and so on. So I hope in the future, people will still be able to see all this electronic information.

Most other interviewees, however, when they spoke about their archives at all, appeared to view them as of interest only to themselves. Renia, for example, said: 'When I am 30 or older I will think "how did I get from there to there?" and I would see. It would be good to see how it goes along – how it all worked in the end'.

Annie appeared to believe that nobody would read through her archives – at least not in their entirety – although she said she enjoyed reading the archived postings of others. When she discovered that at least one blogger was willing to read her blog in its entirety she was surprised and somewhat perturbed:

> There was a guy advertising a LiveAid ticket for free as long as he came and stayed... I said 'read my blog to see if you want to do it' so he read my entire blog. The entire thing. Really creeps me out. He came down and he was awesome – a really cool guy – but he knew everything about me and I was just like 'woah'. I didn't really think anyone would pay that much attention to go all the way back through it and really really read it.

Betty in part justified not editing her old posts because 'I don't think anyone would scroll back and read it all', although she had noted earlier in the interview that 'people who are acquaintances of yours begin to have quite an intimate knowledge of what's going on in your life', and

Charles left up his early political postings (albeit 'filed away' separately from his then-current blog) because 'I couldn't see why anybody would want to' read them. For Harriet, her belief that few readers read back into the archive was a source of occasional frustration: 'I appreciate that not everybody has been reading [my blog] since the beginning but sometimes people do comment on things that if they even read back two posts they would have the whole story'. And for Phillippa this piqued her vanity:

> I think it's more the egotistical thing of 'I thought that was a particularly good piece of writing and I want it to be set in stone for whatever it was' and then having to realise that well it's not. It's a live document – it's changing all the time and moving on and so does the world so that's just the way it is. So I had to let go of that quickly. Because when you write something – you would know as a journalist or a writer – if you write a book then you have this object. You've got this book – it's there and can be passed around and read again or whatever. Whereas with this it can be accessed definitely but it probably won't be.

Elaine repeatedly stressed that her blog was produced primarily as a writing exercise for herself, so she said that she did go back, read and re-edit old entries, but said in the case of year-old entries that she did so believing that no one would ever read them. It appears clear from this that these interviewees are focused on primary rather than secondary reception of their blogging texts.

When interviewees' perceptions of blogging practice changed radically, they did not therefore attempt to systematically re-edit what they had written to reflect this change – they stopped blogging on their present sites, either leaving their archived text online or attempting to have the text removed or hidden. A few then started new blogs elsewhere.

Even when blogs are abandoned, however, they can have an 'afterlife'. Of the 11 blogs by the bloggers interviewed that subsequently appeared to have been permanently abandoned or hidden from public view, most or all of the archives of five remained visible at the time of writing. When George was dismissed from his job, he made the blogger archives of what he posted harder for a casual browser to find and started a new blog with a similar name. He said during the interview that he could not bring himself to remove the archives completely, however. Of the sites where the archives appear to have been deliberately hidden from public view or removed, the two LiveJournal sites were inaccessible to the public but two of the four blogger sites which had been closed are archived partially or fully via archive.org. In these cases, their content does not appear in casual web searches but anyone who knows the addresses of their weblogs can see what they had said. It is also possible (if unlikely) that readers of any of these weblogs may have used one of the many free tools available to archive web pages onto their hard disks for their private use.

The way in which archives like archive.org operate is seldom discussed in the press or online outside specialist circles. Only one interviewee, Simon, spoke of the existence of such third-party archives and it is not likely that many bloggers are aware of how to manipulate their weblogs in order to keep their sites from being archived in this way. When asked about her attitude towards such archival sites or caches, Frances said: 'I wasn't actually aware you could request cached content to be removed'. Site authors can request that their site should not appear in their indexes using the accepted technical code for this purpose,[5] but it is not always clear how to implement this on any given social media site (except by making postings themselves friends-only, which users may not want to do). In addition, requesting that search engines should not index pages does not guarantee that they will not be indexed – it is a convention that is not always followed. Even privacy protection functions provided by websites designed to prevent access to pages from anyone other than authorised users are not always effective (Thomas, 2008).

The lack of emphasis on archives among some of those interviewed could be linked to the uncertainty over whether blogging practice bears a closer relation to orality or written speech, which was alluded to earlier. This was not directly probed in the interviews, but in the case of at least one interviewee, Isobel, blogging was clearly framed as an oral activity. She said she was not happy to pursue political arguments on her blog because 'if I had to actually sit down and write a coherent argument about why I believed X, Y and Z. It would just ruin the sort of spontaneity'.

To partially substantiate the blurring of the framing of blogging between orality and written forms that was suggested in some blogging literature, I counted the frequency of appearance of the words 'I wrote' (24 times) when associated with weblogging in the interview transcripts and compared this to the frequency of 'I said' and 'I talked' (15 times altogether). Twice both oral and written framings appeared to be used at the same time, which seems to highlight the ambiguity in bloggers' perceptions of their practice. Harriet mentioned 'a recent post where I talked about forgiveness' and Betty said she had decided: 'I would write . . . and it would be, not formal exactly but careful about you know, how I talked about other people'.

To the extent that blogging is experienced as oral, it may also be perceived as sharing speech's normal properties of transitoriness and this may consequently also concentrate the producers' attention on primary rather than secondary reception of their blogs.

In the previous chapter it was noted that many bloggers appeared to orient their practice in relation to an imagined and somewhat idealised audience, and to overlook – possibly deliberately – other unintended audiences. Similarly, the evidence outlined in this section appears to suggest that many bloggers either overlook the possibility that their archives will be read by anyone other than themselves (possibly because blogging seems more an oral than a written practice) or they imagine such reading as taking place in a distant future time by themselves or by a well-disposed posterity.

Conclusion

In the interviews conducted with bloggers, it emerged that a substantial minority of those interviewed had changed their attitude towards their blogging practice after starting blogging – sometimes more than once. However, this was not (as one might have expected) generally to do with reactions to privacy breaches. The bloggers I interviewed did not attempt to edit their past blog postings to make these consistent with changed framings of blogging practice, even when past postings embarrassed them. And, even when they abandoned their blogs altogether, they often left the text of those blogs online rather than seeking to have them removed.

The examination of interviewees' attitudes towards their blogs' archives provides two chief potential explanations for this behaviour. Firstly, it appeared that several perceived a norm that they should not edit past entries which may also have influenced bloggers not to attempt to remove weblogs from view that they were 'finished with'. This may also be related to the sense that weblogs are an open-ended project – some appear to have finished blogging since they have not posted for several months, but they evidently did not feel they needed to formally announce an end. Even such an announcement does not appear binding – several bloggers posted that they were finishing and then recommended blogging without further explanation. Perhaps because of this open-endedness, bloggers appear reluctant to take the final step of removing their blogs completely. At the time of the fieldwork, any such decision would have been final and irrevocable (Blogger, n.d.; LiveJournal, 2007).[6]

Secondly, it appeared that they generally did not expect readers to read the archives of their blogs – they appeared to be focused on their blogs' 'primary reception' or, to a lesser extent, on their own reading at some point in the future. Thus, it may not have appeared necessary for them to make later posts consistent in content or style with earlier ones. This focus on the present may be related to a perception of blogging as an oral rather than a written form that has been tentatively identified.

It is often implied that if a communicative practice's technical characteristics are well understood then those who practice it must be intending to take advantage of those characteristics. The analysis conducted in this study suggests, by contrast, that unsought or perceived undesirable technical characteristics of the weblog can be overlooked by users, deliberately ignored or simply put up with. Although it seems clear that weblogs automatically archive all the content that producers write, making it readable for an indefinite period (and they all include by default a keyword search function on the front page of the blog itself), blogger attitudes in the sample towards the existence of this archive were mixed and both their awareness of the potential reception of their archived postings at a future date and their willingness to edit their archives to protect their self-presentation appear to be subject to both technological and social biases.

Constitutive bias seems to emerge primarily because the sheer volume of text produced in the course of months or years of blogging makes producers feel it would be impractical to make alterations. Where a blog's contents were felt to pose a significant challenge to the producer's current self-presentation, the only solutions that were perceived to be practical were to change the status of the blog by removing it entirely, by making it 'friends-only' or by moving it elsewhere. Any of these would be seen as a draconian solution to any but the most problematic releases of social information. The influence of social norms was discerned because some bloggers said they felt it would be wrong to edit past entries.

Some interviewees for this study did value the archival function provided by weblogging, although for differing reasons, as one might expect given the differing attitudes towards potential readers that have been identified. Some spoke of the usefulness of blog archives as a benefit to themselves; relatively few spoke of the benefit of the archival function for future readers. However, many interviewees appeared to have given little thought to the archives of their blogs at all, suggesting that these would be of little interest to most of their readers and reporting that they seldom looked at their archives themselves.

While for some the availability of an ongoing archive represents an opportunity to reflect on their own personal journeys, the manner in which archives that include social information about a weblog's author persist through time can represent a threat to what Goffman describes as the need to maintain face by presenting an image that is internally consistent (Goffman, 1967, p. 6). The self-presentation that has been archived may be inconsistent with a current self-image maintained in other contexts or that which is currently expressed on the blog (or both). The acceptability of the expressions preserved therein can depend on the temporal context in which they were originally situated – personal views can change as do societal mores. I have not uncovered research into the ways in which blog readers may interpret and take into account the blend of past and present postings they encounter in their reading, and this study did not include questions dealing with this point, but as Mayer-Schönberger (2009) suggests: 'secondary reception' of blog postings may be particularly problematic.

Weblog postings, once made, can be edited by the producer or removed at any point and it was expected at the outset of this study that bloggers might continuously or periodically modify or remove archived material in order to maintain a consistent self-presentation as the conceptual framework suggests would take place. This did not appear to occur frequently, however. The analysis of the interview data and the weblogs themselves suggests that a small amount of retrospective modification did take place, but generally only when grammatical or spelling mistakes were spotted. Interviewees showed little awareness of the possibility that what they wrote might also be archived by third-party sites.

As outlined earlier in the chapter, the 'objective' memorability of postings on any given service and the manner in which social media services' interfaces make it easier or more difficult to look back into the accessible past vary considerably. Outside of blogging studies there appears to have been little academic research into issues of secondary reception in social media. Nonetheless, despite its somewhat different technological affordances, a qualitative study of Facebook and its users referenced earlier comes to similar conclusions to those I have outlined:

> For all users, oneself and those one connect with, what one was cannot be crafted again or adjusted through Facebook. Not only does its design de-privilege ways in which this might be done, but

users – users in our study anyway – also show lack of desire for this: no-one looks back. After all, if one attempts to do so, one's efforts need to be accounted for in the present and that causes complexity and complaint. Thus one is brought back to heel; one is brought back to a fixed 'now', the endless durée of Facebook.

(Harper et al , 2012, p. 17)

This suggests that, at the very least, further studies of the temporal aspects of social media self-presentation are called for.

6
Towards a Radically Open Society

In earlier chapters we have explored how the rising volumes of social media postings may expose users to harm when they are viewed by unanticipated audiences and at unanticipated times. But it is also worth considering why, despite these risks and despite the ready availability of a multitude of other means of social interaction, social media use continues to grown in breadth and depth.

Of course, as the final chapter will explore, social media use has some clearly perceived benefits and gratifications that potentially explain some of this explosion of activity. Over and above this, however, this chapter aims to outline some of the cultural, technological and commercial forces that appear to be driving not only the adoption of SNSes but also an increase in the breadth of information being shared on such services. To summarise the argument I will develop in this chapter, technological affordances of digital communication tools were recognised and exploited by engineers and entrepreneurs, many of whom who appear to have been influenced by a set of (counter)*cultural attitudes* towards self-expression and what we now call 'sharing', which can be traced back in part to the US counterculture from the late 1960s and 1970s. These values (at least as adopted by key social media organisations) have proved consistent with particular *commercial imperatives* and, together, these lead to advertising messages and *technological biases* that push people towards greater online self-disclosure or, as corporations would suggest, greater openness and sharing. In the large parts of the world where social media are becoming near-ubiquitous in certain groups, the *network effects* that result can make it difficult for people to disengage or even minimise their use. Lastly, I will outline several ways in which it seems that *technological trajectories* appear likely to increase the volume of social media data (and thereby almost inevitably multiply the opportunities for social media-related harm).

How did we get here? A brief history of the social media industry

Although it was conceived primarily as an information appliance, the internet has always been a social medium. As Hafner and Lyon remark, 'the ARPANET's creators didn't have a grand vision for the invention of an Earth circling message handling system. But once the first couple of dozen nodes were installed, early users turned the system of linked computers into a personal as well as professional communications tool' (Hafner & Lyon, 1996, p. 189). For much of the early involvement of the internet however, it supported mediated interpersonal interaction aimed at a limited set of specific others (email), mediated quasi-interaction aimed at an indefinite range of potential recipients but not envisioning a dialogue (the webpage) and telelogic communication, envisioning a dialogue but one more or less framed by a set topic or community (the messageboard).[1] What the personal homepage and then personal weblogs added initially was the placement of the individual and their identity at the centre of an internet-mediated practice.[2] These two practices might not be conventionally grouped alongside the use of social media services like Facebook and Twitter, but they are important forerunners. It is at this point that the kinds of risks of self-disclosure to undefined or ill-defined audiences discussed in this book began to emerge.

With the emergence of SNSes – starting with sixdegrees.com in 1997 but popularised by Friendster 2002 (d. boyd & Ellison, 2007), three new elements have gradually been added to self-disclosure sites and practices which have deepened and broadened the risks of their use. The first and most obvious additional element is simply the greatly increased scale of participation. While in the US fewer than one in 10 internet users has ever maintained a personal weblog (Pew Internet & American Life Project, n.d.-a) and fewer than one in five in the UK (Dutton & Blank, 2013),[3] numbers that do not appear to be rising, two-thirds of US and UK internet users use social media (Dutton & Blank, 2013; Pew Internet & American Life Project, n.d.-a). While the adoption of Facebook (for example) may now be slowing in both the US and UK (Bercovici, 2013), thanks largely to increases in internet adoption worldwide, the number of people using Facebook each month continues to rise – from 1 billion in September 2012 to 1.28 billion in March 2014 (Facebook, 2013a). This number excludes the millions of people who use other SNSes – in China, for example, where Facebook is not available, as of January 2014 an estimated 278 million people were using social networking websites and 281 million were using microblogging sites (CNNIC, 2014).

The second new element is the trend in SNS towards an insistence on the users indicating their real names. Revelation of personal information is generally only harmful if it is attributed (rightly or wrongly) to specific individuals. Thus, while personal weblogs and home pages by their nature do involve the sharing of personal information, the frequent use of pseudonyms and other anonymising practices by those who maintain them is an attempt to minimise potential harm.[4] Increasingly, this option is no longer available for SNS users. There are a number of reasons driving this change – some straightforwardly utilitarian, others perhaps more questionable. Some of the more popular SNSes like Facebook are becoming virtual phonebooks for their users and, there may be social pressure on users from their peers not to use pseudonyms. Those who run SNSes also suggest that the use of pseudonyms can lead to antisocial behaviour. Google's chairman, when asked why Google was demanding users of its Google+ SNS use their real names, reportedly suggested that the internet 'would be better if we knew you were a real person rather than a dog or a fake person. Some people are just evil and we should be able to ID them and rank them downward' (Banks, 2011). It is also the case, however, that the commercial value of the data that we share about ourselves on an SNS is greater when it can be attached to an individual and related to other activities of that individual.

The fact that Facebook demands users' real names and articulates connections between activities across its service means that there is much more room for potentially harmful leakage when those with a hidden stigma use it to find others. In one case, changes in Facebook privacy settings revealed to parents that their children were gay when their membership of a gay choir was inadvertently made public (Fowler, 2012) Google's preference for real names and its knowledge of even pseudonymous users' 'real' identities has caused the Google+ service to inadvertently 'out' a number of transgendered individuals (Blue, 2014).

Moreover, in several countries – notably China – laws have been passed requiring SNS users to register using their real names or government identity numbers (Chen, 2012), presumably in part to further dissuade SNS users from expressing political opposition online and to assist in the prosecution of dissenters.

The third new element is what I referred to in Chapter 3 as the increased interlinking of computer-mediated communication. As I noted there, computer-mediated communication using a web (or web-like) platform is bound to be more interlinked than, say, emails without web addresses included once were, but the rise of SNSes has greatly accelerated this trend, as they tend to be more densely interlinked than the rest of the internet. This is not merely a technological accident – as will be discussed below, it is a design choice made to maximise revenue for these sites.

From the 'new communalism' to the rhetoric of 'sharing'

It is outside the scope of this text to provide an extensive discussion of recent sociological discussion about identity in modern society. However, it is notable that a number of leading sociologists (Bauman, 2001; Beck & Beck-Gernsheim, 2001; Giddens, 1991; Lash & Friedman, 1991; Rose, 1999) have suggested in different ways that one of the principal characteristics of late modernity is the need for individuals to define their identities reflexively – a task that online technologies which enable self-expression may appear suited to address. Chandler, for example, suggests that through self-reflexive writing home page authors can 'change ourselves to who we really want to be' (1998).

Why explore one's identity before an audience, however? Giddens (1990) and Illouz (2007) have suggested there is an increasing pressure in modern society to share intimate life details in a variety of contexts in order to build relationships with others. Rose, too notes that 'truthful rendering into speech of who one is, to one's parents, one's teachers, one's doctor, one's lover, and oneself, is installed at the heart of contemporary procedures of individualization' (Rose, 1999, p. 244).

Beyond these overarching sociological considerations, however, I wish to examine a very particular set of social norms around computer-mediated communication which appear to run counter to dominant societal norms. While we are generally admonished to 'think before we talk', and the work of scholars like Goffman is predicated on the notion that impression management is central to interpersonal communication, this alternative set of norms suggests we should express ourselves online openly and honestly. Perhaps the most influential exponent of this philosophy is Mark Zuckerberg, Facebook's founder. While we accept as normal the notion that we present one version of the self to one's co-workers and another to one's family or close friends, Zuckerberg questions that: ' "You have one identity", he says emphatically three times in a single minute during a 2009 interview' (Kirkpatrick, 2010, p. 199), and Facebook has been designed accordingly. At an early point in its development, for example, Zuckerberg rejected suggestions that adult users should be able to have both a work profile and a 'fun social profile'. 'The days of you having a different image for your work friends or co-workers and for the other people you know are probably coming to an end pretty quickly', he says (ibid., p. 199). According to

Kirkpatrick who interviewed the Facebook CEO several times for his book, Zuckerberg's objections are not merely pragmatic (or indeed commercially motivated) but are moral: 'Having two identities for yourself is an example of a lack of integrity' (ibid., p. 199).

This point of view is not an isolated one. It can be found expressed in different ways by many early adopters and opinion performers online, both in their advice about how people should express themselves online and in their own online practice. For example, one high-profile blogger, Tony Pierce, insisted in 'How to Blog' that you must 'say exactly what you want to say no matter what it looks like on the screen' (Pierce, 2004). Another, Mark Bernstein, said in '10 tips on Writing the Living Web': 'Write honestly. Don't hide, and don't stop short' (M. Bernstein, 2002). Many early web pioneers clearly internalised these norms, including Justin Hall, dubbed 'the founding father of personal blogging' and who, starting in 1994, wrote about his father's suicide, his shingles and his sex life, among many other things (Rosen, 2004). Julie Petersen, who worked with Hall at *Wired* magazine wrote about an affair on her personal website as it unfolded (Petersen, 1995).

These attitudes remain widespread online today and were expressed by a number of the bloggers I interviewed. Harriet, for example, explicitly contrasted the (relative) freedom of expression on her blog with the limitations she felt in everyday social interaction:

It's my blog. And it's about how I feel at this particular time. I can't be all singing all dancing cartwheeling. Sometimes I've got to be down. And I think maybe that's one of the things I learned about myself in the blogging. People even in real life – and it does happen sometimes on the blog – expect you to be all singing all dancing cracking the jokes keeping everybody else upbeat and sometimes I just go 'fuck it I don't want to be'. And I'll say it. [...] And people relate to that as well. And if they don't well tough shit.

Two of the interviewees went even further, asserting not just that they should be able to say what they wanted but that they felt that they (and other bloggers) were under pressure to be more open in their weblog writing than is normally permitted in everyday social interaction. This seems to be consistent with the framing of blogging as suggested by Frances, who said: 'my whole life is on there pretty much':

There are really no rules and you can post whatever the hell you like and because it's your site you don't have to – there are no rules so you can say whatever you like and who gives a shit about what that person over there thinks?

Charles insisted that while his own weblog writing was 'my public face', 'true blogging' requires you to write 'as if nobody's reading'. To the extent this is so, the rhetoric of freedom may paradoxically make some writers feel *less* free to avoid self-disclosure.

Alongside the 'openness' norm and related to it is the norm that suggests that one should be truthful in one's accounts about one's self. For example, Renia, whose blog discussed some of the most personal material including self-harm and a suicide attempt, appeared to feel this most strongly. She said:

> I tend to try to leave it as much as I can because I think it might be wrong to alter it just because I am a bit embarrassed.
>
> *If you did something you were really ashamed of would you blog about it?*
>
> I would tell them, yeah. I would say 'look this is what I did'. I would try to put it in a slightly good light but I wouldn't hold back – I would tell them the truth.

And Harriet remarked: 'if you're going to write about yourself – I try to be honest with my posts – not just being honest about myself but about what I'm doing – because otherwise what's the point?'

Marwick observes in her study of Twitter users that – rhetorically at least – many of them also adhere to this norm, insisting as one of them put it: 'when I tweet, I tweet honestly, I tweet passionately. Pure expression of my heart' (A. Marwick & boyd, 2011, p. 119). Some of her own evidence like the quote above and my own fieldwork with bloggers suggests, however, not merely that 'Twitter users negotiate multiple, overlapping audiences by strategically concealing information, targeting tweets to different audiences and *attempting to portray* both an authentic self and an interesting personality' (ibid., p. 124) – emphasis mine – but that some at least have internalised the authenticity norm and attempt not merely to appear but actually to *be* authentic in their postings.

To thoroughly explore the origins of this set of norms around CMC would be a task for another book, but thanks in particular to the work of Fred Turner (2005, 2006) a key potential influence can be identified. The story begins in the late 1960s with the movement he dubs the 'New Communalism', which 'bubbled up from a wide variety of cold war–era cultural springs, including beat poetry and fiction, Zen Buddhism, action painting, and, by the mid-1960s, encounters with psychedelic drugs' (Turner, 2005, p. 493). Crucially for our discussion, it 'hoped to return Americans to a more emotionally authentic and community-based way of life' by transforming ourselves and our relations with others to achieve a 'transcendent collectivity' (ibid., pp. 493–494). The Farm, a commune in Summertown, Tennessee established in 1971, was one attempt to achieve this – there, in the words of one of its members: 'everyone was expected to "say what they saw" about anyone else. Your mind had to be an open book. A mental nudist colony' (Coate, 1987). By 1983, the commune had collapsed but three years later, three of its members would become key managers of an early virtual community, The Well. While the San Francisco-based bulletin board never had more than a few thousand members, it was to become hugely influential online as it attracted journalists, numerous virtual community pioneers including Howard Rheingold, the author of 'the Virtual Community' (2000), and the founders of the Electronic Frontier Foundation (EFF) and of *Wired* magazine, among others. And according to Turner, 'by the mid-1980s, the New Communalist movement had largely melted away, yet the "Community Imperative" and its ideal of virtual, as well as material, collectivity lived on in the software, management structures, and day-to-day rhetoric of the WELL' (Turner, 2005, p. 503).

Another and more radical but related set of ideas that appear to be emerging are lifelogging and the 'quantified self' (QS) community (http://quantifiedself.com/), whose chief promoters and organisers are Gary Wolf and Kevin Kelly (both from *Wired* magazine and long-time members of The Well). Adherents seek to take advantage of the increasing availability and sophistication of recording and measurement tools to monitor themselves in their everyday lives and, in the case of the QS, to use those data as a means of self-improvement. These embryonic groups do not yet have a coherent set of norms around how and whether the data that they collect about themselves and others should be shared. However, to the extent that these ideas popularise the use of automated tracking and recording devices connected (as they usually are) to the internet, it seems inevitable that they would contribute to greater circulation of personal information online and via social media.

These narratives have been exploited by commercial organisations as counter-narratives to conventional concerns about privacy. These include both the companies that provide SNSes and members of the larger 'ecosystem' of companies with a commercial interest in encouraging consumer internet use and data sharing (internet providers, mobile phone and computer vendors). As John (2013) analyses, a variety of

138 Sharing Our Lives Online

forms of self-presentation, creative expression and phatic communication have been grouped together and relabelled 'sharing'. Not only does this word itself have a positive connotation that conceals the potential harm from oversharing, it also neatly rhymes with caring, thus:

> In a blog entry from 2009, we are told that 'the Share button enables you to take content from across the Web and share it with your friends on Facebook, where it can be re-shared over and over so the best and most interesting items get noticed by the people you care about'.
>
> (Facebook, 2009)
>
> Disregarding the fact that if the content you have shared is 're-shared over and over' then it is unlikely that you will even know the people who are noticing it, let alone care about them, the connotation of this quote is quite clear: your sharing is an expression of your caring.
>
> (John, 2013, p. 176)

He goes on to find very similar phrasing used by three other SNSes, and it is not merely SNS companies themselves but also the hundreds of other companies with a stake in greater interpersonal-mediated communications who are reinforcing this framing – he notes: 'in a British ad campaign from 2011, mobile telephony company T-Mobile ran the slogan "Life's for Sharing". One ad, for example, tells us that "Some things in life you just have to share"' (ibid., p. 176).

In a particularly Orwellian use of language, in 2011 Facebook introduced a feature that would automatically post status updates on users' behalf when they read or interacted with sites that had implemented this technology. It dubbed this feature 'frictionless sharing' – because who wants to cause friction? In this case it appears, notwithstanding this clever piece of branding, that the public has yet to warm to the idea (Greenfield, 2012), but Facebook has a history of pushing boundaries, retreating in the face of concerted opposition but often successfully returning to similar proposals in a new guise when concern has subsided (van Dijck, 2013).

Sometimes, companies claim that they are merely responding to changing attitudes, not driving them. Fitzpatrick reports that Zuckerberg describes a kind of deterministic law of ever-increasing sharing, akin to Moore's Law that (correctly) predicted an exponential growth in the number of transistors on a silicon chip over time. 'In a decade, he believes, 1000 times more information about each individual member may flow through Facebook. This hypothesis has corollaries he finds intriguing. Says he: "people are going to have the have a device with them at all times that's [automatically] sharing. You can predict that"' (Kirkpatrick, 2010, p. 313).

Companies are now using the changes that they claim are observable in people's privacy norms to seek loosening of privacy laws. Netflix, for example, successfully challenged a US law that prohibited them from sharing information about the films and TV programmes users were watching without seeking consent each time, by noting that users of Facebook and Spotify were already doing such sharing (Van Dijck, 2013, p. 66).

All of this fits conveniently with the claims alluded to in Chapter 2 that 'digital natives' have a more relaxed attitude to privacy than older generations (Palfrey & Gasser, 2008) and the implication that they might continue to care less about their privacy as they age. As I noted in that chapter, there is room to doubt that this is the case, however, and more fundamentally, as I will address in the concluding chapter, we must ask as a society not just whether we will in future come to tolerate or even enjoy a society with greater self-disclosure, but whether that state of affairs would in some higher sense be good for us.

This also overlooks the possibility that there might be important differences in attitudes towards online privacy between different cultures. Certainly some studies comparing the US to China, Japan and Germany suggest potential points of difference (Capurro, 2005; Krasnova, Veltri & Gunther, 2012; Lu, 2005). For example, a five-nation survey about sharing privacy and trust found, amongst other things, that while overall 35 per cent of respondents said they liked to be anonymous when using social networking services, the proportion in Japan was over 50 per cent (De Rosa, Cantrell, Havens, Hawk & Jenkins, 2007). International social networking services have an interest in equalising attitudes towards privacy protection and pushing all of them in a more permissive direction. Van Dijck suggests that Facebook 'has played an important role in spreading (American) social norms into other national user communities worldwide' (ibid., 2013, p. 57).

Technological biases

It is not merely through advertising messages that companies can encourage self-disclosure – they can also use software defaults and the way in which choices are presented to the user – what Feenberg refers to as 'constitutive bias' (Feenberg, 2008) – see Chapter 3.

The power of defaults to affect individuals' behaviour has also been increasingly recognised thanks to the popularity of books like *Nudge* (Thaler & Sunstein, 2008). While the specific effectiveness of any given default setting can vary depending on context, there are very striking examples from the world of technology. One study of Wifi routers, for example, found that only 28–57 per cent of users acted to change the default settings on their routers to give them a different name than the default even though experts, manufacturers and the government all suggest that they do so (Shah & Sandvig, 2008).

Bucher, in her analysis of the way that Facebook, for example, presents privacy controls, provides a clear and striking example of both modes of persuasion in action:

> The platform itself configures personal profiles for connection by setting the default in the basic privacy settings of users personal profiles to 'everyone'. The privacy settings explicitly state that changing the defaults will 'prevent you from connecting with your friends'; conversely by keeping the default you will 'help' your friends from all spheres and passages of life 'to find you'.
>
> (Bucher, 2012)

Thus, while users are free to choose the setting they like, Facebook has done everything possible to nudge them towards the company's preferred choice, consistent with Zuckerberg's stated goal – to build a web where 'the default is social' (Shiels, 2010).

And the nudging does not merely move towards a set limit – as noted in Chapter 4, social media services, and Facebook in particular, tend to keep 'moving the goalposts'. Once users are accustomed to a certain level of disclosure, their tolerance can be tested again with a new shift in settings. McKeon demonstrates this convincingly in graphical form, showing how with each 'improvement' in Facebook's privacy settings, more information became visible by default (2010) – the Electronic Freedom Foundation has done a similar exercise in textual form (Opsahl, 2010).

If there were any doubt that this is a conscious strategy, it is worth noting that Facebook employees are themselves publishing scholarly research in this area – for example, they themselves have experimented to find ways to encourage newcomers to contribute more on Facebook. They found (unsurprisingly) that, among other things, 'newcomers who see their friends contributing go on to share more content themselves' (Moira, Cameron & Thomas, 2009, p. 1), making it all the more important that they continue to push ever-increasing self-disclosure.

Commercial imperatives

Facebook grandly starts its statement of principles by saying it was built 'to make the world more open and transparent, which we believe will create greater understanding and connection' (Facebook, n.d.-a), and Google claims when designing new features that they 'take great care to ensure that they will ultimately serve *you*, rather than our own internal goal or bottom line' (Google, n.d.). Once social media organisations become publicly held businesses, however (and all the major social media services except Wikipedia either are or seek to be public companies), they come under overwhelming pressure to maximise the profits of their companies – ideally quarter by quarter or at least plausibly in the medium term. As Dror, in his analysis (2013) of these manifestoes concludes, even if we assume that the intentions of these founders are genuine they will only be able to follow through on these promises as long as they deliver these profits.

Exactly what this implies in terms of corporate practices can be harder to establish, because of differences in business models between social media companies, because in the present fast-changing environment, business models are apt to change and, at a deeper level, because of corporate confidentiality. Academics who study the structure and business models of the social media industry (Cha, 2013; Van Dijck, 2013) have identified advertising as the single largest source of revenue for most such services but within that overall umbrella it is not clear, for example, how important is the precision of user targeting that social media services claim to be able to provide towards maximising revenue, or the extent to which now or in the future social media companies will rely on revenues from selling user behaviour data to market researchers, advertisers and data brokers. Given the importance of these organisations to our everyday lives, the fact that the ways in which they make their money are only understood in their broadest sense should concern us all. We can, however, make some reasonable generalisations based on known market conditions.

Facebook, for example, derives more than 80 per cent of its income from advertising (Cutler, 2013). While the sheer volume of traffic to sites like Facebook ensures a level of revenue, it is the ability of social media sites to identify users' exact interests and characteristics – in part because of what they consciously reveal about themselves online – that is the key selling point of advertising on such sites, and drives them to continuously refine their understanding of their users (Sengupta, 2013). According to one study, sites that sold advertising that is targeted based on known reader characteristics could charge 2.68 times as much for it than sites that did not have such information (Beales, 2009). This is just part of a wider trend among the media to target consumers in ever more sophisticated ways (Turow, 2005). However restrictive the privacy controls chosen by users, they don't protect users' data from access by the hosting companies themselves – the extent to which their data are protected is up to the privacy policies of these companies and, where relevant, national laws (as long as these are respected).

As Van Dijck perceptively remarks, SNS owners use 'a sort of newspeak when claiming that technology merely enables or facilitates social activities; however, "making the Web social" in reality means "making sociality technical." Sociality coded by technology renders people's activities formal, manageable, and manipulable, enabling platforms to engineer the sociality in people's everyday routines' (Van Dijck, 2013, p. 12). One key business objective of SNSes is to maximise use and activity. By the increasing use of automated interlinking, the sharing of what seems to be a single piece of information (a picture of a party) can trigger multiple sharing 'events' (there was a party at a given location, and Tom, Dick and Harry attended a party), each of which may in turn trigger a reaction and thereby a reason to return to the service that the information is hosted on to post that reaction.

Linked to this, the recoding of social interactions into technologically mapped data points makes it easier for SNSes to algorithmically analyse and manipulate our behaviour. For example, once a social network service knows that you have held parties at a bar several times over the period of a month, it can sell the opportunity to change your mind in regard to a nearby alternative venue. At present, the privacy policies of social media companies (or simply their technological capabilities) may preclude these kinds of intrusive use, but the sophistication of the technology for behavioural data analysis continues to advance and, in their search for new revenue streams in an uncertain business environment, social media companies may move further and further in this direction. Certainly, in common with other business organisations, they have every incentive to maximise the amount of data they can gather in case these become valuable in future. For example, Fitbit, which makes devices that measure physical activity (and encourages you to share these data with your friends on social networks) is also working with health insurers so the price of your health coverage in the US may in future be linked to your level of physical activity – as long as you volunteer to share these data (and your employer might penalise you if you don't) (Olson & Tilley, 2014).

Network effects

As use of SNSes becomes widespread within a given social group, non-participation becomes more and more difficult. When network services like Facebook offer a wide variety of functions – not just status updates and picture sharing but messaging and party or event coordination features – those who are not connected can miss out on a variety of social opportunities. Once connected, however, there is evidence that alongside the technological biases that encourage self-disclosure, peer expectations may also pressure even reluctant users to share. For example, as one US teenager explained:

> to combat nagging questions from friends and classmates, she has started creating a 'light version' of her life that she'll regularly share on Facebook just so that her friends don't pester her about what's actually happening. Much to her frustration, she finds that sharing at least a little bit affords her more privacy than sharing nothing at all.
>
> (d. boyd, 2014)

One recent survey found that 24 per cent of US Facebook users strongly disliked the 'temptation or pressure to share too much information about yourself', and 12 per cent strongly disliked the 'pressure to post comments that will be popular and get lots of comments/likes' (Smith, 2014). Not only has Facebook made location sharing a default feature for mobile users of its messenger service (without warning users who download the software), but if you wish to use Facebook to see your friends' locations via Facebook in order to meet them, you also have to make your own locations visible to them – thus adding peer pressure to make locations available (Dzyre, 2014).

If people become uncomfortable with the way that social media encourages them to share, can they not simply reduce what they say or opt out altogether? Clearly, in principle they can. However, there can be significant social costs to the individual of such a move, as Mayer-Schönberger (2009) has remarked. We have already seen in Chapter 5 that people can become attached to the cumulative records of their digital selves that are archived as they participate in social media. In addition, both for privacy reasons and for reasons of competitive advantage, social media companies can be reluctant to make it easy for users to take their data with them when they go or move them to another service. They do all they can to discourage withdrawal – as Bates explains, if you deactivate your Facebook account:

> In a stroke of evil genius, Facebook then confronts you with pictures of your friends and messages saying how much they will 'miss you'. Swallowing the lump in your throat, you then have to opt out of Facebook emails – or the site will continue to taunt you with messages about parties and events you are now missing. Even then, deactivation does not actually get rid of your account but leaves it 'hanging in a cloud', waiting for you to scurry back. Deletion is more terminal and the social networking site doesn't make it easy. You have to search Facebook's servers for how to do it and then send in a request, which has to be confirmed by email. Facebook insists that within two weeks every single trace of you will be gone from its servers, with no chance of getting it back. But even then you will still have a presence on the website if any of your Facebook friends continue to put up photos of you.

Just as importantly, withdrawal from a social media service is often not just an individual choice but affects one's relations with others. Numerous case studies of those who have attempted to withdraw from social networks attest to the friction this can cause (Baumer et al., 2013; Portwood-Stacer, 2013; Turkle, 2011; Van Dijck, 2013). Withdrawal from the network can be read as a withdrawal from those who are connected to you through it. Take the case of Bruce, who chose to withdraw from Facebook for political reasons:

> People in his network got offended that he was willing to sacrifice his personal online relationships with them over a political issue. Bruce's aunt expressed sadness that they couldn't interact on Facebook any more. A friend with whom Bruce had used Facebook to stay in touch accused him of being self-centered for 'throwing away' the relationship they had had, just for some ideological stance against Wikileaks. The friend also thought Bruce was being 'self-promoting' by quitting, to show off how 'badass' he was for being able to quit.
>
> (Portwood-Stacer, 2013, p. 1042)

Although numerous other means of communication remain available, it seems that people can be surprisingly resistant to being forced to use them, as this informant from another study of Facebook non-use illustrates:

One acquaintance deactivated his account without warning anyone first, and the fact that he was suddenly not contactable through Facebook dismayed a lot of people. [...] a lot of his friends were not in the same country as him and used Facebook as a primary mode of communication; although they could email him, this was not the norm and many said they didn't want to do that.

(Baumer et al., 2013, p. 6)

Van Dijck tells a similar story – when Pete in a family she studied quit Facebook, he was most troubled by:

the negative reactions from his friends, relatives, and club members who complained they now had to send him separate e-mails to garner his attention ... Pete felt locked in by omnipresent connective media, both technically and socially; paradoxically, he felt caught in the trap of a normative online sociality he had himself helped create over the years.

(Van Dijck, 2013, p. 154)

Moreover, in the social media-saturated milieu that many – particularly the young – increasingly inhabit, failing to participate can be seen as deviant. For example, 'Both users and non-users use words like "strange", "weird", "crazy", "frustrating", and "anti-social" to describe people who choose not to be on Facebook' (Portwood-Stacer, 2013, p. 1049).

Technological trajectories

The technology that has without a doubt contributed most to the explosion of social media services and the increasing circulation of data through them is the smartphone. Before the smartphone, if you wished to write something online you had to have a computer with you, and if you wanted to take a picture, you needed to be carrying a digital camera. Smartphones (and more recently tablet devices) are always with their owners and enable short textual updates, video or still images to be uploaded and shared with a few taps of the finger – with location data automatically appended. Because they tend to be always on, they are also ideal for a variety of forms of what Facebook terms 'frictionless sharing' – the tracking and later distribution of location data, for example.

Globally, per capita smartphone penetration has soared from 7 per cent in 2010 to an estimated 22 per cent in 2013, and tablets were expected to be in the hands of 6 per cent of the population by the end of 2013 (Heggestuen, 2013). Despite this rapid growth, there is clearly plenty of room for further diffusion of this technology – 44 per cent of Americans still did not have one as of mid-2013. As these technologies continue to diffuse (and since social media sharing is one of the key selling points for these devices), one can expect a great deal more social media activity in the coming years. The age at which such devices are likely to be available is also dropping – one study in 2013 in the UK found that on average children received their first mobile phone at 11 years old but 9 per cent of parents bought their children a phone at five years old (Press Association, 2013b).

Smartphones have developed and diffused rapidly thanks to reductions in the price and size of key components like camera and batteries and corresponding increases in digital storage space and processing power. Their popularity has driven the cost of the components they use down still further, and this in turn has enabled new forms of digitally connected device and a new term to describe their emergence – the 'Internet of Things'. The dream of having a multitude of digital devices communicating with one another in the home is as old as personal computing itself – before anyone considered that people might want a word processor at home, early personal computer designers thought they might want to control their home lighting, audio and security cameras using computer networks (Friedman, 2005). To date the industry has had little success in marketing these devices, but Google's purchase of Nest, a maker of 'smart home devices', for $3.2bn suggests this is a strategic direction, at least for this influential tech giant (Carroll, 2014). Just as personal videoconferencing remained forever the 'technology of the future' until Skype and ubiquitous broadband came along and made it free of charge, so the cost of building in connectivity to everyday appliances is declining to the point where there will be no reason not to provide, say, a camera when you buy a doorbell and connect it online. A billion digital cameras were built into new mobile devices in 2012 alone, and adding a simple camera to any device costs around $10 (*The Economist*, 2013) – enabling devices to connect to a wireless network costs a further $5 (Mims, 2013). Alongside the smartphone, we are being offered internet-connected watches and, as this book is written, Google Glass – internet-connected eyeglasses with built-in cameras and recording equipment. Although we have been assured that the latter has been designed not to be well adapted to surreptitious surveillance, anything that makes even the overt recording of everyday interactions more 'frictionless' has the potential to be dangerous.

Other companies will surely take advantage of the capabilities on offer and may not necessarily offer similar safeguards. The Narrative Clip, for example, is a device a bit more than one centimetre square, costing $279 at the time of writing, that takes pictures automatically, twice per minute all day long (http://getnarrative.com/). In 2014, it is already possible to purchase a drone for $1200 which can fly for 20–25 minutes, controlled from a smartphone, hover by itself and take still pictures or video (Eaton, 2014). Amber Case, a 'cyborg anthropologist', envisions a world of 'invisible buttons' – areas in space that trigger actions when you or a device that belongs to you passes through or touches them (Knowles, 2012). It's not hard to envision, for example, a 'smart' door to a bar that lets you enter only if you have a sufficiently high number of Twitter followers.

And inexpensive sensors can do more than simply hear and see you – they may also monitor your heart rate and even brain wave activity to 'enhance' your everyday interactions. InteraXon (http://www.interaxon.ca/) has demonstrated a headband that reads brain waves to change the font of an email message depending on the emotional state of the writer (Knowles, 2012). Wouldn't it be convenient to have friends able to provide you with sympathy on your favourite social network when you are feeling low without your even needing to tell them why? There are many more examples of the planned or actual use of monitoring of emotional states to, for example, sell products when you are at your most vulnerable (Morozov, 2013).

It is not necessary to imagine the ubiquitous or malicious use of such devices and services to become alarmed at harms that might emerge – if even a sizeable minority of people and places became hyper-connected in this way, it could be hard for the rest of us to avoid being implicated in the social media chatter that they might generate. And of course companies and governments might take the use of these technologies as a further sign that we are no longer interested in protecting our privacy.

Conclusion

Discussion about why people on social media are revealing more about themselves and to more people than ever before often returns in the end to a narrative of personal (ir-)responsibility. 'Nobody is forced to say what they say online', it is argued, 'and appropriate privacy settings are available to control others' access to what they say if they want to use them'. In earlier chapters, we have examined some of the reasons people may simply fail to understand or choose to overlook some of the risks they run in publishing their information online. This chapter sheds light on the economic, technical and social factors that create an environment where online self-disclosure and peer disclosure is ever easier and encouraged at every turn.

This is not to say, of course, that individuals don't bear some responsibility for their actions when they reveal material online in an ill-advised way. Nor would I wish to suggest that individual users are powerless in the face of these pressures. There is evidence that some people are resisting some of these social media trends, by reducing their social media use or withdrawing altogether (Baumer et al., 2013; Portwood-Stacer, 2013; Van Dijck, 2013), by attempting to organise and change social media practices and governance (as with http://europe-v-facebook.org/) or through various tactics that undermine, subvert or ignore norms and rules. Though Facebook requires users to give their real names and only have one account per user, one study found an estimated 8 per cent of the names given on Facebook appeared to be false (Gross, Acquisti & Heinz III, 2005). Children under 13 are not supposed to join Facebook, but a pan-European survey found on average that one in five children between 9 and 12 had joined using a false age (rising to 46 per cent in the Czech Republic) (Livingstone, Ólafsson & Staksrud, 2011), and a similar US survey found that 36 per cent of online 12 year olds lied about their age to access a website (Madden et al., 2013, p. 76). boyd, Marwick and others describe numerous tricks that teenagers use to stay in touch with their friends without revealing material they wish to keep from teachers and parents (d. boyd, 2014; d. m. boyd & Marwick, 2011; Oolo & Siibak, 2013). Nonetheless, the majority of users tend to 'go along' rather than expend the energy required to subvert in these ways (and there may also be risks attached to such subversion – social media companies can simply delete profiles of people who fail to adhere to the rules, with no accountability or appeal). One survey found that no more than a quarter of teenagers posted false information to protect their privacy, though 58 per cent had used inside jokes and coded messages (Madden et al., 2013, p. 103).

In the last chapter, I will balance the scepticism and concern raised about social media in this book with a consideration of some of the benefits that we nonetheless can derive from their appropriate use and offer some recommendations to help minimise the risks while enabling us all to enjoy the benefits.

7
Conclusion

This chapter is in four parts. The first part briefly summarises the earlier chapters and suggests how this work challenges conventional wisdom about Web 2.0 and privacy. The second part balances the concerns raised through the rest of this book about the potential harms from self-disclosure on social media with an overview of the many potential benefits that also accrue to users. In the third part I outline several possible interventions by governments, educators and social media companies themselves to minimise the risks posed by the use of such services without curtailing their benefits. Lastly, I set out an agenda for future research and call for a new debate to take place about how we as a society should come to terms with social media.

Overview

Just as in economics there is a notional *homo economicus* – a rational actor who always acts in their own self-interest – so one can describe an idealised social media user. When something significant happens in their lives, they first consider whether it would be appropriate to share this with others online, they select a social media service that offers them the functionality that they need, and that they had taken care to fully understand both functionally and in terms of its privacy policies. They then post the carefully crafted message that they wish, restricting its circulation using privacy controls to only those people they are sure would not misread what they posted or circulate it to others who might do so. They carefully consider possible concerns of others caught up in their narrative, and they make a note to return to what they posted after a period of time to ensure that nothing has materially changed in their lives or the lives of those around them that might place what they posted in a different and unflattering light. Whenever they encounter someone, and that encounter or the interaction that results might cause them embarrassment or harm if revealed, they request that the other party or parties not post the encounter on any social media and they checked afterwards to ensure that such a request has been respected.

Of course, articulated in this fashion it becomes clear that these days it is all but impossible to behave in this way and fully protect oneself on social media, even though social media companies do provide some privacy tools. What I have attempted to show in the course of this book are some of the subtle ways that potentially excessive or inappropriate self-disclosure and disclosure of others are encouraged and why protective measures may be overlooked or may be ineffective or impractical.

In Chapter 4, I showed how social media services may know a lot about the audiences – potential and actual – for any piece of content but to the extent they reveal it to users at all they generally do so only if the user specifically seeks out that information rather than proactively making users aware of their audiences. Because the audience's composition and reaction to what is shared is not 'given off', everyday users often appear to address what they publish to an idealised sympathetic audience and do not look for evidence that would disconfirm the sense they have of support for them and interest in what they have to say. The complexity and fast-changing nature of social media privacy controls also makes it difficult for users to master them and to be confident that their skills remain current.

In Chapter 5, I analysed the way in which social media services vary in the length of time they retain what users post and the ease with which past postings can be found, but point out that even what may appear to have entirely disappeared or is at least substantially hidden by a social media service's user interface may nonetheless be 'remembered' or sought out by those with a sufficient commercial or personal interest to dig it out. It can be very difficult to anticipate which things one posts might turn out to be problematic because of changes in future circumstances, and the sheer volume of material that people generate over time makes it difficult if not impossible to go back and 'cleanse' one's social media record. In any case, evidence suggests that people seldom look back at their own historical postings and that they might be reluctant to edit or remove them, seeing them as potentially valuable memories even if they are not necessarily consulted.

In Chapter 6 I examined the roots of the 'open society' and the forces that are helping to push us more in that direction. I suggested some of the intellectual roots of the ideology of openness and examined how social media companies and the technology companies who work with them draw on that ideology, use sophisticated rhetoric to market it and back up its persuasive force with the passive but nonetheless effective power of default settings to nudge users further towards self-disclosure. An overview of technological developments in the near term suggests it will become ever easier for us to share on social media and for others (both individuals and institutions or indeed objects) to use social media to share information about us.

In the face of all of these pressures, it is hardly surprising that we continue to see what may appear to be an irrational surge in self-disclosure and the disclosure of others' personal information. It is perhaps surprising that we do not see more. That said, it is important to note that a certain amount of self-disclosure and disclosure about others' lives is not merely unavoidable but indeed is essential for everyday existence. To suggest that such self-disclosure should not take place online would be neither sensible nor, in the end, practicable.

The benefits of social media use

Clearly, the social media offer subjective rewards — a review of the psychological literature suggests that they fulfil (or at least offer to fulfil) users' need to belong and need to present themselves to others (Nadkarni & Hofmann, 2012). But there are also numerous ways in which it has been plausibly argued that the social media bring tangible benefits to the individual and to society.

Perhaps the most extensively studied benefit of social media use – in particular the use of SNSes – is the way it can maintain participants' social capital – the connections people have to others who can help them. The argument and evidence are outlined in more detail elsewhere (Hampton, Goulet & Purcell, 2011; Steinfield, Ellison, Lampe & Vitak, 2010) but briefly, it is suggested that SNS services help their users keep their friends. The ability to maintain links with close friends and family is important of course, particularly to derive emotional support, but such close ties are in any case generally maintained effectively by other means. What SNSes add, crucially, is that, 'the lightweight interactions made possible by such features as newsfeeds lowers the costs of maintaining all of the weak ties formed on the SNS, meaning that connections that might have otherwise faded away over time can remain vital' (Steinfield et al., 2010, p. 11). In addition, as noted in the previous chapter, large SNSes like Facebook can act as up-to-date address books for their users, enabling them to continue to reach weak ties whose locations, email addresses and telephone numbers may change.

Those to whom one has weak ties may be less inclined to help when a social network user requests aid (Stefanone, Kwon & Lackaff, 2011), but the number of weak ties people have is much greater and because those with whom you are strongly linked tend to share similar backgrounds, access to weak ties is important when you are looking for new information or for help in novel situations (looking for a new job, for example) (Granovetter, 1973).

On that point, I have already noted in Chapter 6 that social network participation is starting to become almost obligatory in some groups – it may also be that employers will gradually come to expect potential employees to have a social media presence. As Marwick records,

> Auren Hoffman, CEO of the reputation management firm RapLeaf, stated in our interview: 'If you were an employer, and someone applied and they didn't have any activity on social networks and that person was 23 years old, you'd think they were the Unabomber. You would be really scared to meet this person without even a bodyguard. I don't even know if that person exists'.
>
> (A. Marwick, 2013)

On the other hand, one survey found that nearly half of US HR professionals 'say that a strong online reputation influences their decisions to a great extent' (cross-tab, 2010, p. 3).

One aspect of improved access to weak ties and, in the case of other social media sites, access to 'user-generated content' is that it might broaden individuals' exposure to different points of view and encourage greater civic and political engagement (Valenzuela, Park & Kee, 2008; Zhang, Johnson, Seltzer & Bichard, 2010). The social media potentially enable a broader range of voices to be heard in political and cultural debates because actors no longer need to attract the attention of the mainstream media in order to reach a potentially large audience (Beckett, 2008) – although in practice it may be that relatively privileged elites are those most likely to use the new social media and to be heard on them (Brake, 2013a, 2013b). The usefulness of social media for coordinating and publicising political and social movements has also received much attention, particularly after the Arab Spring (Farrell, 2012).

Not only do SNSes allow you to maintain links with weak ties that users encounter outside of the service, they also enable users to find others who share interests or characteristics. People do not generally turn to SNSes to make new friends but research into the potential benefits of virtual community suggests that for people who have 'stigmatised concealable' identities – for example, people who are Lesbian, Bisexual, Gay and Transgendered (LBGT) in communities where this is not accepted – can benefit from the ability to find others in similar situations and exchange information and receive emotional support (Gudelunas, 2012; McKenna & Bargh, 1998).[1]

Social media participation is often framed as being 'aboutnothing' – merely the exchange of trivia to maintain bonds (Miller, 2008) – and undoubtedly this is true of much social media communication. However, as we have noted above it can also be used for political communication and it appears often to be overlooked in the literature on social media that, for many, social media participation is for them an important creative outlet – that they enjoy taking the raw material of their everyday lives and interactions and turning them into a form of art. This may be through storytelling, the remixing of circulating creative content or sharing of photographs for an artistic as well as a documentary purpose. Indeed, as noted in Chapter 4, I found in my fieldwork with personal bloggers that the satisfaction of a creative impulse for some was more important than the communication of particular events in their lives.

Gauntlett, in *Making is Connecting*, suggests three key reasons why the kind of everyday creativity enabled by social media should be celebrated and encouraged. He asserts that creative expression is well suited to produce personal happiness, that interpersonal relationships fostered in informal groups (like those formed around creative practices) build social capital which can benefit society, and by using tools that enable individual creativity, people are helped to 'give shape and character to their own lives' (Gauntlett, 2011, p. 169).

Striking the right balance

The reaction of some – particularly parents and schools – to the risks that social media use can pose is simply to try to block or curtail the use of social media altogether, or to monitor online use and punish inappropriate or unwise use. One US study found over half of the school districts surveyed banned access to social network services in school (National School Boards Association, 2007). There may be sound pragmatic reasons for banning access to SNSes in schools and workplaces to ensure that students and workers are focused on the task at hand, but there are three key reasons why I would suggest that banning social media simply in order to reduce their negative impact on its users is misguided. Firstly, as noted above, there are a variety of significant benefits to the use of social media and social network services. As boyd has forcefully argued, 'by prohibiting teens from engaging in networked publics, we create a participation divide, both between adults and teens and between teens who have access and those who do not' (d. boyd, 2008b, p. 137). Livingstone and I have also reflected that The UN Convention on the Rights of the Child includes the right to freedom of assembly and expression, and SNS participation may now be an important way in which this freedom can be exercised (Livingstone & Brake, 2009). Secondly, parents and educators cannot work effectively alongside children and young people to help them to learn how to use social media better if they are also seen by young people to be trying to prevent their use altogether. Only half of children in an EU study said that teachers had talked to them generally about what they do online, or suggested ways to behave towards other people (Livingstone, Haddon, Gorzik & Ólafsson, 2011, p. 36).

Lastly, and relatedly, given the ubiquity of tools available for social media access in most developed countries, attempts to prevent their use are not likely to succeed; instead, there is the risk that young people may feel unable to turn to parents and teachers when they encounter problems. A substantial minority of young people are already evading existing controls (Livingstone, Ólafsson & Staksrud, 2011; Madden et al., 2013, p. 76), and there is already evidence that some young people may feel they have nobody to turn to when they run into difficulties online. The same EU survey, for example, found that when children received sexual messages that upset them online, 40 per cent did not talk about this to anyone (Livingstone, Haddon, Gorzik et al., 2011, p. 33).

If we cannot and should not attempt to make problems with social media go away by banning access to these services, we need to concentrate on achieving a reasonable balance between risk and opportunity, recognising – as Livingstone and Helsper suggest – that you cannot enable digital opportunities without exposing users to some level of risk (Livingstone & Helsper, 2010). Instead, in this case, as technology and social practices change and evolve we must follow a course of what Tufekci calls 'privacy optimization' (2008, p. 35). How is this to be achieved?

At an individual level, better education in digital literacy is necessary, but it is not enough. I also suggest that improvements in the way that social media companies design their interfaces and regulate their practices are likely to be of crucial importance, since for the reasons described in this book, individuals may struggle unaided to 'do the right thing' in the current environment.

Education

When governments (and schools, whose policies are often led by them) think about education and social media, their attention has tended to be focused on a narrow range of issues under the rubric of 'internet safety' (see, e.g., http://www.thinkuknow.co.uk/ and http://www.fbi.gov/fun-games/kids/kids-safety). Their primary concern seems to be protecting young people from internet predators by attempting to ensure that they do not share personally identifiable information online (an increasingly futile endeavour given the ubiquity of SNSes and their insistence on 'real identities'). As I outlined in Chapter 2, while internet predation does exist and it is of course important to attempt to prevent this, governments should think much more broadly about the potential risks associated with social media and who is at risk.

Rather than focusing on 'internet safety', governments should attempt to instil a broader critical 'digital literacy' agenda (Livingstone, 2003) across education, from primary school all the way through to university. This would focus not merely on preventing harm but also on maximising benefits and enabling a critical understanding of the commercial and other institutional contexts in which digital communication takes place. Those teaching courses in journalism and related fields (and, subsequently, those in journalism organisations who set standards of behaviour) have a particular responsibility to encourage potential journalists to think carefully not just about the actual 'publicness' of social media material they are considering recirculating or commenting on but its intended audience. The widespread use of material by journalists that was intended to be private but which was thoughtlessly or inadvertently circulated publicly cannot but have a corrosive effect on the public's own respect for individual privacy.

Outside of the school environment, libraries and government employment agencies as well as public service media organisations should provide individuals of all ages (and particularly although not exclusively parents) with advice and guidance to help and encourage them to think about the consequences of their social media use and the form it takes as part of a more general critical awareness of the role of media in society. This should not concentrate solely on prevention – given the potential benefits outlined above, one could argue that the elderly are *under*-using social media – 74 per cent of those over 65 in the US have never used a social network site as of September 2013, for example (Brenner, 2013; Pew Internet & American Life Project, n.d.-b). Not only might the elderly have difficulties maintaining ties through infirmity, which social media could address, but appropriate social media use could give them new opportunities for creativity and political expression.

Parents should take the opportunity to guide children while giving them the space to learn rather than monitoring them, blocking their access and punishing their mistakes.

The role of the social media industry

As I have suggested in Chapter 6, in relation to privacy protection, social media companies generally offer users control over what they share but in practice, while they have a very good idea of the audiences for any user's content they don't use this knowledge to help posters visualise their audiences. This undermines the perceived need for controls, encouraging users to post without fear (thus increasing traffic and profitability) but sets up a situation where harm is more likely to occur. Meanwhile they continue to encourage ever wider sharing through advertising messages and the interfaces to their services.

There is no shortage of proposed technical remedies available in the academic literature. If companies took potential harms to their users' happiness and reputations anything like as seriously as they take, say, the circulation of copyrighted images or child pornography on their services, dramatic improvements could certainly result. Here are a few ideas that they might implement that seem likely to 'nudge' their users away from potentially harmful practices.

Audiences

Many of the problems that are encountered in social media interaction might be avoidable if users had a better sense of their audiences (and of the intended audiences of others' postings) by default and as they post, and if software platforms included some algorithmically led guidance for users.

Many social media services offer users a blunt privacy instrument – either all of their postings will be visible to the whole internet or they will be limited to a preset list of 'friends', all of whom must also be users of the same service. Being able to group 'friends' and select individually the privacy level of any given posting (as Facebook and Google+ allow) would give users greater control and avoid situations as with Twitter where participants' dominant use may be for purely public disclosures but where they may occasionally be drawn into private discussions unthinkingly.

On services that do allow this more fine-grained control of access, both the scale and the sensitivity of the audience could be more clearly indicated to users as they post. Perhaps, for example, any posting that you make that would be public could be given a light pink background in or around the posting box, changing to yellow for posting that reaches (or potentially reaches) 50 friends and green for fewer? Postings whose recipients include parents, employers or partners could be similarly colour coded (even if only as an option).

There have been repeated studies of inadvertent exposure of sensitive information online which have simply searched for references to alcohol, illegal drugs and other controversial material (Bohnert & Ross, 2010; Hinduja & Patching, 2008; Nielsen BuzzMetrics, 2007; Wang et al., 2011). To forestall some of the more obvious potential harms, perhaps social media organisations could themselves automatically check posts before they are placed online and, if the content matches key phrases, alert the poster that what they are about to post could get them into trouble. Of course some of these warnings could be inaccurate, but as long as the providers did not prevent users from posting the content being warned about and the warnings could be disabled if desired, this could be a useful aid for posters.

Lastly, to minimise harm from third-party posting of information or harmful recirculation, if facial recognition software were sufficiently reliable, users who do not wish to be included in others' photos (or do not wish their children to be visible) could ask to be notified if others publish pictures containing them, even if those pictures are not 'tagged' and therefore linked explicitly back to them. Researchers have already been working on ways of 'marking' private spaces like toilets or bedrooms so automated recording devices will know not to record in them (Templeman, Korayem, Crandall & Kapadiay, 2014). Similarly, users might be given an option to request that when others who know them mention their name in a posting the poster would be prompted to ask their permission. Lastly, although it could violate privacy if recipients of postings were made aware of exactly who else was able to read that posting, it might help people judge whether what they read was not intended for a large audience if they had a visual cue to tell them the rough size of the audience a poster had intended (perhaps using the same colour code system as suggested above).

Time

As discussed in Chapter 5, the extent to which social media material is preserved varies greatly. Nonetheless, and in particular where postings are public and might remain visible for an extended period, better tools for control over digital 'remembering' may be called for.

Social media providers could, by default, request that archives of postings be automatically purged from search engines after a certain interval of time has elapsed unless the owner of such data chooses otherwise, and providers could give tools that would make it easier for users to hide large numbers of their postings at once using certain criteria (their date or the presence of keywords, for example). Mayer-Schönberger devotes a substantial part of *Delete* to a discussion of possible remedies to the problems caused by digital remembering (Mayer-Schönberger, 2009).

Regulation

As with anything that increases the 'friction' of sharing, social media providers will likely question the need for such measures in the first instance and may be reluctant to implement anything similar to what I've described. In any event, exactly what measures would be technically possible and effective is something social media providers are best placed to answer. Nonetheless, governments, educators and members of the public all have a role in persuading social media providers to behave more responsibly. As we have seen in Chapter 6, social media companies wield a great deal of power over their users, whether they seek to or not, and just as we regulate 'conventional' media organisations because of the public interest in properly run media so we should have the right to regulate social media – not in order to inhibit free speech but in order to empower users to make better decisions.

One way to hold the larger social media companies to account might be to use surveys to measure the extent to which posters on a given service have experienced some kind of clash due to inadvertent exposure and (equally as importantly) to measure the extent to which readers of postings on a service have encountered sensitive material they believed they were not intended to see. Services could then be given targets to reduce these potential harms by whatever means worked best.

On the other hand, there is ample evidence that governments and governmental agencies – particularly but not exclusively in authoritarian regimes – may be tempted to exploit their commercial or legal power over social media providers to track and monitor their citizens. Where possible, the public and politicians responsible for governmental oversight must be vigilant and seek to ensure that this use is proportionate. In countries where citizens do not have an adequate voice, it falls to the social media industry itself to act responsibly and to resist requests for data from organisations which seem likely to abuse them and/or at least to reveal when such requests are taking place. Groups like the Global Network Initiative (http://www.globalnetworkinitiative. org/) working with Google, Microsoft, Yahoo and Facebook appear to be a useful first step.

Need for research

Although in the last few years a sizeable, global and interdisciplinary group of internet researchers has emerged, there are still some important gaps in our understanding of social media. The broadest such gap is in our knowledge of internet users older than university age. Because until recently social media use has been seen as the domain of young people and because university students are a resource that is easy for researchers to tap, we know much more about university students' internet use than about any other group. As I noted in Chapter 5, we know from survey evidence that people's internet use tends to change at different life stages. We don't know enough about, for example, the attitudes of middle-aged or older people towards social media – more qualitative research in this area is necessary. Another area seemingly lacking in research is the attitude of the social media user as reader. To what extent is encountering material about others they did not intend you to see an important if an acknowledged motivation in social media consumption? How often and why do people attempt to cause conflict online by deliberately recirculating discreditable material? To what extent and under what circumstances are social media users inclined to forgive or overlook discreditable information about others they encounter online and does it appear that attitudes differ between age groups or at different life stages? These are just a few of the fundamental questions that would help to inform our understanding of social media interaction but that remain largely unanswered.

Where do I stand?

I believe that unless there is an overriding public interest, everyone, whether a private citizen or a journalist or public body, must be mindful of the rights of those we encounter to conduct their lives privately, according to their interpretation of privacy, which may be stricter than our own. We must therefore always be aware that what we share about ourselves may also implicate others. We must never assume that because people have published something 'openly' online that it is therefore something that they are happy for anyone to be informed about. Given the potential length of digital memory and the increasing volumes of digital exposure, we will undoubtedly increasingly find evidence of people's past indiscretions and discreditable behaviour. While everyone must take responsibility for their actions, we will also increasingly be called upon to forgive or to overlook past indiscretions. In particular, if the public and the press acting on their behalf continue to demand unassailable personal moral rectitude and a complete lack of personal hypocrisy in our politicians and leaders, we will find nobody left willing to enter public life. If there is one thing that we must learn in order to live with lengthier and more complete memories, it is that all of us can change and grow.

Need for wider debate

Discussion of the implications of the burgeoning use of social media and in particular of negative consequences tends to be either moralistic ('young people today have no sense of shame') or fatalistic ('soon there will be no way to lead one's life in private thanks to Facebook'). Neither attitude is helpful. Certainly we need to recognise individuals' responsibility to protect the privacy of others, but we should not assume that revealing information about oneself or others is the product of shamelessness or carelessness given the difficulties people are bound to face in navigating a new environment of social interaction. Equally, we need not simply accept fatalistically the environment of maximum personal exposure that technology and the influence of the social media industries appear to be nudging us towards. While it is difficult to refuse technologies altogether, governments can regulate their development and use and whether in small groups or as a society as a whole we can debate and then agree on (or agree to disagree on) norms of social interaction. We can take into consideration new technological capabilities but be mindful of the consequences of their use and we can agree limits in the interests of a more harmonious society. The time for a thorough debate on these issues is now, while the novelty of these technologies and services makes us aware of them. Otherwise, like the proverbial frog in a pan of water on a stove, we will not notice we are cooking until it is too late to jump out.

If matters merely drift, I can foresee two futures. In the first, we all know much more about what used to be considered private in the lives of those around us and this knowledge gives us a better sense of the differing values and experiences of others. In response to this, we become less judgemental of others and happier to reveal our own frailties. In the latter, greater knowledge of each other's once private actions does not lead to greater toleration. Instead, it leads us to an uncomfortable new equilibrium where from early in life we are constrained to define ourselves in a socially acceptable way and to act in all but the most private of situations in such a way that nobody who is important to us and nobody with power over us would disapprove. I would like to believe that the first future may come to pass, but I fear that the second is a more realistic prospect, and even if we eventually learn how to live in a radically open society, the path from our present one to this hoped-for future seems likely to be a tempestuous one. It is better, therefore, that we find ways to slow the march of 'progress' towards radical openness to give us time to adapt – or at least to march with our eyes open.

Methodological Appendix

The fieldwork cited in this book that I conducted with personal webloggers was originally performed to inform my doctoral thesis (2009). I sought in this research to understand personal weblogging as a socially constructed practice and thus relied primarily on interviews with the bloggers themselves rather than on an analysis of their texts. As I noted in the concluding chapter, I am concerned that research into social media practices tends to focus on young people and university students, so I purposely made my interview sample as diverse as possible given logistical constraints.

Google was used to find recently updated blogs hosted using Blogger or LiveJournals that were listed as being from around London, UK (to facilitate face-to-face interviews) and that offered personal information accessible to any internet user (because users' attitudes towards their potential audiences were part of the study). Search engines try to prioritise their results using 'relevance' measures that tend to bring the most popular sites matched to the top of the page, so the first 200 search results were disregarded in an attempt to provide a sample of more typical weblogs. An online questionnaire was emailed to the authors of 237 of these websites, both to solicit their permission to be interviewed and to provide demographic information to aid in the selection of interviewees. A purposive sample (Chadwick, Bahr & Albrecht, 1984, pp. 65–66) was chosen from the 150 who answered in an attempt to maximise relevant variety in those interviewed – 75 were invited to interview and 23 were successfully interviewed. The sample constructed for this study used the demographic information offered to ensure a range of ages (between 16 and 64), educational backgrounds, self-reported social classes, occupations and perceived audience sizes among interviewees.[1] The number of bloggers interviewed was defined in part by the sense during the fieldwork that a point of saturation had been reached, and by the assertion by Bauer and Gaskell (Bauer & Gaskell, 2000, p. 43) that somewhere between 15 and 25 interviews is the upper limit for a single researcher to be able to analyse sensitively.

Between July and September of 2005 I conducted face-to-face semi-structured interviews, each lasting between 60 and 90 minutes.

A considerable amount of contextual information was available about each blogger's practices and was drawn upon in the preparation for each interview. Although the text of the blogs of each interviewee was not formally analysed, I read current and archived postings on their blogs to familiarise myself with the lives of the interviewees to the extent they were revealed and with the style and the content of their blogs. I was also able to refer to the answers they gave to the questions on the survey that they had responded to earlier.

In the course of the interviews themselves, my blogging experience (four years at the time of the fieldwork) also helped to build a rapport with the interviewees – especially since at the time the interviews were conducted, blogging was still a fairly unusual practice and many of these bloggers would rarely if ever have had the chance to discuss blogging face to face. I provided the address of my 'personal' weblog (http://blog.org/) in my first email contact, in part to assure interviewees that I was 'one of them'. I was able in most cases to draw on this experience to understand and, where appropriate, to use the weblogging-specific argot of interviewees, which may also have put them at their ease.

All interviews were transcribed and the resulting texts were analysed thematically (Flick, 2006) through an interactive process of open and selective coding.

Notes

1 Introduction

1. Although in fact messages in net.motss have been archived back to 1986 and are accessible (with the poster's email addresses) on the web at http://groups.google.com/group/net.motss/
2. Details of this research are outlined in the methodological appendix.

2 What Is Risky about Online Self-Disclosure and Who Is at Risk?

1. Text-based online spaces that enabled live chat and where people often were only identified by pseudonyms.
2. Although Turkle now takes a much more critical position on online self-expression via social network sites (Turkle, 2011).
3. Section V of the Telecommunications Act of 1996 http://transition.fcc.gov/Reports/tcom1996.txt.
4. http://www.law.cornell.edu/uscode/text/47/231.
5. This difference may in part be due to the US poll asking about children in general and the UK poll asking about attitudes towards the parents' own children.

3 How and Why Social Media Interaction Is Different

1. Although he resisted the label of symbolic interactionist himself (Winkin, 1988, pp. 235–236).
2. The 'confined self' relates to his study of interaction in 'total institutions' like asylums and prisons and is not applicable to this study. Another theme is the 'production of self'. Goffman's view of the self is essentially dualistic, with a self-as-performer reacting to different situations to produce the self-as-character. This is not directly applicable to this book but highlights the importance of interpersonal interaction to self-construction, which in turn helps to explain why people seek out multiple venues to interact with others.
3. Although any social media network can be subverted or interpreted in unexpected ways by its users – LinkedIn, for example, contains a 'peace through anarchy' group and a 'porn and hentai' group at the time of writing.
4. Also popularly termed 'many to many' communication because, unlike the mass media, it is accessible to 'many' users and can nonetheless reach 'many' people.

5. The Social Identity model of Deindividuation Effects (Postmes et al., 1998).
6. He discusses bias in earlier works (Feenberg, 1999, pp. 178–183; 2002b, pp. 80–82) using slightly different terminology (what is here termed 'constitutive bias' he dubbed 'substantive' bias, while 'implementation bias' is earlier styled 'formal' bias). The thrust of his argument is the same, however.

4 Imagining the Reader

1. As social media activity is increasingly via mobile devices with multimedia capabilities, tools like Vine and Keek have sprung up enabling audio- and video-based social media sharing but the ease and speed with which text can be produced and consumed suggests it may continue to dominate social media interaction.
2. Most such tracking relies on the analysis of visitors' IP addresses – this is for a variety of reasons an imprecise measure (Winder, 2011).
3. Although this particular issue has now been resolved by Facebook, which no longer has regional networks.
4. This (and all other names of interviewees from this study) is a pseudonym.
5. It was difficult to define what might count as sensitive, however, and no systematic content analysis was done.
6. It is difficult to be precise about how identifiable a weblogger might be from their weblog postings without knowing about what others might already know about them in other contexts – a mention of a seemingly commonplace detail could reveal a blogger's identity to a person familiar with that detail.
7. See, for example, Nathaniel Hawthorne: 'Some authors, indeed, do far more than this, and indulge themselves in such confidential depths of revelation as could fittingly be addressed, only and exclusively, to the one heart and mind of perfect sympathy' (Hawthorne, 1850, p. 1).

5 Time and Memory in Social Media

1. boyd (2008b) refers similarly to digital data's persistence, replicability and searchability, adding 'scalability' – the fact data can be shared across great distances and between many people.
2. I am not aware of research by others into social media consumption that addresses this particular issue but, as you will see later in the chapter, I have been able to touch on it in my own research on bloggers.
3. Although if a picture is not viewed it will stay on the company's servers for a month, and law enforcement officers can ask for a picture to be retained.
4. Indeed, there have been archives made of deleted tweets both for academic purposes (Almuhimedi et al., 2013) and as a means of drawing attention to the ethical issues (Hughes, 2011) raised by collecting such tweets.
5. See http://www.robotstxt.org/ for more about how this works.
6. It is now possible to remove one's blog from public view without deleting it altogether, but in the case of LiveJournal, this would by default involve

changing the privacy status of each post individually and this option was not available for Blogger users at the time that fieldwork was being conducted. The relevant web pages explaining how to remove one's blog do not suggest making it completely private as an alternative. In any case, even when blogs are deleted from their host servers their texts may remain available via third-party services.

6   Towards a Radically Open Society

1. See discussion: 'Thompson: new forms of interaction and the role of the imagination' in Chapter 3.
2. One could connect this to some extent to earlier internet-mediated forms like the Multi User Dungeon (MUD) and MOO, but these appear to have been generally used for identity experimentation rather than the expression of users' 'real' identities (Turkle, 1996a, 1996b) and they never achieved mass-market acceptance, although arguably Minecraft builds on many of the same themes. Also, before the existence of the World Wide Web, a program called 'finger' that worked across the internet provided simple information about users (whether or not they were online, for example) and accessed '.plan' and '.project' files that could be edited by users – an early service analogous to a personal home page (Indiana University Information Technology Services, 2006).
3. Taking the 11 and 23 per cent adoption figures from the two surveys and adjusting for the fact that 76 per cent of US bloggers polled said they do so to 'document their personal experiences and share them with others' (Lenhart & Fox, 2006).
4. This does not provide perfect protection, however. It is difficult to be clear about how identifiable a social media user might be from their pseudonymous postings without knowing about what others might already know about them in other contexts – a mention of a seemingly commonplace detail could reveal their identity to a person familiar with that detail, for example. It is also worth noting that people tend to use the same pseudonyms across different services, thus allowing the curious to cross-index multiple sources of information and identify the person behind the pseudonym. One large-scale content analysis found that 'a vast majority of users from our datasets can be uniquely identified among a population of 1 billion users, relying only on their username' (Fischer-Hubner et al., 2011, p. 5). Companies like Rapleaf have used a variety of techniques to gather demographic and other information about individuals and associate them with their email addresses and social network profiles, even when these are pseudonymous (Steel, 2010).

7   Conclusion

1. Of course it should be noted that the same process can also reinforce identities that may be stigmatised for good reasons – for example where those with anorexia encourage each other to starve themselves (Haas, Irr, Jennings & Wagner, 2011; Neumyer, 2014).

Methodological Appendix

1. I provided more details on the methods used to construct a sample for this research in this presentation (Brake, 2007), and an appendix of user profiles can be downloaded separately at davidbrake.org/ intervieweesummarybloggers.xls.

Bibliography

Acquisti, A. & Gross, E. F. (2006). Imagined Communities Awareness, Information Sharing, and Privacy on the Facebook. Paper presented at the Privacy Enhancing Technologies Workshop, Cambridge, UK. Retrieved from http://www.heinz.cmu.edu/~acquisti/papers/acquisti-gross-facebook-privacy-PET-final.pdf

Almuhimedi, H., Wilson, S., Liu, B., Sadeh, N. & Acquisti, A. (2013). Tweets are Forever: A Large-Scale Quantitative Analysis of Deleted Tweets. Paper presented at the CSCW 2013, San Antonio, Texas, USA. Retrieved from http://www.cs.cmu.edu/~shomir/cscw2013_tweets_are_forever.pdf

Andrews, L. B. (2012). *I know who you are and I saw what you did: Social networks and the death of privacy* (1st Free Press hardcover ed.). New York: Free Press.

Angwin, J. (2010, 30 July). The Web's New Gold Mine: Your Secrets. *Wall Street Journal.* Retrieved from http://online.wsj.com/article/SB10001424052748703940904575395073512989404.html

Armstrong, H. B. (2002, 26 February). Collecting Unemployment. Retrieved 25 May 2004, from http://www.dooce.com/archives/daily/02_26_2002.html

Bakardjieva, M. & Smith, R. (2001). The internet in everyday life: Computer networking from the standpoint of the domestic user. *New Media & Society*, 3(1), 67–83. doi: 10.1177/1461444801003001005

Ball-Rokeach, S. J. & Reardon, K. (1988). Monologue, dialogue, and telelog: Comparing an emergent form of communication with traditional forms. In S. Pingree, R. P. Hawkins & J. M. Wiemann (eds.), *Advancing communication science: Merging mass and interpersonal processes* (pp. 135–161). Newbury Park, CA: Sage.

Banks, E. (2011, August 28). Eric Schmidt: If You Don't Want To Use Your Real Name, Don't Use Google+. Retrieved 28 December 2013, from http://mashable.com/2011/08/28/google-plus-identity-service/

Barlow, J. P. (1996, February 8). A Declaration of the Independence of Cyberspace. Retrieved 25 January 2004, from http://www.eff.org/~barlow/Declaration-Final.html

Bauer, M. & Gaskell, G. (2000). *Qualitative researching with text, image and sound: A practical handbook for social research.* London: SAGE.

Bauman, Z. (2001). *The individualized society.* Cambridge, UK; Malden, MA: Polity Press.

Baumer, E. P. S., Adams, P., Khovanskaya, V. D., Liao, T. C., Smith, M. E., Sosik, V. S. et al. (2013). Limiting, Leaving, and (re)lapsing: An Exploration of Facebook Non-use Practices and Experiences. Paper presented at the Proceedings of the SIGCHI Conference on Human Factors in Computing Systems, Paris, France. Retrieved from http://ericbaumer.com/wp-content/uploads/2013/04/CHI2013-FBLL-13-camera.pdf

BBC News Online (2003, 28 February). Internet Abduction Man Jailed. Retrieved 12 January 2010, from http://news.bbc.co.uk/1/hi/england/2809369.stm

BBC News Online (2004a, 12 February). Ex-marine Admits Abduction. Retrieved 12 January 2010, from http://news.bbc.co.uk/1/hi/england/manchester/ 3481219.stm

BBC News Online (2004b, 3 November). US Blogger Fired by her Airline. Retrieved 6 February 2009, from http://news.bbc.co.uk/1/hi/technology/3974081.stm

BBC News Online. (2009, 14 October). Fraud Fugitive in Facebook Trap. Retrieved 20 September 2009, from http://news.bbc.co.uk/1/hi/world/americas/8306032. stm

BBC News Online. (2012, 2 April). Privacy Backlash Over Girls Around Me Mobile App. Retrieved 29 August 2013, from http://www.bbc.co.uk/news/technology-17582975

Beales, H. (2009). The Value of Behavioral Targeting. Retrieved from http://www. networkadvertising.org/pdfs/Beales_NAI_Study.pdf

Beck, U. & Beck-Gernsheim, E. (2001). *Individualization: Institutionalized individualism and its social and political consequences*. London: Sage.

Beckett, C. (2008). *SuperMedia: Saving journalism so it can save the world*. Malden, MA: Blackwell.

Beevolve (2012, 10 October). An Exhaustive Study of Twitter Users Across the World. Retrieved 30 August 2013, from http://www.beevolve.com/twitter-statistics/

Bercovici, J. (2013, 30 October). Facebook Admits It's Seen a Drop in Usage among Teens. Retrieved 26 December 2013, from http://www.forbes.com/sites/ jeffbercovici/2013/10/30/facebook-admits its-seen-a-drop-in-usage-among-teens/

Bernstein, M. (2002, 16 August). 10 Tips on Writing the Living Web. Retrieved 20 September 2010, from http://www.alistapart.com/articles/writeliving/

Bernstein, M. S., Bakshy, E., Burke, M. & Karrer, B. (2013). Quantifying the Invisible Audience in Social Networks. Paper presented at the ACM SIGCHI Conference on Human Factors in Computing Systems (CHI 2013), Paris, France. Retrieved from http://hci.stanford.edu/publications/2013/invisibleaudience/ invisibleaudience.pdf

Bilton, N. (2012, 6 May). Disruptions: Indiscreet Photos, Glimpsed then Gone. Retrieved 20 September 2013, from http://bits.blogs.nytimes.com/2012/05/06/ disruptions-indiscreet-photos-glimpsed-then-gone/

Birdwhistell, R. L. (2011). *Kinesics and Context: Essays on Body Motion Communication*. Philadelphia: University of Pennsylvania Press.

Blogger (n.d.). How Do I Delete a Blog? Retrieved 2 April 2009, from http://help. blogger.com/bin/answer.py?hl=en&answer=41387

Blue, V. (2014, 22 January). Google Outed Me. Retrieved 23 January 2014, from http://www.zdnet.com/google-outed-me-7000025416/

Bohnert, D. & Ross, W. H. (2010). The influence of social networking web sites on the evaluation of job candidates. *Cyberpsychology, Behavior, and Social Networking*, 13(3), 341–347. doi:10.1089/cyber.2009.0193.

boyd, d. (2008a). Taken Out of Context: American Teen Sociality in Networked Publics. PhD, University of California, Berkeley. Retrieved from http://ssrn. com/abstract=1344756

boyd, d. (2008b). Why youth (heart) social network sites: The role of networked publics in teenage social life. In D. Buckingham (ed.), *Youth, identity, and digital media* (pp. 119–142). Cambridge, MA: MIT Press.

boyd, d. (2014). *It's complicated: The social lives of networked teens.* New Haven, CT: Yale University Press. Retrieved from http://www.danah.org/books/ItsComplicated.pdf

boyd, d. & Ellison, N. B. (2007). Social network sites: Definition, history, and scholarship. *Journal of Computer-Mediated Communication*, 13(1), 210–230. doi: 10.1111/j.1083-6101.2007 00393.x.

boyd, d. m. & Marwick, A. (2011). Social Privacy In Networked Publics: Teens' Attitudes, Practices, and Strategies. Paper presented at the A Decade in Internet Time: Symposium on the Dynamics of the Internet and Society, Oxford, UK. http://papers.ssrn.com/sol3/papers.cfm?abstract_id=1925128

Brackenbury, I. & Wong, T. (2012). Online Profile & Reputation Perceptions Study. Retrieved from http://go.microsoft.com/?linkid=9797356

Brady, M. (2006). Blogs: Motivations Behind the Phenomenon. Paper presented at the Information, Communication & Society, York, UK.

Brake, D. R. (2007). Constructing a Purposive Interview Sample of Bloggers. Paper presented at the Internet Research 8.0 – Let's Play, Vancouver, Canada. Retrieved from http://www.slideshare.net/davidbrake/constructing-a-purposive-interview-sample-of-bloggers

Brake, D. R. (2009). 'As if nobody's reading'?: The Imagined Audience and Sociotechnical Biases in Personal Blogging Practice in the UK. PhD, The London School of Economics and Political Science, London, UK. Retrieved from http://etheses.lse.ac.uk/4/

Brake, D. R. (2013a). Are we all online content creators now? Web 2.0 and digital divides. *Journal of Computer-Mediated Communication*. doi: 10.1111/jcc4.12042

Brake, D. R. (2013b). Journalists, user generated content and digital divides. In J. Gordon, G. Stewart & P. Rowinski (eds.), *Br(e)aking the news: Journalism, politics and new media* (pp. 253–270). Oxford, UK: Peter Lang.

Branaman, A. (1997). Goffman's social theory. In E. Goffman & C. C. Lemert (eds.), *The Goffman reader* (pp. xlvi–lxxxii). Malden, MA; Oxford: Blackwell.

Brandimarte, L., Acquisti, A. & Loewenstein, G. (2013). Misplaced confidences: Privacy and the control paradox. *Social Psychological and Personality Science*, 4(3), 340–347. doi: 10.1177/1948550612455931.

Brandtzaeg, P. B., Luders, M. & Skjetne, J. H. (2010). Too many Facebook 'Friends'? Content sharing and sociability versus the need for privacy in social network sites. *International Journal of Human-Computer Interaction*, 26(11–12), 1006–1030. doi: 10.1080/10447318.2010.516719.

Bratteteig, T. (2008). Does it matter that it is digital? In K. Lundby (ed.), *Digital storytelling, mediatized stories: Self-representations in new media* (pp. 271–84). New York: Peter Lang.

Brenner, J. (2013, 5 August). Pew Internet: Social Networking (full detail). Retrieved 5 August 2013, from http://pewinternet.org/Reports/2013/social-networking-sites/Findings.aspx

Brooks, L. & Anene, V. (2012, 29 July). Information Disclosure and Generational Differences in Social Network Sites. Paper presented at the AMCIS 2012. Retrieved from http://aisel.aisnet.org/amcis2012/proceedings/SocialIssues/10

Broughton, A., Higgins, T., Hicks, B. & Cox, A. (2012). Workplaces and Social Networking: The Implications for Employment Relations. Retrieved from http://www.acas.org.uk/media/pdf/f/q/1111_Workplaces_and_Social_Networking-accessible-version-Apr-2012.pdf

Brown, D. (2007, 6 February). The 'Holly and Jess' chat-room plot. *The Times*. Retrieved from http://www.timesonline.co.uk/tol/news/uk/crime/article1336929.ece

Bucher, T. (2012). Programmed Sociality: A Software Studies Perspective on Social Networking Sites. PhD, University of Oslo, Oslo. Retrieved from http://tainabucher.com/wp-content/uploads/2009/08/Bucher_Ph.D.diss_.pdf

Buchwalter, C. (2005). The Blog Universe: Influencers, Early Adopters and Online Tenure Rolled into One. Paper presented at the Word of Mouth Marketing Association. Retrieved from http://www.womma.org/metrics/pres/womma_research_buchwalter.pdf

Bureau of Justice Statistics (2011). Identity Theft Reported by Households, 2005–2010. Retrieved from http://bjs.gov/content/pub/pdf/itrh0510.pdf

Calvert, C. (2000). *Voyeur nation: Media, privacy, and peering in modern culture*. Boulder, CO: Westview Press.

Capurro, R. (2005). Privacy. An intercultural perspective. *Ethics and Information Technology*, 7(1), 37–47. doi: 10.1007/s10676-005-4407-4. Retrieved from http://www.capurro.de/privacy.html

Careerbuilder (2009). Forty-five Percent of Employers Use Social Networking Sites to Research Job Candidates, CareerBuilder Survey Finds. Retrieved from http://www.careerbuilder.com/share/aboutus/pressreleasesdetail.aspx?id=pr519&sd=8%2f19%2f2009&ed=12%2f31%2f2009&siteid=cbpr&sc_cmp1=cb_pr519_

Carey, J. W. (2005). Historical pragmatism and the internet. *New Media & Society*, 7(4), 443–455.

Carroll, R. (2014, 14 January). Google Buys Nest Labs for $3.2bn in Bid for Smart Home-devices Market. Retrieved 26 April 2014, from http://www.theguardian.com/technology/2014/jan/13/google-nest-labs-3bn-bid-smart-home-devices-market

Carter, J. & Behram, F. T. M. (2009). Gaydar: Facebook friendships expose sexual orientation. *First Monday*, 14(10). Retrieved from http://firstmonday.org/htbin/cgiwrap/bin/ojs/index.php/fm/article/view/2611/2302

Cassell, J. & Cramer, M. (2007). High Tech or High Risk: Moral Panics about Girls Online Digital Young, Innovation, and the Unexpected (pp. 53–75). Retrieved from http://www.mitpressjournals.org/doi/abs/10.1162/dmal.9780262633598.053

Cha, J. (2013). Business models of most-visited U.S. social networking sites. In A. B. Albarran (ed.), *The social media industries* (pp. 60–85). New York: Routledge.

Chadwick, B. A., Bahr, H. M. & Albrecht, S. L. (1984). *Social science research methods*. Englewood Cliffs, NJ: Prentice-Hall.

Chaffin, M. & Jones, L. (2011). Declining Rates of Child Sexual Abuse and What This Really Means. Retrieved from http://www.nationalcac.org/online-training/webinar-chaffin-jones-01-2011.html

Chandler, D. & Roberts-Young, D. (1998, 19 April 2000). The Construction of Identity in the Personal Homepages of Adolescents. Retrieved 19 June 2014, from http://www.aber.ac.uk/media/Documents/short/strasbourg.html

Chen, L. Y. (2012, 28 December). China Passes Law Requiring People Identify Selves Online. Retrieved 2 July 2013, from http://www.bloomberg.com/news/2012-12-28/china-passes-rules-requiring-people-identify-themselves-online.html

Choi, J. H.-j. (2006). Living in cyworld: Contextualisation of cyworld blogging in Korea. In A. Bruns & J. Jacobs (eds.), *Uses of blogs* (pp. 173–186). New York: Peter Lang.

Chou, H.-T. G. & Edge, N. (2012). 'They Are Happier and Having Better Lives than I Am': The impact of using Facebook on perceptions of others' lives. *CyberPsychology, Behavior & Social Networking*, 15(2), 117–121. doi: 10.1089/cyber.2011.0324.

Clark, L. S. (2013). *The parent app: Understanding families in the digital age*. Oxford University Press.

Clayton, R. B., Nagurney, A. & Smith, J. R. (2013). Cheating, breakup, and divorce: Is Facebook use to blame? *Cyberpsychology, Behavior, and Social Networking*. doi: 10.1089/cyber.2012.0424.

Clinton, H. R. (2013). Internet Rights and Wrongs: Choices & Challenges in a Networked World. Retrieved from http://www.state.gov/secretary/rm/2011/02/156619.htm

CNNIC (2013). 32nd Statistical Report on Internet Development in China (July 2013). Retrieved from http://www1.cnnic.cn/IDR/ReportDownloads/

CNNIC (2014). 33rd Statistical Report on Internet Development in China (January 2014). Retrieved from http://www1.cnnic.cn/IDR/ReportDownloads/

Coate, J. (1987, unknown). Life on the Bus and Farm: An Informal Recollection. Retrieved 2 April 2009, from http://cervisa.com/stories/farm.txt

Common Sense Media. (2010). Protect Our Privacy – Protect Our Kids Poll (Adults). Retrieved from http://www.privacylives.com/common-sense-media-poll-three-out-of-four-parents-say-social-networks-aren%E2%80%99t-protecting-kids%E2%80%99-online-privacy/2010/10/08/

Conniff, M. (2005, 29 September 2005). Just What is a Blog, Anyway? Retrieved 18 November 2005, from http://www.ojr.org/ojr/stories/050929/

Cosenza, V. (2012, June). World Map of Social Networks. Retrieved 13 August 2012, from http://www.vincos.it/world-map-of-social-networks/

cross-tab (2010). Online Reputation in a Connected World. Retrieved from go.microsoft.com/?linkid=9709510

Culnan, M. J. & Markus, M. L. (1987). Information technologies. In F. M. Jablin (ed.), *Handbook of organizational communication: An interdisciplinary perspective* (pp. 420–443). Newbury Park, CA; London: Sage.

Cutler, K.-M. (2013, 30 January). Facebook's Q4 Revenue Rises 40% To $1.59B, Shares Down Slightly in After-Hours. Retrieved 27 June 2013, from http://techcrunch.com/2013/01/30/facebooks-q4-revenue-rises-40-to-1-59b-shares-decline-7-percent-in-after-hours/

Das, S. & Kramer, A. (2013). Self-Censorship on Facebook. Paper presented at the International AAAI Conference on Weblogs and Social Media, Boston. Retrieved from http://www.cmuchimps.org/publications/122-self-censorship_on_facebook/pub_download

Dateline (2008, 9 January). To Catch a Predator. Retrieved 23 August 2012, from http://www.msnbc.msn.com/id/10912603/

DeLamater, J. & Myers, D. (2010). *Social Psychology*. Belmont, CA: Wadsworth Cengage Learning.

De Rosa, C., Cantrell, J., Havens, A., Hawk, J. & Jenkins, L. (2007). Sharing, Privacy and Trust in Our Networked World. Retrieved from http://www.oclc.org/reports/sharing/default.htm

diasp.eu (2013, 16 August). How Many Users Are in the DIASPORA Network? Retrieved 16 August 2013, from https://diasp.eu/stats.html

Dibbell, J. (1993, 23 December). A Rape in Cyberspace: How an Evil Clown, a Haitian Trickster Spirit, Two Wizards, and a Cast of Dozens Turned a Database into a Society the Village Voice. Retrieved from http://www.juliandibbell.com/texts/bungle_vv.html

Dickinson, G. (2009, 1 February). 14-times Olympic Gold Medal Winner Michael Phelps Caught with Cannabis Pipe News of the World. Retrieved from http://www.hightimes.com/read/14-times-olympic-gold-medal-winner-michael-phelps-caught-cannabis-pipe

Doctorow, C. (2002, 31 May). My Blog, My Outboard Brain. Retrieved 21 February 2008, from http://www.oreillynet.com/pub/a/javascript/2002/01/01/cory.html

Dong, F. (2012). Controlling the internet in China: The real story. *Convergence: The International Journal of Research into New Media Technologies.* doi: 10.1177/1354856512439500.

Doostdar, A. (2004). 'The Vulgar Spirit of Blogging': On language, culture, and power in Persian weblogistan. *American Anthropologist,* 106(4), 651–662. Retrieved from http://www.swiss.ai.mit.edu/6.805/admin/admin-fall-2005/weeks/doostdar-vulgar_spirit_of_b.pdf

Dror, Y. (2013). 'We are not here for the money' Founders' manifestos. *New Media & Society.* doi: 10.1177/1461444813506974.

Duggan, M. & Smith, A. (2013). Social Media Update 2013. Retrieved from http://pewInternet.org/Reports/2013/Social-Media-Update.aspx

Duhigg, C. (2012). Psst, you in Aisle 5. *New York Times.* Retrieved from http://www.nytimes.com/2012/02/19/magazine/shopping-habits.html

Dutton, W. H. & Blank, G. (2011). Next Generation Users: The Internet in Britain. Retrieved from http://www.oii.ox.ac.uk/microsites/oxis/

Dutton, W. H. & Blank, G. (2013). Cultures of the Internet. Retrieved from http://www.oii.ox.ac.uk/microsites/oxis/

Dzyre, N. (2014). 5 Essential Things You Should Know about Facebook Nearby Friends. Retrieved 27 April 2014, from http://www.hongkiat.com/blog/facebook-nearby-friends/

Eaton, K. (2014, 1 January). Civilian photography, now rising to new level. *New York Times.* Retrieved from http://www.nytimes.com/2014/01/02/technology/personaltech/review-the-phantom-2-vision-photo-drone-from-dji.html

Einarsen, S. (2011). *Bullying and harassment in the workplace: Developments in theory, research, and practice* (2nd edn.). Boca Raton, FL: CRC Press.

Elmer-Dewitt, P. (1995). On a screen near you: Cyberporn. *Time,* 146, 38–45. Retrieved from http://www.time.com/time/magazine/article/0,9171,134361,00.html

Erikson, E. H. (1956). The problem of ego identity. *Journal of the American Psychoanalytic Association,* 4, 56–121. doi: 10.1177/000306515600400104.

Evans, M. (2009). Wife of Sir John Sawers, the future head of MI6, in Facebook security alert. *The Times.* Retrieved from http://technology.timesonline.co.uk/tol/news/tech_and_web/article6644199.ece

Facebook (2009). Keeping Count of Sharing Across the Web. Retrieved from https://blog.facebook.com/blog.php?topic_id=167544352390

Facebook (2013a, March). Company Info. Retrieved 26 April 2014, from https://newsroom.fb.com/company-info/

Facebook (2013b, 6 August). News Feed FYI: A Window into News Feed. Retrieved 1 February 2014, from https://http://www.facebook.com/business/news/News-Feed-FYI-A-Window-Into-News-Feed

Facebook (n.d.-a). Facebook Principles. Retrieved 30 December 2013, from http:// www.facebook.com/principles.php

Facebook (n.d.-b). How News Feed Works. Retrieved 4 September 2013, from https://http://www.facebook.com/help/www/327131014036297/

Farrell, H. (2012). The consequences of the Internet for politics. *Annual Review of Political Science*, 15(1), 35–52. doi: 10.1146/annurev-polisci-030810-110815.

Feenberg, A. (1999). *Questioning technology*. London: Routledge.

Feenberg, A. (2002a). Democratic Rationalization: Technology, Power, and Freedom. Dogma. Retrieved from http://dogma.free.fr/txt/AF_democratic-rationalization.htm

Feenberg, A. (2002b). *Transforming technology: A critical theory revisited*. New York; Oxford: Oxford University Press.

Feenberg, A. (2008). From critical theory of technology to the rational critique of rationality. *Social Epistemology*, 22(1), 5–28. doi: 10.1080/02691720701 773247.

Findlaw (2013). A Quarter of Young People have Facebook or Other Social Media Postings they May Later Regret, Says New FindLaw.com Survey. Retrieved from http://company.findlaw.com/press-center/2013/a-quarter-of-young-people-have-facebook-or-other-social-media-pos.html

Finkelhor, D., Mitchell, K. J. & Wolak, J. (2000). Online Victimization: A Report on the Nation's Youth. Retrieved from http://www.unh.edu/ccrc/pdf/jvq/ CV38.pdf

Finn, J. (2004). A survey of online harassment at a university campus. *Journal of Interpersonal Violence*, 19(4), 468–483. doi: 10.1177/0886260503262083.

Fischer-Hubner, S., Hopper, N., Perito, D., Castelluccia, C., Kaafar, M. A. & Manils, P. (2011). How Unique and Traceable are Usernames? Privacy Enhancing Technologies (Vol. 6794, pp. 1–17): Springer Berlin Heidelberg. Retrieved from http://arxiv.org/abs/1101.5578

Fitzpatrick, M. G. (2006, 26 July). Deleting Online Predators Act of 2006. Retrieved 22 August 2012, from http://www.c-spanvideo.org/appearance/ 595663226

Fletcher, H. (2008). Human flesh search engines: Chinese vigilantes that hunt victims on the web. *The Times*. Retrieved from http://technology.timesonline. co.uk/tol/news/tech_and_web/article4213681.ece

Flick, U. (2006). Coding and categorizing. In U. Flick (ed.), *An introduction to qualitative research* (3rd edn., pp. 295–319). London: Sage.

Florencio, D. & Herley, C. (2011). Sex, Lies and Cyber-crime Surveys. Retrieved from http://research.microsoft.com/apps/pubs/default.aspx?id=149886

Fowler, G. A. (2012, 13 October). When the most personal secrets get outed on Facebook. *Wall Street Journal*. Retrieved from http://online.wsj.com/news/ articles/SB10000872396390444165804578008740578200224

Friedman, T. (2005). *Electric dreams: Computers in American culture*. New York: New York University Press.

Froomkin, A. M. (2000). The death of privacy? *Stanford Law Review*, 52, 1461–1543. Retrieved from http://personal.law.miami.edu/~froomkin/articles/ privacy-deathof.pdf

Gangadharan, S. P. (2012). Digital inclusion and data profiling. *First Monday*, 17(5–7). doi: 10.5210/fm.v17i5.3821. Retrieved from http://firstmonday.org/ojs/index.php/fm/article/view/3821/3199

Gartner. (2012). Gartner Says Monitoring Employee Behavior in Digital Environments is Rising. Retrieved from http://www.gartner.com/newsroom/id/2028215

Gauntlett, D. (2011). *Making is connecting: The social meaning of creativity, from DIY and knitting to YouTube and Web 2.0*. London: Polity Press. Retrieved from http://www.makingisconnecting.org/

Gawker. (2012, n.d.). Our Titles – Gawker. Retrieved 13 August 2012, from http://advertising.gawker.com/gawker/

Gellman, B. & Poitras, L. (2013, 7 June). U.S., British intelligence mining data from nine U.S. Internet companies in broad secret program. *Washington Post*. Retrieved from http://www.washingtonpost.com/investigations/us-intelligenceminingdatafromnine-us-internet-companies-in-broad-ecret-program/2013/06/06/3a0c0da8-cebf-11e2-8845-d970ccb04497_story.html

Genette, G. (1997). *Paratexts: Thresholds of interpretation*. Cambridge: Cambridge University Press.

Gergen, K. J. (1985). The social constructionist movement in modern psychology. *American Psychologist*, 40(3), 266–275. doi: 10.1037/0003-066X.40.3.266.

Gershon, I. (2011). Un-Friend my heart: Facebook, promiscuity, and heartbreak in a neoliberal age. *Anthropological Quarterly*, 84(4), 865–894. Retrieved 19 June, 2014, from http://www.academia.edu/266205/Un-Friend_My_Heart_Facebook_Promiscuity_and_Heartbreak_in_a_Neoliberal_Age

Giddens, A. (1987). *Erving Goffman as a systematic social theorist social theory and modern sociology* (pp. 109–139). Cambridge: Polity in Association with Blackwell.

Giddens, A. (1990). *The consequences of modernity*. Cambridge: Polity in association with Blackwell.

Giddens, A. (1991). *Modernity and self identity: Self and society in the late modern age*. Cambridge: Polity Press in Association with Basil Blackwell.

Gillespie, T. (2012, 22 February). The Dirty Job of Keeping Facebook Clean. Retrieved 23 April 2014, from http://socialmediacollective.org/2012/02/22/the-dirty-job-of-keeping-facebook-clean/

Goffman, E. (1959). *The presentation of self in everyday life*. New York: Anchor Books.

Goffman, E. (1963a). *Behavior in public places: Notes on the social organization of gatherings*. New York; London: Free Press of Glencoe; Collier-Macmillan.

Goffman, E. (1963b). *Stigma: Notes on the management of spoiled identity*. Harmondsworth: Penguin.

Goffman, E. (1967). *Interaction ritual: Essays in face-to-face behavior*. London; Chicago: The Penguin Press: Aldine.

Goffman, E. (1971a). *Relations in public: Microstudies of the public order*. London: Allen Lane.

Goffman, E. (1971b). The territories of the self. In E. Goffman (ed.), *Relations in public: Microstudies of the public order* (pp. 28–61). London: Allen Lane.

Goffman, E. (1986 [1974]). *Frame analysis: An essay on the organization of experience*. Boston, MA: Northeastern University Press.

Goo, S. K. (2012, 16 May). Facebook: A Profile of Its 'Friends'. Retrieved 18 August 2012, from http://pewresearch.org/pubs/2262/facebook-ipo-friends-profile-social-networking-habits-privacy-online-behavior

Goode, E. & Ben-Yehuda, N. (2009). *Moral panics: The social construction of deviance* (2nd edn.). Chichester, UK; Malden, MA: Wiley-Blackwell.

Google. (n.d.). What We Believe. Retrieved 30 December 2013, from http://www.google.co.uk/about/company/philosophy/

Granka, L. A., Joachims, T. & Gay, G. (2004). Eye-tracking Analysis of User Bbehavior in WWW Search. Paper presented at the Proceedings of the 27th annual international ACM SIGIR conference on Research and development in information retrieval, Sheffield, UK.

Granovetter, M. (1973). The strength of weak ties. *American Journal of Sociology*, 78(6), 1360–1380. Retrieved from http://links.jstor.org/sici?sici=0002-9602%28197305%2978%3A6%3C1360%3ATSOWT%3E2.0.CO%3B2-E

Greenberg, A. (2010, 19 July 2010). Researchers Show How Twitter, Twitpic Make Stalking Simple. Retrieved 20 July 2010, from http://blogs.forbes.com/firewall/2010/07/19/researchers-show-how-twitter-twitpic-make-stalking-simple/

Greenfield, R. (2012, 21 September). Frictionless Sharing Hits the Skids at Facebook. Retrieved 30 December 2013, from http://www.thewire.com/technology/2012/09/facebook-realizes-nobody-wants-share-everything-all-time/57109/

Grodin, D. & Lindlof, T. R. (1996). *Constructing the self in a mediated world.* Thousand Oaks: Sage.

Gross, R., Acquisti, A. & Heinz III, H. J. (2005). Information Revelation and Privacy in Online Social Networks. Paper presented at the Proceedings of the 2005 ACM workshop on Privacy in the electronic society, Alexandria, VA.

Gudelunas, D. (2012). There's an app for That: The uses and gratifications of online social networks for gay men. *Sexuality & Culture*, 16(4), 347–365. doi: 10.1007/s12119-012-9127-4.

Haas, S. M., Irr, M. E., Jennings, N. A. & Wagner, L. M. (2011). Communicating thin: A grounded model of Online Negative Enabling Support Groups in the pro-anorexia movement. *New Media & Society*, 13(1), 40–57. doi: 10.1177/1461444810363910.

Habermas, J. (1970). *Technology and Science as 'Ideology' toward a rational society: Student protest, science, and politics.* Boston, MA: Beacon Press.

Hafner, K. & Lyon, M. (1996). *Where wizards stay up late: The origins of the Internet.* New York: Simon & Schuster.

Halavais, A. (2005, 28 October 2005). Blogging in the Plural. Retrieved 18 November 2005, from http://alex.halavais.net/?p=1281

Hampton, K., Goulet, L. S. & Purcell, K. (2011). Social Networking Sites and Our Lives. Retrieved from http://www.pewinternet.org/Reports/2011/Technology-and-social-networks.aspx

Hanscom, M. (2003, 27 October 2003). Of Blogging and Unemployment. Retrieved 25 May 2004, from http://www.michaelhanscom.com/eclecticism/2003/10/of_blogging_and.html

Hansen, C. (2005, 10 November). Catching Potential Internet Sex Predators. Retrieved 12 January 2010, from http://www.msnbc.msn.com/id/9927253/

Hargie, O. & Dickson, D. (2004). *Skilled interpersonal communication: Research, theory, and practice* (4th edn.). London: Routledge.

Hargrave, A. M. & Livingstone, S. (2007). Harm and Offence in Media Content: Updating the 2005 Review. Retrieved from http://stakeholders.ofcom.org.uk/binaries/research/telecoms-research/annex6.pdf

Harper, R., Whitworth, E. & Page, R. (2012). Fixity: Identity, Time and Duree on Facebook. Paper presented at the Internet Research 13, University of Salford. Retrieved from http://research.microsoft.com/apps/pubs/default.aspx?id=169221

Hawthorne, N. (1850). *The custom-house the Scarlet Letter: A romance* (pp. 1–54). Boston: Ticknor, Reed & Fields. Retrieved from http://etext.lib.virginia.edu/toc/modeng/public/Eaf135.html

Heggestuen, J. (2013, 15 December). One in Every 5 People in the World Own A Smartphone, One in Every 17 Own A Tablet. Retrieved 31 December 2013, from http://www.businessinsider.com/smartphone-and-tablet-penetration-2013-10

Heidegger, M. & Lovitt, W. (1977). *The question concerning technology, and other essays*. New York; London: Harper and Row.

Hevern, V. W. (2004). Threaded identity in cyberspace: Weblogs & positioning in the dialogical self. *Identity*, 4(4), 321–335. Doi: 10.1207/s1532706xid0404_2.

Hill, K. (2013, 19 December). Data Broker was Selling Lists of Rape Victims, Alcoholics, and 'Erectile Dysfunction Sufferers'. Retrieved 20 December 2013, from http://www.forbes.com/sites/kashmirhill/2013/12/19/data-broker-was-selling-lists-of-rape-alcoholism-and-erectile-dysfunction-sufferers/

Hiltz, R. S., Johnson, K. & Turoff, M. (1986). Experiments in group decision making: Communication process and outcome in face to face versus computerized conferences. *Human Communication Research*, 13, 225–252. doi: 10.1111/j.1468-2958.1986.tb00104.x.

Himmer, S. (2004). The labyrinth unbound: Weblogs as literature. In S. Herring, I. Kouper, L. A. Scheidt & E. L. Wright (eds.), *Into the blogosphere: Rhetoric, community, and culture of weblogs*. Retrieved from http://blog.lib.umn.edu/blogosphere/labyrinth_unbound.html

Hinduja, S. & Patchin, J. W. (2012). Cyberbullying: Neither an epidemic nor a rarity. *European Journal of Developmental Psychology*, 9(5), 539–543. doi: 10.1080/17405629.2012.706448.

Hinduja, S. & Patchin, J. W. (2008). Personal information of adolescents on the Internet: A quantitative content analysis of MySpace. *Journal of Adolescence*, 31(1), 125–146. doi:10.1016/j.adolescence.2007.05.004.

Hodkinson, P. (2007). Interactive online journals and individualisation. *New Media & Society*, 9(4), 625–650. doi: 10.1177/1461444807076972.

Hoffman, D. L. & Novak, T. P. (1995). A Detailed Analysis of the Conceptual, Logical, and Methodological Flaws in the Article: 'Marketing Pornography on the Information Superhighway'. Retrieved from http://ceres.imt.uwm.edu/cipr/image/147.pdf

Hogan, B. (2010). The presentation of self in the age of social media: Distinguishing performances and exhibitions online. *Bulletin of Science, Technology & Society*, 30(6), 377–386. doi: 10.1177/0270467610385893.

Hollenbaugh, E. E. & Everett, M. K. (2013). The effects of anonymity on self-disclosure in blogs: An application of the online disinhibition effect. *Journal of Computer-Mediated Communication*, 18(3), 283–302. doi: 10.1111/jcc4.12008.

Holmes, J. (2009). MYTHS AND MISSED OPPORTUNITIES – Young people's not so risky use of online communication. *Information, Communication & Society*, 12(8), 1174–1196. Retrieved from http://www.informaworld.com/10.1080/13691180902769873

Howard, P. N. & Hussain, M. M. (2011). The upheavals in Egypt and Tunisia: The role of digital media. *Journal of Democracy*, 22(3), 35–48. Retrieved from http://www.journalofdemocracy.org/upheavals-egypt-and-tunisia-role-digital-media

Hudson, L. (2013). Shame with Caution: Mad at some Jerk? Think Twice Before Sending that Tweet. Wired. Retrieved from http://www.wired.com/underwire/2013/07/ap_argshaming/

Hughes, S. A. (2011, 4 August). Undetweetable Archives Deleted Tweets, Gets Warning from Twitter (Update). Retrieved 3 April 2013, from http://www.washingtonpost.com/blogs/blogpost/post/undetweetable-archives-deleted-tweets-gets-warning-from-twitter/2011/08/04/gIQAlqlBuI_blog.html

Illouz, E. (2007). *Cold intimacies: The making of emotional capitalism*. Cambridge: Polity.

Indiana University Information Technology Services. (2006, 11 May 2005). In Unix, How Do I Make Plan and Project Files That Will Show Up when People Finger My Account? Retrieved 9 April 2006, from http://kb.iu.edu/data/afky.html

Information Commissioner's Office. (2011). Quick Guide to the Employment Practices Code. Retrieved from http://www.ico.org.uk/for_organisations/data_protection/topic_guides/employment

Intersperience. (2011, 23 May). PRESS RELEASE: Twenty-Somethings Top Online Friends' League Table. Retrieved 18 August 2012, from http://www.intersperience.com/news_more.asp?news_id=34&current_id=1

Jagatic, T. N., Johnson, N. A., Jakobsson, M. & Menczer, F. (2007). Social phishing. *Communications of the ACM*, 50(10), 94–100. Retrieved from http://portal.acm.org/citation.cfm?id=1290958.1290968

Jansen, B. J. & Spink, A. (2006). How are we searching the World Wide Web? A comparison of nine search engine transaction logs. *Information Processing & Management*, 42(1), 248–263. Retrieved from http://www.sciencedirect.com/science/article/pii/S0306457304001396

Jarvis, J. (2011). *Public parts: How sharing in the digital age improves the way we work and live*. New York: Simon & Schuster.

Jogin, T. (2003, 15 July 2003). Winer Watcher. Retrieved 12 October 2008, from http://jogin.com/weblog/archives/2003/07/15/winer_watcher

John, N. A. (2013). Sharing and Web 2.0: The emergence of a keyword. *New Media & Society*, 15(2), 167–182. doi: 10.1177/1461444812450684.

Jourard, S. M. & Lasakow, P. (1958). Some factors in self-disclosure. *The Journal of Abnormal and Social Psychology*, 56(1), 91–98. doi: 10.1037/h0043357.

Julius, A. (2003). *T.S. Eliot, anti-Semitism and literary form* (Rev. edn.). London: Thames & Hudson.

Kaplan Test Prep (2013, 31 October). Facebook Checking is No Longer Unchartered Territory in College Admissions: Percentage of Admissions Officers Who Visited an Applicant's Profile on the Rise. Retrieved 2 February 2014, from http://press.kaptest.com/press-releases/kaplan-test-prep-survey-more-college-admissions-officers-checking-applicants-digital-trails-but-most-students-unconcerned

Karat, C.-M., Halverson, C., Horn, D. & Karat, J. (1999). Patterns of Entry and Correction in Large Vocabulary Continuous Speech Recognition Systems. Paper presented at the Proceedings of the SIGCHI conference on Human Factors in Computing Systems, Pittsburgh, PA, USA.

Katz, J. E. & Rice, R. E. (2002). *Social consequences of internet use*. Cambridge, MA: MIT Press.

Katz, M. L. & Shapiro, C. (1985). Network externalities, competition, and compatibility. *The American Economic Review*, 75(3), 424–440. Retrieved from http://www.jstor.org/stable/1814809

Kendall, L. (2007). Shout into the wind, and it shouts back: Identity and interactional tensions on LiveJournal. *First Monday*, 12(9). Retrieved from http://firstmonday.org/htbin/cgiwrap/bin/ojs/index.php/fm/article/view/2004/1879

Kessler, S. (2013, 12 September). Meet Your Future Memory Aid: The Internet. Retrieved 15 December 2013, from http://www.salon.com/2013/09/12/meet_your_future_memory_the_internet_newscred/

Kiesler, S. B. (1997). *Culture of the internet*. Mahwah, NJ: Lawrence Erlbaum Associates Publishers.

Killoran, J. B. (2002). Homepage, Homebound: Web Log, We Blog: Web Genres for Personal Civic (Dis-)Engagement. Paper presented at the Rhetoric Society of America, Las Vegas. Retrieved from http://myweb.brooklyn.liu.edu/jkillora/research/2002rsa.html

Kinder, L. (2013, 10 September). Twitter gaffes: The embarrassing, the shameful and the stupid. *The Daily Telegraph*. Retrieved from http://www.telegraph.co.uk/culture/tvandradio/bbc/10298777/Twitter-gaffes-the-embarrassing-the-shameful-and-the-stupid.html

King, S. A. (1996). Researching internet communities: Proposed ethical guidelines for the reporting of results. *The Information Society*, 12(2), 119–128. Retrieved from http://dx.doi.org/10.1080/713856145

Kirkpatrick, D. (2010). *The Facebook effect: The inside story of the company that is connecting the world* (1st Simon & Schuster hardcover edn.). New York: Simon & Schuster.

Kitzmann, A. (2003). That different place: Documenting the self within online environments. *Biography-an Interdisciplinary Quarterly*, 26(1), 48–65.

Knowles, J. (2012, 9 December). Why 2013 Will Be the Year of the Internet of Things. Retrieved 31 December 2013, from http://thenextweb.com/insider/2012/12/09/the-future-of-the-internet-of-things/

Kosinski, M., Stillwell, D. & Graepel, T. (2013). Private Traits and Attributes Are Predictable from Digital Records of Human Behavior. Proceedings of the National Academy of Sciences. doi: 10.1073/pnas.1218772110.

Kotenko, J. (2013, 24 August). Want to Get Fired? Apparently these People Publicly Using the #ihatemyjob Hashtag Do. Retrieved 20 September 2013, from http://www.digitaltrends.com/social-media/these-people-are-totally-getting-fired-for-being-social-media-idiots/

Kowalski, R. M., Limber, S. & Agatston, P. W. (2008). *Cyber bullying: Bullying in the digital age*. Oxford: Blackwell.

Kowalski, R. M. & Limber, S. P. (2007). Electronic bullying among middle school students. *Journal of Adolescent Health*, 41(6, Supplement), S22–S30. doi: 10.1016/j.jadohealth.2007.08.017.

Krasnova, H., Veltri, N. F. & Gunther, O. (2012). Self-disclosure and privacy calculus on social networking sites: The role of culture. *Business & Information Systems Engineering*, 4(3), 127–135. doi: 10.1007/s12599-012-0216-6.

Krasnova, H., Wenninger, H., Widjaja, T. & Buxmann, P. (2013). Envy on Facebook: A Hidden Threat to Users' Life Satisfaction? Paper presented at the Wirtschaftsinformatik, Universität Leipzig. Retrieved from http://www.wi2013.de/proceedings/WI2013-Track 11-Krasnova.pdf

Kruger, J., Epley, N., Parker, J. & Ng, Z. (2005). Egocentrism over e-email: Can we communicate as well as we think? *Journal of Personality and Social Psychology*, 89(6), 925–936. doi: 10.1037/0022-3514.89.6.925.

Lally, E. (2002). *At home with computers*. Basingstoke: Berg.

Langer, E. J., Blank, A. & Chanowitz, B. (1978). The mindlessness of ostensibly thoughtful action: The role of 'placebic' information in interpersonal interaction. *Journal of Personality and Social Psychology*, 36(6), 635–642. doi: 10.1037/0022-3514.36.6.635.

Lash, S. & Friedman, J. (1991). *Modernity and identity*. Oxford; Cambridge, MA: Blackwell.

Lenhart, A. (2006). Unstable Text: An Ethnographic Look at How Bloggers and Their Audience Negotiate Self-Presentation, Authenticity and Norm Formation. Master of Arts in Communication, Culture and Technology, Georgetown University, Washington, DC. Retrieved from http://lenhart.flashesofpanic.com/Lenhart_thesis.pdf

Lenhart, A. & Fox, S. (2006). Bloggers: A Portrait of the Internet's New Storytellers. Retrieved from http://www.pewinternet.org/Reports/2006/Bloggers.aspx

Lessig, L. (2006a). *Code: And other laws of cyberspace, version 2.0* (2nd edn.). New York: Basic Books (The Perseus Books Group). Retrieved from http://codev2.cc/

Lessig, L. (2006b). What things regulate. In L. Lessig (ed.), *Code: And other laws of cyberspace: Version 2.0* (Rev. edn., pp. 120–137). Basic Books (The Perseus Books Group). Retrieved from http://codev2.cc/

Lie, M. & Sørensen, K. H. (1996). Making technology our own?: Domesticating technology into everyday life. In M. Lie & K. H. Sørensen (eds.), *Making technology our own?: Domesticating technology into everyday life* (pp. 1–30). Oslo; Boston: Scandinavian University Press.

Litt, E. & Birnholtz, J. (2014, 7 January). [Statistics on intentionality from your 'Awkward Encounters of an "other" kind' study].

Litt, E., Spottswood, E., Birnholtz, J., Hancock, J., Smith, M. E. & Reynolds, L. (2014). Awkward Encounters of an 'Other' Kind: Collective Self-Presentation and Face Threat on Facebook. Paper presented at the CSCW, Baltimore, MD. Retrieved from http://socialmedia.northwestern.edu/files/2013/10/AwkwardFacebookPhotoReadyVersion1.pdf

LiveJournal (2007, 10 May). How Do I Delete/Undelete My Journal or Community? Retrieved 9 November 2008, from http://www.livejournal.com/support/faqbrowse.bml?faqid=16

LiveJournal (2008, 24 June). How Do I Make all My Journal Entries Friends-Only, Private, or Public? Retrieved 6 August 2008, from http://www.livejournal.com/support/faqbrowse.bml?faqid=120&q=edit+journal+privacy&lang=

Livingstone, S. (2003). The Changing Nature and Uses of Media Literacy. Retrieved from http://www.lse.ac.uk/collections/media@lse/mediaWorkingPapers/ewpNumber4.htm

Livingstone, S. (2008). Taking risky opportunities in youthful content creation: Teenagers' use of social networking sites for intimacy, privacy and self-expression. *New Media & Society*, 10(3), 393–411. doi: 10.1177/1461444808089415. Retrieved from http://eprints.lse.ac.uk/27072/

Livingstone, S. & Brake, D. R. (2009). On the rapid rise of social networking sites: New findings and policy implications. *Children and Society*, 24(1), 75–83. doi: 10.1111/j.1099-0860.2009.00243.x Retrieved from http://eprints.lse.ac.uk/30124/

Livingstone, S., Haddon, L., Gorzig, A, & Olafsson, K (2011a). Risks and Safety on the Internet: The Perspective of European Children: Full Findings. Retrieved from http://www.eukidsonline.net/

Livingstone, S. & Hargrave, A. M. (2006). *Harm and offence in media content: A review of the evidence*. Bristol: Intellect.

Livingstone, S. & Helsper, E. J. (2010). Balancing opportunities and risks in teenagers' use of the internet: The role of online skills and internet self-efficacy. *New Media & Society*, 12(2), 309–329.

Livingstone, S., Ólafsson, K. & Staksrud, E. (2011). Social Networking, Age and Privacy. EU Kids Online, Retrieved from http://eprints.lse.ac.uk/35849/.

Lloyds TSB (n.d.). Social Media and Identity Theft. Retrieved 24 June 2013, from http://www.lloydstsb.com/help-guidance/security/social-networking.asp

Lu, Y.-H. (2005). Privacy and data privacy issues in contemporary China. *Ethics and Information Technology*, 7(1), 7–15. doi: 10.1007/s10676-005-0456-y.

Ludwig, S. (2013, 9 August). Yikes: This New App Saves Snapchats without Letting the Sender Know. Retrieved 15 August 2013, from http://venturebeat.com/2013/08/09/app-to-save-snapchat-messages/

Lunden, I. (2013, 30 October). Facebook's Mobile Tipping Point: 48% of Daily Users Are Now Mobile-Only (But No Mention of BlackBerry). Retrieved 1 January 2014, from http://techcrunch.com/2013/10/30/nearly-half-48-of-daily-users-of-facebook-are-now-mobile-only-says-ceo-zuckerberg/

MacAskill, E. (2007, 14 November). Yahoo forced to apologise to Chinese dissidents over crackdown on journalists. *The Guardian*. Retrieved from http://www.guardian.co.uk/technology/2007/nov/14/news.yahoo

Madden, M., Lenhart, A., Cortesi, S., Gasser, U., Duggan, M. & Smith, A. (2013). Teens, Social Media, and Privacy. Retrieved from http://www.pewinternet.org/2013/05/21/teens-social-media-and-privacy/

Madjeski, M., Johnson, M. & Bellovin, S. M. (2011). The Failure of Online Social Network Privacy Settings. Retrieved from http://mice.cs.columbia.edu/getTechreport.php?techreportID=1459

Magnanti, B. (2009, 15 November). Now I'm Not Anonymous... Retrieved 12 January 2010, from http://web.archive.org/web/20110413163220/http://belledejour-uk.blogspot.com/2009_11_01_archive.html

Maple, C., Short, E. & Brown, A. (2011). Cyberstalking in the United Kingdom: An Analysis of the ECHO Pilot Survey. Retrieved from http://www.beds.ac.uk/—data/assets/pdf_file/0003/83109/ECHO_Pilot_Final.pdf

Maple, C., Short, E., Brown, A., Bryden, C., & Salter, M. (2012). Cyberstalking in the UK: Analysis and recommendations. *International Journal of Distributed Systems and Technologies*, 3(4), 34-51. doi: 10.4018/jdst.2012100104.

Margolis, Z. (2009, 15 November 2009). Sexblogger's Tale: How My Life Changed Forever. Retrieved 12 January 2010, from http://www.guardian.co.uk/commentisfree/2009/nov/15/sex-blog-zoe-margolis

Markoff, J. (2002, 9 November). Pentagon plans a computer system that would peek at personal data of Americans. *New York Times*. Retrieved from http://www.nytimes.com/2002/11/09/politics/09COMP.html

Marvin, C. (1988). *When old technologies were new: Thinking about electric communication in the late nineteenth century*. New York: Oxford University Press.

Marwick, A. E. (2008). To catch a predator? The MySpace moral panic. *First Monday*, 13(6). Retrieved from http://firstmonday.org/htbin/cgiwrap/bin/ojs/index.php/fm/article/view/2152/1966

Marwick, A. (2013). *Status update: Celebrity, publicity, and branding in the social media age*. New Haven, CT: Yale University Press.

Marwick, A. & boyd, d. (2011). I tweet honestly, I tweet passionately: Twitter users, context collapse, and the imagined audience. *New Media & Society*, 13(1) doi: 10.1177/1461444810365313.

Marwick, A. E., Murgia-Diaz, D. & Palfrey, J. G., Jr. (2010). Youth, Privacy and Reputation (Literature Review). Retrieved from http://ssrn.com/paper=1588163

Mayer-Schönberger, V. (2009). *Delete: The virtue of forgetting in the digital age*. Princeton, NJ: Princeton University Press.

McCown, F., Diawara, N. & Nelson, M. L. (2007). Factors Affecting Website Reconstruction from the Web Infrastructure. Paper presented at the Proceedings of the 7th ACM/IEEE-CS joint conference on Digital libraries.

McKenna, K. Y. A. & Bargh, J. A. (1998). Coming out in the age of the Internet: Identity 'de-marginalization' from virtual group participation. *Journal of Personality and Social Psychology*, 75, 681–694.

McKeon, M. (2010, 19 May). The Evolution of Privacy on Facebook. Retrieved 27 April 2014, from http://mattmckeon.com/facebook-privacy/

Mehrabian, A. (1977). *Nonverbal communication*. Piscataway, NJ: Transaction Publishers.

Meyrowitz, J. (1985). *No sense of place: The impact of electronic media on social behavior*. Oxford; New York: Oxford University Press.

Microsoft. (2013). Data Privacy Day Privacy Survey 2013. Retrieved from http://download.microsoft.com/download/5/3/8/53890306-627C-4EFE-8E61-7FE593B013F0/DPD Privacy Survey 2013 Executive Summary_Final.pdf

Mikhailova, A. (2006, 6 August). By day she worked on Harry Potter. But by night . . . *Sunday Times*. Retrieved from http://www.timesonline.co.uk/tol/news/uk/article601445.ece

Miller, V. (2008). New media, networking and phatic culture. *Convergence*, 14(4), 387–400. doi: 10.1177/1354856508094659.

Milne, G. R. & Culnan, M. J. (2004). Strategies for reducing online privacy risks: Why consumers read (or don't read) online privacy notices. *Journal of Interactive Marketing*, 18(3), 15–29. doi: 10.1002/dir.20009. Retrieved from http://www.sciencedirect.com/science/article/pii/S1094996804701085

Mims, C. (2013, 5 December). 2014 Is the Year of the Internet of Things – No, Seriously, We Mean It This Time. Retrieved 31 December 2013, from http://qz.com/154064/2014-is-the-year-of-the-internet-of-things-no-seriously-we-mean-it-this-time/

Mitchell, K. J., Jones, L. M., Finkelhor, D. & Wolak, J. (2013). Understanding the decline in unwanted online sexual solicitations for U.S. youth 2000–2010: Findings from three Youth Internet Safety Surveys. *Child Abuse & Neglect*. doi: 10.1016/j.chiabu.2013.07.002. Retrieved from http://www.sciencedirect.com/science/article/pii/S0145213413001828

Moira, B., Cameron, M. & Thomas, L. (2009). Feed Me: Motivating Newcomer Contribution in Social Network Sites. Paper presented at the Proceedings of the SIGCHI Conference on Human Factors in Computing Systems, Boston, MA.

Morozov, E. (2011). *The net delusion: How not to liberate the World*. London: Penguin.

Morozov, E. (2013, 2 December). I Know What Will Cheer You Up: Emotion-detecting Advertising is Coming. Beware. Retrieved 16 December 2013 from http://www.slate.com/articles/technology/future_tense/2013/12/emotion_detecting_advertising_regulators_aren_t_ready_for_it.html.

Mortensen, T. (2004). Dialogue in Slow Motion: The Pleasure of Reading and Writing Across the Web. Paper presented at the Blogtalk 2, Vienna. Retrieved from http://tilsett.hivolda.no/tm/blogtalk2004.doc

Muise, A., Christofides, E. & Desmarais, S. (2009). More information than you ever wanted: Does Facebook bring out the green-eyed monster of jealousy? *CyberPsychology & Behavior*, 12(4), 441–444.

myjobgroup.co.uk (2010). Social Media in the Workplace. Retrieved from http://www.myjobgroup.co.uk/socialmediawhitepaper/

Nadkarni, A. & Hofmann, S. G. (2012). Why do people use Facebook? *Personality and Individual Differences*, 52(3), 243–249. doi: 10.1016/j.paid.2011.11.007.

Nardi, B., Schiano, D. & Gumbrecht, M. (2004). Blogging as Social Activity, or, Would You Let 900 Million People Read Your Diary? Paper presented at the ACM conference on Computer supported cooperative work, Chicago, IL.

National School Boards Association (2007). Creating & Connecting – Research and Guidelines on Online Social – and Educational – Networking. Retrieved from http://www.nsba.org/

Neumyer, S. (2014, 16 January). Thinstagram. Retrieved 1 February 2014, from https://medium.com/the-magazine/1ed639152e34

Nie, N. H. (2001). Sociability, interpersonal relations, and the Internet: Reconciling conflicting findings. *American Behavioral Scientist*, 45(3), 420–435(416).

Niedzviecki, H. (2009). *The peep diaries: How we're learning to love watching ourselves and our neighbors*. San Francisco: City Lights Books.

Nielsen BuzzMetrics (2007). A Qualitative Study of Online Discussions About Teen Alcohol & Drug Use. Retrieved from http://www.caron.org/caron-research-reports/

Nosko, A., Wood, E. & Molema, S. (2010). All about me: Disclosure in online social networking profiles: The case of Facebook. *Computers in Human Behavior*, 26(3), 406–418.

Nussbaum, E. (2004, 11 January). My so-called blog. *New York Times Magazine*. Retrieved from http://www.nytimes.com/2004/01/11/magazine/11BLOG.html

Nyst, C. (2013, 27 November). The Five Eyes Fact Sheet. Retrieved 23 April 2014, from https://http://www.privacyinternational.org/blog/the-five-eyes-fact-sheet

Ofcom (2011). Children and Parents: Media Use and Attitudes Report. Retrieved from http://stakeholders.ofcom.org.uk/market-data-research/media-literacy-pubs/

Ofcom (2013). The Communications Market 2013. Retrieved from http://stakeholders.ofcom.org.uk/market-data-research/market-data/communications-market-reports/cmr13/

Olson, P. & Tilley, A. (2014, 5 May). The quantified other: Nest and fitbit chase a lucrative side business. *Forbes*. Retrieved from http://www.forbes.

com/sites/parmyolson/2014/04/17/the-quantified-other-nest-and-fitbit-chase-a-lucrative-side-business/

Olweus, D. (2012). Cyberbullying: An overrated phenomenon? *European Journal of Developmental Psychology*, 9(5), 520–538. Retrieved from 10.1080/17405629.2012.682358.

Oolo, E. & Siibak, A. (2013). Performing for one's imagined audience: Social steganography and other privacy strategies of Estonian teens on networked publics. *Cyberpsychology: Journal of Psychosocial Research on Cyberspace*, 7(1). doi: 10.5817/CP2013-1-7. Retrieved from http://www.cyberpsychology.eu/view.php?cisloclanku=2013011501&article=7

Opsahl, K. (2010, 28 April). Facebook's Eroding Privacy Policy: A Timeline. Retrieved 27 April 2014, from https://http://www.eff.org/deeplinks/2010/04/facebook-timeline/

O'Reilly, T. (2006, 10 December). Web 2.0 Compact Definition: Trying Again. Retrieved 14 September 2012, from http://radar.oreilly.com/2006/12/web-20-compact-definition-tryi.html

Palfrey, J. & Gasser, U. (2008). *Born digital: Understanding the first generation of digital natives*. New York: Basic Books.

Patchin, J. W. & Hinduja, S. (2010). Trends in online social networking: Adolescent use of MySpace over time. *New Media & Society*, 12(2), 197–216. doi: 10.1177/1461444809341857. Retrieved from http://nms.sagepub.com/cgi/content/abstract/12/2/197

Patchin, J. W. & Hinduja, S. (2012). Cyberbullying: An update and synthesis of the research. In J. W. Patchin & S. Hinduja (eds.), *Cyberbullying prevention and response: Expert perspectives* (pp. 13–35). New York: Routledge.

Petersen, J. (1995). Letters from the Dead. Retrieved 11 November 2005, from http://web.archive.org/web/20001025145952/www.awaken.org/trans/let2.html

Pew Internet & American Life Project (2006). Digital Footprints. Retrieved from http://pewinternet.org/Shared-Content/Data-Sets/2006/December-2006–Digital-Footprints.aspx

Pew Internet & American Life Project (n.d.-a). Trend Data (Adults): What Internet Users Do Online. Retrieved from http://pewinternet.org/Trend-Data-(Adults)/Online-Activites-Total.aspx

Pew Internet & American Life Project (n.d.-b). Trend Data (Adults): Who's Online: Internet User Demographics. Retrieved from http://pewinternet.org/Trend-Data-(Adults)/Whos-Online.aspx

Pfaffenberger, B. (1996). 'If I want it, it's OK': Usenet and the (outer) limits of free speech. *The Information Society*, 12(4), 365–386.

Pierce, T. (2004, 16 June). How to Blog. Retrieved 20 September 2010, from http://www.tonypierce.com/blog/2004/06/how-to-blog-by-tony-pierce-110-1.htm

Plummer, K. (1996). Symbolic interactionism in the twentieth century: The rise of empirical social theory. In B. S. Turner (ed.), *The Blackwell companion to social theory* (pp. 223–251). Oxford; Cambridge, MA: Blackwell Publishers.

Pool, I. d. S. (1977). *The social impact of the telephone*. Cambridge, MA; London: M.I.T. Press.

Portwood-Stacer, L. (2013). Media refusal and conspicuous non-consumption: The performative and political dimensions of Facebook abstention. *New*

Media & Society, 15(7), 1041–1057. doi: 10.1177/1461444812465139. Retrieved from http://nms.sagepub.com/content/15/7/1041.abstract

Postmes, T., Spears, R. & Lea, M. (1998). Breaching or building social boundaries? SIDE-effects of computer-mediated communication. *Communication Research*, 25, 689–715.

Prensky, M. (2001). Digital natives, digital immigrants. *On the Horizon*, 9(5), 1–2. Retrieved from http://www.marcprensky.com/writing/Prensky - Digital Natives, Digital Immigrants – Part1.pdf

Press Association (2013a, 27 August). Most Babies Make Facebook Debut Within an Hour of Being Born. Retrieved 2 February 2014, from http://www.huffingtonpost.co.uk/2013/08/27/baby-photos-facebook-hour-birth_n_3821257.html

Press Association (2013b, 23 August). Nearly one in 10 children gets first mobile phone by age five, says study. *The Guardian*. Retrieved from http://www.theguardian.com/money/2013/aug/23/children-first-mobile-age-five

Purcell, R., Pathé, M. & Mullen, P. E. (2004). Stalking: Defining and prosecuting a new category of offending. *International Journal of Law and Psychiatry*, 27(2), 157–169. Retrieved from http://www.sciencedirect.com/science/article/pii/S016025270400007X

Reed, A. (2005). 'My blog is me': Texts and persons in UK online journal culture (and anthropology). *Ethnos*, 70, 220–242.

Rettberg, J. W. (2008). *Blogging*. Cambridge; Malden, MA: Polity.

Rheingold, H. (2000). *The virtual community: Homesteading on the electronic frontier* (Rev. edn.). Cambridge, MA: MIT Press. Retrieved from http://www.rheingold.com/vc/book/

Rice, R. E. (1993). Media appropriateness: Using social presence theory to compare traditional and new organizational media. *Human Communication Research*, 19(4), 451–484.

Rimm, M. (1994). Marketing pornography on the information superhighway: A survey of 917,410 images, descriptions, short stories, and animations downloaded 8.5 million times by consumers in over 2000 cities in forty countries, provinces, and territories. *Georgetown Law Journal*, 83, 1849–1915. Retrieved from http://www.sics.se/~psm/kr9512-001.html

Rose, N. (1999). *Governing the soul: The shaping of the private self*. London: Routledge.

Rosen, J. (2004, 19 December). Your blog or mine? *New York Times Magazine*. Retrieved from http://www.nytimes.com/2004/12/19/magazine/19PHENOM.html?ei=5090&en=0f68277267a43d84&ex=1261198800&partner=rssuserland&pagewanted=all&position=

Rosen, J. (2005). *The naked crowd: Reclaiming security and freedom in an anxious age* (1st edn.). New York: Random House.

Ruffner, M. & Burgoon, M. (1981). *Interpersonal communication*. New York: Holt, Rinehart, and Winston.

SalahEldeen, H. M. & Nelson, M. L. (2012). Losing My Revolution: How Many Resources Shared on Social Media have been Lost? Paper presented at the Theory and Practice of Digital Libraries 2012, Paphos, Cyprus. Retrieved from http://www.cs.odu.edu/~mln/pubs/tpdl-2012/tpdl-2012.pdf

Schacter, D. L. (2003). *How the mind forgets and remembers: The seven sins of memory*. London: Souvenir.

186 *Bibliography*

Schwartz, M. (2012). Fire in the Library. Technology Review. Retrieved from http://www.technologyreview.com/article/39317/

Sengupta, S. (2013, 10 April). Facebook Refines Ad Targeting. Retrieved 27 June 2013, from http://bits.blogs.nytimes.com/2013/04/10/facebook-refines-ad-targeting/?_r=0

Serfaty, V. (2004). *The mirror and the veil: An overview of American online diaries and blogs*. Amsterdam: Rodopi.

Shah, R. C. & Sandvig, C. (2008). Software defaults as de facto regulation: The case of the wireless internet. *Information, Communication & Society*, 11(1), 25–46. Retrieved from http://www.informaworld.com/10.1080/13691180701858836

Shank, G. (1993). Abductive multiloguing: The semiotic dynamics of navigating the net. *The Arachnet Electronic Journal on Virtual Culture*, 1(1). Retrieved from http://www.ibiblio.org/pub/academic/communications/papers/ejvc/SHANK.V1N1

Shapiro, C. & Varian, H. R. (1999). *Information rules: A strategic guide to the network economy*. Boston, MA: Harvard Business School Press.

Sheridan, L. P. & Grant, T. (2007). Is cyberstalking different? *Psychology, Crime & Law*, 13(6), 627–640. doi: 10.1080/10683160701340528.

Shiels, M. (2010, 22 April). Facebook's Bid to Rule the Web as It Goes Social. Retrieved 30 December 2013, from http://news.bbc.co.uk/1/hi/8590306.stm

Short, J., Williams, E. & Christie, B. (1976). The Social Psychology of Telecommunications, Wiley. Retrieved from http://books.google.ca/books?id=Ze63AAAAIAAJ

Siklos, R. (2005, 18 July). News corp. to acquire owner of MySpace.com. *The New York Times*. Retrieved from http://www.nytimes.com/2005/07/18/business/18cnd-newscorp.html

Silver, D. (2000). Looking backwards, looking forward: Cyberculture studies 1990–2000. In D. Gauntlett (ed.), *Web.studies: Rewiring media studies for the digital age* (pp. 19–30). London: Arnold. Retrieved from http://rccs.usfca.edu/intro.asp

Silverstone, R. & Mansell, R. (1996). The politics of information and communication technologies. In R. E. Mansell & R. Silverstone (eds.), *Communication by design: The politics of information and communication technologies* (pp. 213–227). Oxford; New York: Oxford University Press.

Smith, A. (2013). Smartphone Ownership 2013. Retrieved from http://pewinternet.org/Reports/2013/Smartphone-Ownership-2013.aspx

Smith, A. (2014). 6 New Facts about Facebook. Retrieved from http://www.pewresearch.org/fact-tank/2014/02/03/6-new-facts-about-facebook/

Solove, D. J. (2008). *Understanding privacy*. Cambridge, MA: Harvard University Press.

Sophos (2007). Sophos Facebook ID Probe Shows 41% of Users Happy to Reveal all to Potential Identity Thieves. Retrieved from http://www.sophos.com/pressoffice/news/articles/2007/08/facebook.html

Sorapure, M. (2003). Screening moments, scrolling lives: Diary writing on the web. *Biography-an Interdisciplinary Quarterly*, 26(1), 1–23.

Spitzberg, B. H. & Cupach, W. R. (2007). The state of the art of stalking: Taking stock of the emerging literature. *Aggression and Violent Behavior*, 12(1), 64–86.

Sproull, L. & Kiesler, S. (1986). Reducing social context cues: Electronic mail in organizational communications. *Management Science*, 32(11), 1492–1512. Retrieved from http://www.jstor.org/stable/2631506

Staksrud, E. (2013). *Children in the online world: Risk, regulation and rights.* London: Ashgate.

Staksrud, E., Ólafsson, K. & Livingstone, S. (2012). Does the use of social networking sites increase children's risk of harm? *Computers in Human Behavior.* doi: 10.1016/j.chb.2012.05.026.

Steel, E. (2010, 25 October). A web pioneer profiles users by name. *The Wall Street Journal.* Retrieved from http://online.wsj.com/news/articles/SB10001424052702304410504575560243259416072

Stefanone, M. A., Kwon, K. & Lackaff, D. (2011). The value of online friends: Networked resources via social network sites. *First Monday,* 16(2). Retrieved from http://www.uic.edu/htbin/cgiwrap/bin/ojs/index.php/fm/article/view/3314

Steinfield, C., Ellison, N. & Lampe, C. (2008). Social capital, self-esteem, and use of online social network sites: A longitudinal analysis. *Journal of Applied Developmental Psychology,* 29(6), 434–445.

Steinfield, C., Ellison, N., Lampe, C. & Vitak, J. (2010). Online Social Network Sites and the Concept of Social Capital. Paper presented at the The Internet Turning 40, Chinese University of Hong Kong. Retrieved from https://Sharing Our Lives Online final draft.docx

Stepanek, M. (2000). Weblining. Bloomberg Businessweek. Retrieved from http://www.businessweek.com/2000/00_14/b3675027.htm

Stutzman, F., Gross, R. & Acquisti, A. (2012). Silent listeners: The evolution of privacy and disclosure on Facebook. *Journal of Privacy and Confidentiality,* 4(2), 7–41. Retrieved from http://repository.cmu.edu/jpc/vol4/iss2/2

Subrahmanyam, K., Kraut, R. E., Greenfield, P. M. & Gross, E. F. (2000). The impact of home computer use on children's activities and development. *Future Child,* 10(2), 123–144.

Sullivan, B. (2012, 6 March). Govt. Agencies, Colleges Demand Applicants' Facebook Passwords. Retrieved 6 March 2012, from http://redtape.msnbc.msn.com/_news/2012/03/06/10585353-govt-agencies-colleges-demand-applicants-facebook-passwords

Sweney, M. (2013, 20 March). Facebook users risk identity theft, says famous ex-conman. *The Guardian.* Retrieved from http://www.guardian.co.uk/media/2013/mar/20/facebook-risks-identity-theft-frank-abagnale

Tan, K. (2013, 20 May 2008). Student Pranks, Earthquakes and Internet Manhunts. Retrieved 2 September 2013, from http://shanghaiist.com/2008/05/20/student_pranks.php

Tate, R. (2008, 13 August). Her Royal Highness of Princeton. Retrieved 20 September 2010, from http://gawker.com/5036818/her-royal-highness-of-princeton

Templeman, R., Korayem, M., Crandall, D. & Kapadiay, A. (2014). PlaceAvoider: Steering First-Person Cameras away from Sensitive Spaces. Paper presented at the NDSS, San Diego, CA. Retrieved from http://www.cs.indiana.edu/~kapadia/papers/placeavoider-ndss14.pdf

Thaler, R. H. & Sunstein, C. R. (2008). *Nudge: Improving decisions about health, wealth, and happiness.* New Haven, CT: Yale University Press.

The Economist (2013). The people's panopticon. *The Economist,* 27–29. Retrieved from http://www.economist.com/news/briefing/21589863-it-getting-ever-easier-record-anything-or-everything-you-see-opens

Thomas, O. (2008, 3 June). Paris Hilton, Lindsay Lohan Private Pics Exposed by Yahoo Hack. Retrieved 3 July 2008, from http://valleywag.com/5012543/paris-hilton-lindsay-lohan-private-pics-exposed-by-yahoo-hack

Thompson, C. (2008, 7 September). Brave new world of digital intimacy. *New York Times Magazine*. Retrieved from http://www.nytimes.com/2008/09/07/magazine/07awareness-t.html

Thompson, J. B. (1995). *The media and modernity: A social theory of the media*. Cambridge, UK: Polity Press.

Tidwell, L. C. & Walther, J. B. (2002). Computer-mediated communication effects on disclosure, impressions, and interpersonal evaluations getting to know one another a bit at a time. *Human Communication Research*, 28(3), 317–348. Retrieved from http://www.scopus.com/scopus/inward/record.url?eid=2-s2.0-0036338851&partner=40&rel=R4.0.0

Tokc-Wilde, I. (2011, 7 May). Workforce surveillance: Is your boss keeping a private eye on you? *The Guardian*. Retrieved from http://www.theguardian.com/money/2011/may/07/workforce-surveillance-employer-employee

Tufekci, Z. (2008). Can you see me now? Audience and disclosure regulation in online social network sites. *Bulletin of Science, Technology and Society*, 28(1), 20–36.

Turkle, S. (1996a). *Life on the screen: Identity in the age of the Internet*. London: Weidenfeld & Nicolson.

Turkle, S. (1996b). Parallel lives: Working on identity in virtual space. In D. Grodin & T. R. Lindlof (eds.), *Constructing the self in a mediated world* (pp. 156–175). Thousand Oaks: Sage.

Turkle, S. (2011). *Alone together: Why we expect more from technology and less from each other*. New York: Basic Books.

Turner, F. (2005). Where the counterculture met the new economy: The WELL and the origins of virtual community. *Technology and Culture*, 46(July 2005), 485–512.

Turner, F. (2006). *From counterculture to cyberculture: Stewart Brand, the Whole Earth Network, and the rise of digital utopianism*. Chicago: University of Chicago Press.

Turow, J. (2005). Audience construction and culture production: Marketing surveillance in the digital age. *The ANNALS of the American Academy of Political and Social Science*, 597(1), 103–121. Retrieved from http://ann.sagepub.com/content/597/1/103.abstract

Twitter (n.d.-a). Types of Tweets and Where They Appear. Retrieved 22 September 2013, from https://support.twitter.com/groups/52-connect/topics/211-tweeting/articles/119138-types-of-tweets-and-where-they-appear

Twitter (n.d.-b). Why is My Twitter Profile in Google Search? Retrieved from https://support.twitter.com/articles/15349-why-is-my-twitter-profile-in-google-search

Ugander, J., Karrer, B., Backstrom, L. & Marlow, C. (2011). The Anatomy of the Facebook Social Graph. Retrieved from http://arxiv.org/pdf/1111.4503

Ullyot, T. (2013, 14 June). Facebook Releases Data, Including All National Security Requests. Retrieved 20 December 2013, from http://newsroom.fb.com/News/636/Facebook-Releases-Data-Including-All-National-Security-Requests

Ungoed-Thomas, J. (2009, 15 November). Belle de Jour revealed as research scientist Dr Brooke Magnanti. *Sunday Times*. Retrieved from http://entertainment.timesonline.co.uk/tol/arts_and_entertainment/books/article6917260.ece

USC Annenberg School Center for the Digital Future. (2013). The World Internet Report 2013. Retrieved from http://www.worldinternetproject.net/

Valenzuela, S., Park, N. & Kee, K. F. (2008). Lessons from Facebook: The Effect of Social Network Sites on College Students' Social Capital. Paper presented at the 9th International Symposium on Online Journalism, Austin, TX.

van Deursen, A. J. A. M., van Dijk, J. A. G. M. & Peters, O. (2011). Rethinking Internet skills: The contribution of gender, age, education, Internet experience, and hours online to medium- and content-related Internet skills. *Poetics*, 39(2), 125–144. doi: 10.1016/j.poetic.2011.02.001. Retrieved from http://www.sciencedirect.com/science/article/pii/S0304422X11000106

Van Dijck, J. (2004). Composing the Self: Of Diaries and Lifelogs. fibreculture(3). Retrieved from http://journal.fibreculture.org/issue3/issue3_vandijck.html

Van Dijck, J. (2007). *Mediated memories in the digital age*. Stanford, CA: Stanford University Press.

van Dijck, J. (2013). *The culture of connectivity: A critical history of social media*. Oxford; New York: Oxford University Press.

Viegas, F. (2005). Bloggers' expectations of privacy and accountability: An initial survey. *Journal of Computer-Mediated Communication*, 10(3). doi: 10.1111/j.1083-6101.2005.tb00260.x.

Villasenor, J. (2011). Recording Everything: Digital Storage as an Enabler of Authoritarian Governments. Retrieved from http://www.brookings.edu/papers/2011/1214_digital_storage_villasenor.aspx

Vitak, J. (2012). The impact of context collapse and privacy on social network site disclosures. *Journal of Broadcasting & Electronic Media*, 56(4), 451–470. doi: 10.1080/08838151.2012.732140.

Voida, A., Newstetter, W. C. & Mynatt, E. D. (2002). When Conventions Collide: The Tensions of Instant Messaging Attributed. Paper presented at the Proceedings of the SIGCHI conference on Human factors in computing systems: Changing our world, changing ourselves, Minneapolis, MN.

Voiskounsky, A. E. (1997). Telelogue conversations. *Journal of Computer-Mediated Communication*, 2(4). doi: 10.1111/j.1083-6101.1997.tb00194.x. Retrieved from http://www3.interscience.wiley.com/journal/120837711/abstract?CRETRY=1&SRETRY=0

Volkenberg, M. v. (2005, 11 July). Dog 'poop' Girl Redux. Retrieved 2 September 2013, from http://populargusts.blogspot.co.uk/2005/07/dog-poop-girl-redux.html

Walker, J. (2005). Final version of weblog definition. In D. Herman, M. Jahn & M.-L. Ryan (eds.), *The Routledge encyclopedia of narrative theory*. London: Routledge. Retrieved from http://jilltxt.net/archives/blog_theorising/final_version_of_weblog_definition.html

Walther, J. B. (1996). Computer-mediated communication: Impersonal, interpersonal, and hyperpersonal interaction. *Communication Research*, 23(1), 3–43.

Walther, J. B. & D'Addario, K. P. (2001). The impacts of emoticons on message interpretation in computer-mediated communication. *Social Science Computer Review*, 19(3), 324–347. doi: 10.1177/089443930101900307.

Walther, J. B. & Parks, M. R. (2002). Cues filtered out, cues filtered in: Computer-mediated communication and relationships. In M. L. Knapp & J. A. Daly (eds.), *Handbook of interpersonal communication* (3rd edn., pp. 529–563). London: SAGE.

Walther, J. B., Van Der Heide, B., Kim, S. Ä., Westerman, D. & Tong, S. T. (2008). The role of friends' appearance and behavior on evaluations of individuals on

Facebook: Are we known by the company we keep? *Human Communication Research*, 34(1), 28–49.

Wandhofer, T., van Eeckhaute, C., Taylor, S. & Fernandez, M. (2012). WeGov Analysis Tools to Connect Policy Makers with Citizens Online. Paper presented at the tGovernment Workshop 2012 (tGov2012), London. Retrieved from http://eprints.soton.ac.uk/349577/

Wang, Y., Norcie, G., Komanduri, S., Acquisti, A., Leon, P. G. & Cranor, L. F. (2011). 'I regretted the minute I pressed share': A Qualitative Study of Regrets on Facebook. Paper presented at the Proceedings of the Seventh Symposium on Usable Privacy and Security, Pittsburgh, PA.

Waskul, D. (1996). Considering the electronic participant: Some polemical observations on the ethics of on-line research. *The Information Society*, 12(2), 129–140. Retrieved from http://www.informaworld.com/10.1080/713 856142

Waugh, R. (2011). Half of Facebook users 'can't keep up' with site's snooping policies as privacy rules change EIGHT times in two years. *The Daily Mail*. Retrieved from http://www.dailymail.co.uk/sciencetech/article-2057000/Half-Facebook-users-sites-snooping-policies-site-changes-privacy-rules-EIGHT-times-years. html

Webroot (2009, 24 June). Webroot®Survey Reveals Social Networkers' Risky Behaviors. Retrieved 24 June 2013, from http://www.webroot.com/En_US/pr/threat-research/corp/survey-reveals-social-networkers-risky-behaviors.html

Weiner, A. (2011, 7 June). Transcript of Weiner's Statement Confessing to Twitter Photo, Past Relationships. Retrieved 22 September 2013, from http://www.nbcnewyork.com/news/local/Weiner-Admits-Confesses-Photo-Twitter-Relationships-123268493.html

Wellman, B., Quan-Hasse, A., Witte, J. & Hampton, K. (2001). Does the Internet increase, decrease, or supplement social capital? Social networks, participation, and community commitment. *American Behavioral Scientist*, 45(3), 436–455(420).

Widyanto, L. & Griffiths, M. (2006). 'Internet Addiction': A critical review. *International Journal of Mental Health and Addiction*, 4(1), 31–51. Retrieved from http://dx.doi.org/10.1007/s11469-006-9009-9

Willard, N. E. (2006). *Cyberbullying and cyberthreats: Responding to the challenge of online social aggression, threats, and distress*. Eugene, OR: Center for Safe and Responsible Internet Use.

Winder, D. (2011, 28 March). Can You Really be Traced from Your IP Address? Retrieved 3 September 2013, from http://www.pcpro.co.uk/features/366349/can-you-really-be-traced-from-your-ip-address

Winkin, Y. (1988). *Erving Goffman: Les Moments et leurs hommes*. Paris: Minuit.

Winston, B. (1998). *Media technology and society: A history: From the telegraph to the internet*. London; New York: Routledge.

Wolak, J., Finkelhor, D. & Mitchell, K. (2004). Internet-initiated sex crimes against minors: Implications for prevention based on findings from a national study. *Journal of Adolescent Health*, 35, 424.e411–424.e420. Retrieved from http://www.unh.edu/ccrc/pdf/CV71.pdf

Wolak, J., Finkelhor, D., Mitchell, K. J. & Ybarra, M. L. (2008). Online 'predators' and their victims. *American Psychologist*, 63(2), 111–128. Retrieved from http://www.childcentre.info/projects/internet/dbaFile15685.pdf

Wu, T. (2010). *The master switch: The rise and fall of information empires*. New York: Alfred A. Knopf.

Ybarra, M. L. & Mitchell, K. J. (2004). Online aggressor/targets, aggressors, and targets: A comparison of associated youth characteristics. *Journal of Child Psychology and Psychiatry*, 45(7), 1308–1316.

Ybarra, M. L., Mitchell, K. J., Finkelhor, D. & Wolak, J. (2007). Internet prevention messages: Targeting the right online behaviors. *Archives of Pediatrics & Adolescent Medicine*, 161(2), 138–145. doi: 10.1001/archpedi.161.2.138.

YouGov. (2007). What does your NetRep Say About You? A Study of How Your Internet Reputation can Influence Your Career Prospects. Retrieved from http://www.viadeo.com/netrep/

Yu, J. (2008, 13 August). Egotistical Princeton Freshman Wants to Rule the World. Retrieved 12 January 2010, from http://www.ivygateblog.com/2008/08/egotistical-princeton-freshman-wants-to-rule-the-world/

Zhang, W., Johnson, T. J., Seltzer, T. & Bichard, S. L. (2010). The revolution will be networked: The influence of social networking sites on political attitudes and behavior. *Social Science Computer Review*, 28(1), 75–92. doi: 10.1177/0894439309335162. Retrieved from http://ssc.sagepub.com/cgi/content/abstract/28/1/75

Zickhur, K. (2013). Location-Based Services. Retrieved from http://pewinternet.org/Reports/2013/Location.aspx

Index

affordances, *see* formal bias
anonymity, 2, 23, 35, 60–2, 82, 91–2,
    106, 133, 139
archiving of social data, 13, 63, 89,
    103–16, 121–9, 157
    see also search engines, time
awareness of readers, 12, 45–7
    see also imagined audience

benefits of SNS use, 14, 151–2
blogs, *see* weblogs

censorship/blocking of social
    media, 153–4
children, 3, 16–24, 154
creativity, 99, 122, 153
cyberbullying, 22–4, 30, 33
cyberstalking, 29–31

defaults, *see* software defaults
digital literacy, 25–6, 80, 154–6
digital natives, 8, 24–6, 139
drivers of SNS use
    commercial promotion, 8, 66, 137–8
    network effects, 143–5
    technological capabilities, 145–7

Facebook, 58, 65, 80–1, 85–9, 104–6,
    111–12, 132–5, 138–45, 158
    examples of risky use, 3–7, 28, 133
    number of friends, 12, 48
    usage statistics and studies, 2–3, 9,
        25–7, 37–9, 59–60, 62, 66–7,
        85–9, 129–30
    see also privacy controls, software
        defaults, Mark Zuckerberg
Feenberg, Andrew, 68–72, 81, 105,
    109, 139
formal bias, 70–1, 75, 80–2, 105, 109,
    128, 139–40

Goffman, Erving, 11–12, 43–54, 61,
    73–5, 84, 99, 129
    see also awareness of readers,
        symbolic interaction
government surveillance, 34–5, 158

harms from SNS use
    embarrassment, 6
    employment-related, 4–5, 31–3
    identity theft and fraud, 28
    interpersonal relationship damage,
        6–7, 36–8
    see also paedophile use of social
        networks

identity, 16, 43, 132, 134
imagined audience, 60–2, 73–100

Lessig, Lawrence, 64–70
Lifelogging, 137
LinkedIn, 44–5, 82, 88

Mayer-Schönberger, Viktor, 55, 101–2,
    129, 143, 158
memory, *see* time
Meyrowitz, Joshua, 49–50
mobile phones/devices, 9, 29, 39, 78,
    121, 138, 143, 145–6
moral panic, 19

network effects, *see* drivers of SNS use
norms, 24, 26, 67, 134–8

paedophile use of social networks, 3,
    17–22
policy, 153–60
primary and secondary reception, 55,
    73, 76, 105, 110–12, 128
privacy controls, 32, 39, 47–8, 59,
    80–1

Printed and bound in the United States of America